From Revolution to Rapprochement:
The United States and Great Britain, 1783—1900

AMERICA AND THE WORLD

EDITOR: Robert A. Divine

The United States and Russia
JOHN GADDIS

From Revolution to Rapprochement:
The United States and Great Britain, 1783–1900
CHARLES S. CAMPBELL

America's Response to China:
An Interpretative History of Sino-American Relations
WARREN I. COHEN

The United States and Germany
MANFRED JONAS

The Cuban Policy of the United States:
A Brief History
LESTER LANGLEY

The United States and the Middle East
CARL LEIDEN and ROBERT STOOKEY

The United States and Japan
CHARLES NEU

The United States and Mexico
KARL M. SCHMITT

The United States and England in
The Twentieth Century
GADDIS SMITH

The United States and France
MARVIN ZAHNISER

From Revolution to Rapprochement:

The United States
and Great Britain, 1783 — 1900

CHARLES S. CAMPBELL
Claremont Graduate School

John Wiley & Sons, Inc.
New York • *London* • *Sydney* • *Toronto*

Library of Congress Cataloging in Publication Data:

Campbell, Charles Soutter, 1911–
   From revolution to rapprochement.

   (America and the world)
   Bibliography: p.
   1. United States—Foreign relations—Great Britain.
2. Great Britain—Foreign relations—United States.
I. Title.

E183.8.G7C29   327.73'042   73–11055
ISBN 0-471-13341-8
ISBN 0-471-13342-6 (pbk)

Printed in the United States of America

10 9 8 7 6 5 4 3 2 1

For Anne

Foreword

Relations with Great Britain dominated the course of American foreign policy from the Revolution through the end of the nineteenth century. The United States won its political independence in the Treaty of Paris in 1783 but, for the next half century, it struggled to free itself from British cultural and economic control. Conflict and tension with the former mother country on both land and sea led to the War of 1812; the quest for economic freedom resulted in frequent clashes in Latin America and the Orient; the British presence in Canada created border disputes in Maine, Minnesota and Oregon that were not resolved until the 1840s. Anglo-American rivalry took many other forms, including a century-long fisheries dispute in the North Atlantic, heated controversy over fur sealing in the Pacific and a bitter contest for influence in Central America in the 1850s. The Civil War raised new issues that kept the old animosities alive until the Treaty of Washington and the Geneva Arbitration in 1872 finally ushered in a period of relative calm, broken briefly by the Venezuelan boundary dispute in 1895 that culminated in a growing rapprochement between the two English-speaking countries at the turn of the twentieth century.

In tracing the deceptively stormy history of Anglo-American relations from 1783 to 1900, Professor Campbell goes beyond the quarrels to show how mutual patience, conciliation and tact enabled the United States and England to settle their differences by peaceful means. Stressing the mutual intertwining of their economies, as well as the cultural and racial ties between the two peoples, he points out the astonishing series of general treaties, special commissions and arbitration agreements that began with Jay's Treaty in the 1790s and culminated in the Treaty of Washington and the subsequent settlement of all outstanding issues by the 1890s. It was, he argues, a remarkable achievement that two such aggressive nations survived so many crises without resorting to armed force. By the middle of the nineteenth century, the United States, relatively content with its continental empire, ceased to threaten British interests in Canada, and England gave up the policy of trying to contain America's restless expansion. For the next 50 years, American and British diplomats gradually liquidated the stubborn disputes they had inherited from the past to achieve the basis for the special relationship that emerged in the twentieth century. By emphasizing the constructive aspect of foreign policy, Professor Campbell has written a perceptive and persuasive account of a genuine diplomatic victory—one in which there were no losers, only winners.

This book is one in a series of volumes tracing the history of American foreign policy toward those nations with which the United States has had significant relations over a long period of time. By stressing the continuity of diplomatic themes through the decades, each author will seek to identify the distinctive character of America's international relationships. It is hoped that this country-by-country approach will not only enable readers to understand more deeply United States diplomatic history but make them aware that past events and patterns of behavior exert a continuous influence on American foreign policy.

ROBERT A. DIVINE

Preface

From the American Revolution through the nineteenth century United States foreign policy was directed mainly at one country: Great Britain. So much was this the case that policy toward Britain can almost be equated with total American foreign policy. The principal reasons for this are clear enough. The Revolution left a bitter and abiding heritage. Britain was not only the world's strongest country but her North American possessions paralleled the breadth of the United States; she had menacing bases along the international boundary, in the Caribbean Sea, and in Central America; and her warships patrolled the waters off the American east and west coasts. Furthermore, during the early years of independence American and British ideologies differed sharply from each other, and this was a major factor in producing a second British-American war, the War of 1812. For many years the United States tried, sporadically, to expand into British North America, and Great Britain tried to check American expansion not only toward the north but toward the south and west as well.

As if all this was not enough, a whole new set of controversies arose over Britain's alleged help for the South during the Civil War. So enraged was the North that a third Anglo-American conflict seemed possible at times during the Civil War and, more particularly, in the late 1860s and early 1870s. Thereafter Britain and America found themselves embroiled over the northeastern fisheries and, before long, over the Bering Sea fur seals too. An unexpected clash in 1895 over the boundary between British Guiana and Venezuela gave rise to one final outburst of ugly talk of war.

With so many reasons for hostility, and so many rancorous

disputes, it is not surprising that Washington was engrossed with Great Britain. The wonder is that despite the two wars, threats of a third war, and decades of animosity, America and Britain achieved a lasting rapprochement around 1900.

I am greatly indebted to Mrs. Catherine Tramz for her unfailing patience and promptness in typing the manuscript, a process that often entailed considerable retyping. I also thank Mrs. Audrey Munro for typing drafts of some chapters. I am grateful to Mr. Robert A. Divine who, as editor, read the manuscript and made helpful suggestions.

CHARLES S. CAMPBELL

Contents

From Revolution to Rapprochement:
The United States and Great Britain, 1783—1900

CHAPTER I

The Continuing Struggle for Independence

IN 1776 THIRTEEN BRITISH COLONIES in North America declared themselves independent, and the American Revolution got fully under way. From the American point of view relations with Great Britain were henceforth between two sovereign countries, but in the British view they were between a motherland and rebellious colonies. During the Revolution Britain did not, of course, recognize the colonies' independence; and when France was so bold as to do so in 1778 she quickly found herself at war with the British. The Netherlands recognized the United States in 1782 but not until 1783, the Revolution over, did Great Britain extend formal recognition.

The history of relations between Great Britain and the United States may begin in either 1776 or 1783. To select the former date, however, would be needlessly partial; and that date is all the more inappropriate in a study giving considerable attention to diplomacy, because the years from 1776 to 1783 were marked by British-American fighting rather than British-American diplomacy. It is true that there was diplomacy of sorts. In 1778 London sent a mission across the Atlantic that tried, unsuccessfully, to persuade the rebels to accept home rule within the empire; and various British-American negotiations took place preliminary to the peace treaty, signed at Paris on September 3, 1783.[1] Nonetheless, full-fledged diplomatic relations between Great Britain

---

[1] Regarding diplomacy during the Revolution see Samuel F. Bemis, *The Diplomacy of the American Revolution* (New York, 1935); Richard B. Morris, *The Peacemakers: The Great Powers and American Independence* (New York, 1965); and Richard W. Van Alstyne, *Empire and Independence, The International History of the American Revolution* (New York., 1965).

and the United States, each formally recognizing the other, began only in 1783.

The omission of detailed consideration of the Revolution should not, of course, cause one to overlook its enduring effects on Anglo-American relations. For many years to come memories of that struggle were bitter in both countries, and relations between them would have been far more tranquil had they not separated so violently and rancorously.

By the treaty of 1783 Great Britain recognized United States independence. The new country was to be bordered on the west by the Mississippi River, on the north by approximately the same river-and-lake line that exists today, and on the south by Spanish Florida. The United States was to have the "liberty" of fishing in British North American waters. She promised that British creditors would not be impeded in collecting their prewar debts and that the federal government would recommend to the states the restoration of the rights and properties of the Loyalists.

The treaty conferred an independence that was limited in reality if not in law. Its most remarkable feature was Britain's cession of the northwest back country between the Ohio River and the Great Lakes, a cession in no way dictated by military necessity. During the years of fighting only tiny bands of American soldiers temporarily ventured into this enormous area, and in 1783 United States authority was nonexistent. Wild animals and Indians allied to the British moved silently through the thick forests, unchallenged by Americans. Moreover south of the lakes and the St. Lawrence River on admittedly American soil stood seven British forts, flying the British flag, manned by British soldiers. For thirteen years after the peace treaty they remained there, a steady menace to the United States.

London had several reasons for keeping these strongholds. For one thing America herself was not carrying out the treaty terms regarding the prewar debts and the Loyalists. (Indeed, the terms regarding the Loyalists were never properly fulfilled.) More important was Britain's and Canada's desire to have time to reorganize the valuable fur trade flourishing north and south of the Great Lakes and now cut in two by the new boundary, and to make better arrangements for the Indians, who had been ignored in the peace treaty. Another consideration was the uncertain future of the sprawling republic, loosely held together under the Articles of Confederation. If it was to break up, Britain wanted to be on the spot to pick up the pieces. Many members of the British ruling class would have been delighted to see the union dissolve. Naturally they resented the American success in the Revolution. They took no care to conceal their rather arrogant, supercilious attitude toward Americans, mere vulgar, uncultured, low-class colonials. Before long, British agents were intriguing with Ethan Allen and others in Vermont to detach that state from the country.

Exercising no authority in an enormous part of her domain, helplessly witnessing British troops occupying her soil, the United States was not yet free of the old motherland. She did not even have regular diplomatic representation with Great Britain. John Adams, it is true, went to London in 1785 as Minister but, accomplishing nothing, he left in disgust in 1788. Great Britain did not bother to send a Minister to the United States until late 1791.

Commercial relations too were unsatisfactory. During the Revolution Americans had eagerly looked forward to freedom from the Navigation Laws, which had bound their commerce narrowly to Great Britain. But freedom proved to have unexpected hardships no less than benefits because Britain had no intention of treating rebels on the same basis as members of the empire. An Order in Council of December 1783 permitted American ships to carry most raw materials, but not manufactured goods, to Great Britain; but they could not go to British North America or to the British West Indies, islands the provisioning of which London had decided to turn over to Canada and the other loyal North American colonies. For Americans this represented a most unwelcome change from the privileged position they had enjoyed in British markets before the Revolution; and the exclusion from the West Indies in particular was a hard blow. Britain refused to make any commercial treaty at all.

Yet the close commercial ties that had been built up during a century and a half could not easily be disrupted; and trade between the two countries continued to be vitally important for each of them. United States exports to Great Britain, consisting almost entirely of agricultural products, declined sharply for a few years, mainly because the British turned to non-American sources for much of their tobacco and rice. The value of exports fluctuated between $4,134,000 in 1786 to $4,901,000 in 1788.[2] Accurate figures are unobtainable, but one may be sure that despite the decline Great Britain was, by far, America's leading market. More accurate statistics are available beginning in 1790 when United States exports to Britain amounted to $7,000,000, over a third of the total exports of $20,000,000.[3]

British exports to the United States—these were overwhelmingly manufactured products—flourished at almost the prewar level during the 1780s. Woolens, hardware, and other manufactures flooded into the United States in 1784 as Americans hastened to restore depleted stocks of once-familiar goods. Britain's manufactured goods were cheaper and better than those of any other country, and only her merchants would extend the long-term credits that Americans needed. The average annual value of British exports to America for the six years ending 1789 was £2,333,643.[4] Almost a fourth of all her exports went to the United States in 1784 (an exceptional year); about a tenth went there in 1786.[5]

The trans-Atlantic commerce was less important to Great Britain than to the United States in those early years. In the 1780s about a twentieth of Britain's imports came from America, whereas over a third of America's imports came from Britain in 1795.[6] And, as has appeared, a smaller percentage of total British exports went to the United States than of total American exports to Britain. Indeed, if one takes into account not merely

---

[2] Douglass C. North, *Growth and Welfare in the American Past, A New Economic History* (Englewood Cliffs, 1966), 60.

[3] U.S. Bureau of the Census, *Historical Statistics of the United States, Colonial Times to 1957* (Washington, 1960), 551.

[4] Emory R. Johnson, *History of Domestic and Foreign Commerce of the United States* . . . (Washington, 1915), I, 123.

[5] Harry C. Allen, *Great Britain and the United States, A History of Anglo-American Relations (1783–1952)* (New York, 1955), 56.

[6] *Ibid.* Samuel F. Bemis, *Jay's Treaty: A Study in Commerce and Diplomacy* (New York, 1924), 33–34, says that in 1790 out of a total of $15,388,409 worth of American imports paying *ad valorem* duties, $13,798,168 worth (about ninety percent) came from Britain.

Great Britain but all places under the British flag, approximately two-thirds of America's foreign trade was with this larger area in 1790.[7] The United States, consequently, had to deal very circumspectly with the former mother country. But the dependence was reciprocal, even if not equal, since Britain could not lightly offend a country that took even a tenth of her exports, and the truly significant point is not which country was more dependent but that for almost all the years under consideration in this book each country was the other's best customer. This intertwining of the two economies was a persistent and potent factor for peace.

George Washington became President in 1789, with the federal government much strengthened by the new constitution. It gave the government powers that might compel Britain to relax her commercial restrictions and, early in the new administration, Congress threatened to curtail British imports. England took alarm. For the first time she deigned to appoint a Minister: George Hammond arrived at Philadelphia, then the capital, in October 1791. In return Thomas Pinckney went to London the next year as the second American Minister. Although the United States did not get the desired trading concessions, she had at least induced Britain to exchange diplomatic relations.

The government used its new powers also against the seven British-occupied forts, for several years without success, however. American armies invaded the Indian country between the Great Lakes and the Ohio in 1790 and again in 1791, each time with disastrous results. So helpless did the United States seem that London considered setting up a permanent neutral Indian buffer state. But instead of accepting this, President Washington directed General Anthony ("Mad Anthony") Wayne—"the chief who never sleeps," the Indians called him—to organize a new army for yet another invasion of the northwest.

Before Wayne was ready, momentous events in Europe undermined Britain's American policy. In February 1793 revolutionary France declared war on Britain. Hoping to strangle her foe with naval power, Britain adopted measures that threatened neutral

[7] Edward C. Kirkland, *A History of American Economic Life* (New York, 1932), 214.

American shipping. She even seized some three hundred American merchant ships trading with French islands in the Caribbean Sea, and she began to impress American sailors for service in her own navy. News of the seizures, which reached Philadelphia in the spring of 1794, coincided with alarmist reports from the back country. Learning that Wayne had taken up winter quarters north of the Ohio River, the Governor-General of Canada ordered, in February 1794, the construction of a new fort on the Maumee River, where it would guard Detroit. Not only were the British refusing to surrender already established posts, they were constructing a new one well to the south of the international line. A week earlier the Governor-General, speaking to some Indians, had injudiciously predicted war with the United States before the year expired. Only thirteen years had passed since the end of the Revolution. Still holding American soil, inspiring the Indians to resistance, refusing to grant commercial concessions, and intriguing with separatists, Great Britain seemed to stand convicted of vindictive hostility.

Anger against her surged up across the United States. Sympathy was strong with France, America's former ally during her struggle for independence and now a sister republic. Calls for military preparation and even war swept the country. This, President Washington was determined to avoid. Hostilities would curtail imports from Britain, duties on which constituted most of the federal income, and the new country, so painfully put together, might fall apart. But the government felt obliged to impose an embargo on shipping for two months; and a bill completely banning commerce with Britain failed by only one vote. As a last-ditch move to avoid war, the administration decided to send a special envoy to London to seek a settlement. Chief Justice John Jay landed in England in early June 1794 and soon opened negotiations with the British Foreign Secretary, Lord Grenville.

Five months later he and Grenville concluded what may be called a second peace treaty. But before then a new crisis had flared up. Moving north in 1794 from his winter headquarters, Wayne clashed with Indians, buttressed by some sixty Canadians, near the new British fort on the Maumee. Defeated at the Battle of Fallen Timbers on August 20, the fleeing tribes ran past the fort. A collision between the pursuing Americans and the British seemed imminent. But both sides held fire, and Wayne withdrew. As one writer has said, "Rarely have two countries come so close to war without plunging into it."[8]

The Jay-Grenville Treaty was signed on November 19, 1794. It was the first (after the treaty of independence) of a long series of Anglo-American treaties that time after time settled serious disputes, some of which might have led to war. Moreover the treaty set a powerful example for arbitration. It provided for four British-American commissions to determine four controverted points: the sum of debts contracted by the United States before the end of the Revolution; the amount of damages to be paid by Britain for her recent seizures of American ships; the identity of the St. Croix River, named in the treaty of 1783 as part of America's northeastern boundary; and the definition of a section of the northwestern boundary left obscure by the same treaty. Other articles regulated commercial relations, although less favorably than Americans would have liked. Trade between the British Isles and the United States was to be nondiscriminatory. American ships would be allowed to trade with the British East Indies and West Indies (but the Senate rejected the latter privilege, which was hedged in with unacceptable restrictions). Trade by land but not by sea with British North America was permitted. Most important of all, Great Britain agreed to evacuate the northwest forts by June 1, 1796. Her fur traders, however, were given the right to move back and forth at will and to carry on their business across the international boundary; and this enabled Britain to maintain a close contact with American Indians that was to complicate her relations with the United States over the next two decades.

The four commissions, meeting at various dates after the treaty's signature, had mixed success. The first broke down, but by a convention of 1802 the United States agreed to pay $2,664,-000 in settlement of the debts. The second awarded the United States about $11,500,000 for the British maritime seizures. The

---

[8]Alfred L. Burt, *The United States, Great Britain and British North America from the Revolution to the Establishment of Peace after the War of 1812* (New Haven, 1940), 140.

third designated the Schoodiac River as the St. Croix of the peace treaty; and the fourth failed to agree on the northwestern boundary, which was not defined until 1818.

The forts were in American hands by the agreed date. Feeling themselves abandoned by the British White Father, the Indians folded their tents and moved west. By the Treaty of Greenville, 1795, they ceded their title to territory comprising most of present-day Ohio. The United States was now the actual as well as nominal sovereign of her entire dominion as defined in 1783. A gigantic step toward full independence had been taken.

The treaty passed over in silence one major point disputed by the two countries: that of neutral rights, a question brought to prominence by the Caribbean seizures at the outset of the European war and one that was to preoccupy Americans for the next twenty years. The United States stood for the doctrine (not yet universally accepted) that a neutral ship had the legal right to carry noncontraband to a belligerent country, except to a blockaded port—"free ships, free goods," the doctrine was often called. Although Great Britain had agreed in the Jay-Grenville Treaty to pay compensation for captures of American ships, she had refused to acknowledge that the American doctrine was international law. Nor had she agreed that impressment was illegal. Thus although the United States had successfully redeemed her national domain by 1796, one of the main tenets she espoused—neutral rights, or freedom of the sea (including freedom from impressment)—had still to be secured. The threat to neutral rights loomed large as the European conflict gathered momentum. This was intolerable to former revolutionaries now running the government because, to their mind, security of American ideology, no less than security of her territory, had to be attained. Partly in order to attain it the United States, or more accurately her dominant Republican party, embarked upon a second war with Great Britain, the War of 1812.

CHAPTER II

Ideology, Politics, and War

THE EUROPEAN WAR, which had broken out in 1793 and which was to engulf all the great powers of Europe as well as the United States before it ended with the battle of Waterloo in 1815, was interrupted by the Peace of Amiens lasting from October 1801 to May 1803. During the first phase of the struggle, from 1793 to 1801, Britain and America experienced the war scare of 1794 mentioned in the first chapter, but after the Jay-Grenville peace treaty they enjoyed several years of improved relations. Instead of England being her antagonist, America moved sharply toward a rupture with France, and in 1798 the two former allies found themselves engaged in an undeclared but violent war on the high seas that lasted until the autumn of 1800. Another crisis with France erupted when that powerful country, now under Napoleon Bonaparte, got title to the Louisiana Territory; it ended when the United States purchased the territory in 1803. Because of these distractions American attention was largely diverted from the old enemy, Great Britain, until about 1803, when the war in Europe resumed.

Another factor, too, was significant. The two administrations of George Washington were followed by the four years of President John Adams. Both these men were Federalists; both were repelled by Jacobin France. Behind the scenes the powerful Secretary of the Treasury, Alexander Hamilton, labored for friendship with Great Britain, partly in order to maintain the commercial ties on which the Federal revenue depended. But in 1801 President Thomas Jefferson and his Republican party took office; James Madison, another Republican and Jefferson's Secretary of State, succeeded him in 1809. Both Jefferson and Madison were instinctively anti-British and less bothered by France's revolutionary excesses than their predecessors had been. Viewing America as a beacon of hope in a darkly monarchical world, they zealously upheld American principles, such as freedom of the seas; to have compromised them would have been, in their way of thinking, a betrayal of republicanism and indeed of the best hopes of mankind itself. Had the Federalists occupied the White House during the critical years from 1803 to 1812 it is probable that they would have followed a less ideological policy than did the Republicans and that the War of 1812 would not have come.

As in the two world wars of the twentieth century, so during most of the years from 1793 to 1812 United States exports to Great Britain boomed. The value of exports to all countries rose from $33,000,000 in 1794 to $108,000,000 in 1807. Much of the rise was accounted for by reexports, that is, goods imported into America (mainly from the French West Indies) and then sent on to Europe; or else goods coming to America from Europe and destined for the West Indies; before long reexports had a greater value than exports originating in the United States. Reexports first became significant in 1796 when they had a value of $26,000,000, as compared with $7,000,000 in 1794. Their value rose sharply to $60,000,000 in 1806 and in 1807.[1] A considerable proportion of total exports went to Britain: $6,000,000 worth (including reexports) in 1794, $17,000,000 worth in 1796, and $23,000,000 worth in 1807. About one-fifth to one-third of all American exports went to that country alone.[2] Exports to France were lower in value: $1,000,000 in 1794, $8,000,000 in 1795, $3,000,000 in 1796, $11,000,000 in 1806, $13,000,000 in 1807, and $3,000,000 in 1808; and thereafter, as British maritime controls clamped down, less than $500,000 in 1809 and in 1810.[3]

A major element of British strategy after 1803 was to curtail

---

[1] U.S. Bureau of the Census, *Historical Statistics of the United States, Colonial Times to 1957* (Washington, 1960), 538. Convenient tables of American foreign trade are in Eli F. Heckscher, *The Continental System, An Economic Interpretation* (Oxford, 1922), 103, 146.

[2] *Historical Statistics*, 551. Sometimes the percentage was less than a fifth; in 1795 it was only an eighth.

[3] *Ibid.*

neutral commerce, almost all of it American, destined for France. Lord Nelson's victory over the French and Spanish fleets at Trafalgar on October 21, 1805 made the British navy supreme, and an effective blockade of France became more feasible. In the same year a decision concerning an American ship, the *Essex*, threatened the reexport trade. A famous British judge, Sir William Scott (later Lord Stowell), in the *Polly* case of 1800, had said that such trade did not violate British law. Now in 1805 another judge, Sir William Grant, declared it contrary to what was known as the Rule of 1756. According to this British Rule, colonial trade that had been reserved to the mother country in peace time could not be handed over to a neutral in war time. Before the war France and Spain had reserved trade with their West Indian colonies to themselves; and Sir William declared that the *Essex* had been in effect on a continuous voyage between two Spanish ports. After the *Essex* decision an American ship, in the European trade, carrying goods destined for, or originating in, the French or Spanish West Indies became good British prize, even if the ship was not headed for a blockaded port and the goods were noncontraband reexported from the United States. The decision's effect was softened, however, by a British Order in Council of May 1806 (often called Fox's blockade, after the Whig Foreign Secretary, Charles James Fox), which in effect permitted the reexport trade in noncontraband to many Continental ports.

Fox's blockade, involving as it did the novel blockade of a coast rather than a port, gave Napoleon, now Emperor of France, a pretext to issue the Berlin Decree of November 1806, which declared the British Isles blockaded and prohibited trade in British goods. Napoleon lacked the navy to blockade Britain, but he could and did seize ships bringing British goods to the Continent. His so-called Continental System amounted to a self-imposed blockade. Though weak on the seas, the Emperor controlled most of Europe, and he intended to seal off its ports from his great adversary. Britain's merchant marine, on which she depended for her vital overseas trade, would, he hoped, be reduced to sailing around the ocean with few places to land; and the economic underpinning of her military and naval power would crumble. Britain, justifying the step as retaliation against an illegal French move, retorted with Orders in Council of January and November 1807. The first banned trade between French ports. The second declared that French-controlled countries were to be treated as if blockaded; however, if an American ship stopped at a British port, paid duty on the goods carried, and got a British license, it might be permitted to proceed to the Continent with some or all of its cargo.[4] In part this Order was a patriotic device to control exports to France; but it was also a means of helping British shipping interests combat American competition. The imposition of duty on American goods raised their price as against British goods, which could then be carried to the Continent in the American ships. Napoleon's answer was the Milan Decree of December 1807: ships paying British duty or going to Britain were lawful prize. Theoretically American ships could go neither to Britain (prohibited by France) nor to much of Europe (prohibited by Britain). Actually France could not stop them from going to Britain, and the British allowed them to trade in noncontraband with the Continent if they first visited a British port—a practice violating the Milan Decree but often overlooked by Napoleon, who wanted the goods.

Were these Decrees and Orders legal? The United States contended that they were not. But the doctrine of the freedom of the seas was neither clearly defined nor universally accepted. The Jay-Grenville Treaty was silent about it. In the course of the nineteenth century older maritime doctrines would be discarded, whereas the freedom of the seas would win general acceptance. But in the early years of the century this was not apparent. The truth is that international maritime law was in transition, fluid and uncertain. As an authority has written, "it can hardly be said that it had any effective existence at the time of the outbreak of the Revolutionary Wars."[5]

Despite the *Essex* decision, and despite the French Decrees and the British Orders, American exports to the Continent held steady at values of $46,000,000, $49,000,000, and $48,000,000

---

[4] The Order in Council of November 1807 was replaced by one of April 26, 1809, which greatly reduced or eliminated the duties.
[5] Walter A. Phillips and Arthur H. Reede, *Neutrality, Its History, Economics and Law, The Napoleonic Period* (New York, 1936), 10; see also *ibid.*, 10–17. The quoted words are Phillips's.

for 1805, 1806, and 1807, respectively. Exports to Great Britain continued to increase: $15,000,000 worth in 1805, $16,000,000 worth in 1806, and $23,000,000 worth in 1807.[6]

But trade with the Continent flourished at British sufferance. To republican ideologues like President Jefferson and Secretary of State Madison, American trade should flourish as a matter of right. Neutral America should be free to carry noncontraband, whether reexports or not, to France as she saw fit. And to men with their anti-British backgrounds, British monitoring of United States behavior was insufferable.

Just as intolerable as trade restrictions was another British practice: the impressment of American seamen. Impressment was a centuries-old custom; and the British, engaged in a desperate struggle with France, considered it indispensable for staffing the royal navy and hence for the nation's survival. How many seamen were impressed from American ships is uncertain, but they numbered in the thousands; and of them thousands were probably Americans. "The practice . . . ," Madison said, "is so far from affecting British subjects alone that, under the pretext of searching for these, thousands of American citizens, under the safeguard of public law and of their national flag, have been torn from their country and from everything dear to them; have been dragged on board ships of war of a foreign nation and exposed . . . to risk their lives in the battles of their oppressors. . . ."[7]

The legality of impressment, like that of the trade controls, was not clear. According to one writer, "Both sides were right, Britain by the old usage, and the United States by a new doctrine then only beginning to take shape: that a country's ships at sea are detached portions of its soil and therefore covered by its sovereignty."[8] The ethics of impressment was obscured by the fact that American ship owners, needing sailors for the merchant

---

[6] *Historical Statistics*, 551.

[7] Madison to Congress, June 1, 1812, James D. Richardson, ed., *A Compilation of the Messages and Papers of the Presidents, 1789–1897* (Washington, 1899), I, 500.

[8] Alfred L. Burt, *The United States, Great Britain and British North America from the Revolution to the Establishment of Peace after the War of 1812* (New Haven, 1940), 212–13; see also Alfred T. Mahan, *Sea Power in its Relations to the War of 1812* (Boston, 1905), I, 2–11.

marine expanding rapidly under the stimulus of wartime profits, actively encouraged desertions by offering higher pay and safer conditions than the British could. Another complication resulted from different views about the legality of expatriation and naturalization. Just as the United States insisted on the universal validity of the newer doctrines of freedom of the seas and immunity of her sailors on her ships, she also stood for another modern doctrine: the right of expatriation at a person's choice and of subsequent naturalization. An Englishman who had become a naturalized American was, the United States held, no more liable to being impressed than a native-born American. But Britain stood by the older view: once an Englishman, always an Englishman. No right of expatriation existed; and consequently a British-born person was liable to impressment.

To summarize, regarding the law pertaining to all these matters—trade controls, impressment, and naturalization—the United States with all the fervor of a revolutionary country espoused newer principles soon to become generally accepted, whereas staid Britain stood for long-held principles soon to be outmoded. The law was in flux. This was at the root of much Anglo-American controversy.

Determined to uphold American ideology, Jefferson refused to compromise. In 1806 James Monroe, then Minister to Great Britain, and William Pinkney, a special envoy, signed an agreement in London by which the British made several conditional concessions. London refused to renounce impressment, although it did promise to give written assurance "that the strictest care shall be taken to preserve the citizens of the United States from any molestation or injury; and that immediate and prompt redress shall be afforded upon any representation of injury sustained by them."[9] Jefferson stood on principle: the impressment of Americans must be stopped root and branch. He objected, too, to a British condition for the agreement, that the United States reject the recently issued Berlin Decree. Consequently he declined to submit the treaty to the Senate for its consideration, though he did ask for further negotiations.

---

[9] Holland and Auckland (the British negotiators) to Monroe and Pinkney, Nov. 8, 1806, *American State Papers, Foreign Relations* (Washington, 1832), III, 140.

A tragedy followed. Acting under orders from an admiral in Halifax, a British warship, the *Leopard*, on June 22, 1807 fired on an American warship, the *Chesapeake*, killing three and wounding eighteen, and forcibly removed four alleged deserters. This was an inexcusable act. The legality of impressment from a merchant ship might be uncertain but its illegality from a public ship was indisputable. London recalled the erring admiral (but did not otherwise punish him) and disavowed his action—but did not abandon impressment. Violent anti-British feeling swept the United States. "Never since the battle of Lexington," Jefferson asserted, "have I seen the country in such a state of exasperation as at present, and even that did not produce such unanimity."[10] War would have come had the President fanned the emotionalism. Instead, he acted with wisdom and restraint by quieting the excitement. Nowhere does Jefferson show to better advantage than in his avoidance of war in 1807. Although certainly an ideologue, he was a flexible one, and it is possible that hostilities would not have come in 1812 had he still been in the White House. All the same, one must ask whether the *Chesapeake* incident would have occurred at all without the failure of Monroe and Pinkney's treaty. For would not an improved atmosphere following agreement have precluded the rash orders to the *Leopard*? Jefferson cannot escape blame for his handling of this affair.

By the end of 1807 principles by which republican America set great store regarding the freedom of the seas, impressment, and expatriation were being flouted by the British—and by the French too, although less effectively in practice. This was unbearable to men like President Jefferson and Secretary of State Madison who did not doubt the universal validity of American ideology as maintained by their Republican party. For them no basic compromise was conceivable.

It will be recalled that the war scare of 1794 had resulted from incidents in the Indian country as well as on the high seas. Although the Treaty of Greenville had ended the Indian trouble in the present-day state of Ohio, by 1807 ominous clouds had

---

[10] Jefferson to Dupont de Nemours, July 14, 1807, Andrew A. Lipscomb and Albert E. Bergh, eds., *The Writings of Thomas Jefferson* (Washington, 1903–1904), XI, 274.

gathered farther west. From then until war started in 1812 Anglo-American contention was to have the same twin focus that it had in the 1790s: on the high seas and the back country of the northwest. In September 1807 not long after the *Chesapeake* affair, and while the British and French maritime measures were taking shape, William Henry Harrison, governor of the Indiana Territory, reported that a powerful Indian leader, Tecumseh, and his brother, the Prophet, were waiting for a British sign to attack. Harrison was, in fact, overly apprehensive; but the threat of war raised by the *Chesapeake* did cause the Canadians to reknit ties with the Indians. "If we do not employ them, there cannot exist a moment's doubt that they will be employed against us," a high official stated.[11] In 1808 the British supplied the Indians with large quantities of "presents," that is, weapons. Although there were fewer presents the next year when the crisis subsided, Indian determination to resist the encroaching American settler was strengthened. Along the western frontier Americans were persuaded that behind the red man was the same sinister British hand that had opposed their westward course before John Jay went to London in 1794. In a sense they were correct, but the basic cause of Indian hostility was not British intrigue but unremitting American expansion.

A great Indian battle comparable to that of Fallen Timbers was to take place in late 1811 and feed the flames of war with Britain, but in 1807 Washington's attention was mainly on the Atlantic Ocean: What should be done about the *Chesapeake*, about impressment, and about the maritime controls? The *Chesapeake* provocation in particular compelled the government to act with vigor. Its response was threefold. An act of July 2, 1807 banned United States ports and waters to British warships; and a Non-Importation Act of December 14 prohibited the importation of certain British goods. Then on December 18 Jefferson argued in a special message to Congress that because of "the great and increasing dangers with which our vessels, our seamen, and merchandise are threatened on the high seas and elsewhere from the belligerent powers of Europe" American ships should

---

[11] Burt, *United States*, 249.

not be allowed to leave the United States.[12] Congress agreed. The Embargo Act of December 22 prohibited the departure of American vessels, except in the coasting trade under bond. For many years Jefferson had looked to economic sanctions as a substitute for war; he was eager to test the theory in practice. Curtailing trade with Great Britain would compel her, he believed, to accept American doctrines. The freedom of the seas and the right of expatriation would be triumphantly and peaceably vindicated.

Nonimportation, to the extent that it included all imports from Britain, put the United States in effect in Napoleon's Continental system. The Emperor could prevent areas he controlled from trading with England, but he could not force Britain's most important commercial partner, the United States, to do the same. To his delight the United States, by her own action, had joined France's self-imposed blockade. On the other hand, the Embargo Act was welcomed by the ruling Tories in England because it ended American commercial competition and exports to France.

Economic sanctions failed to work out as Jefferson hoped. Britain did not revoke her Orders in Council until several years later, and by then the American measures of 1807 had been repealed. Indeed the ironical result of the sanctions was to weaken the United States more than Great Britain. The abrupt curtailment of foreign trade struck the country a devastating blow. Exports fell from a value of $108,000,000 in 1807 to a mere $22,000,000 the next year, while imports declined over the same years from a value of $139,000,000 to $57,000,000.[13] Unemployment mounted alarmingly. Bankruptcies were rife. In New York City, according to a contemporary, "The ships were dismantled; their decks were cleared, their hatches were battened down. Not a box, not a cask, not a barrel, not a bale was to be seen on the wharves, where the grass had begun to grow luxuriantly."[14] Stacks of southern and western staples—cotton, tobacco,

---

[12] Jefferson to Congress, Dec. 18, 1807, Richardson, *Messages and Papers*, I, 433.

[13] *Historical Statistics*, 538. In 1808 $3,000,000 worth of exports went to the United Kingdom, $7,000,000 to all Europe. *Ibid.*, 551.

[14] John B. McMaster, *A History of the People of the United States, from the Revolution to the Civil War* (New York, 1883–1914), III, 415.

hemp, and others—piled up, cut off from their European markets. As imports declined, so did customs receipts and, therefore, the federal revenue. Economic disaster had its political effect so that the Federalist vote surged ahead in the elections of 1808, although not sufficiently to win the presidency. The next March, Jefferson left the White House to return to his native Virginia, a discredited man. James Madison, his faithful Secretary of State, but a less flexible and a weaker man, succeeded him as President.

It is important to note that these calamities were unnecessary from the standpoint of national interest conceived in military and economic terms. The security of the United States was not enhanced one whit by cutting off foreign trade—on the contrary. Nor, of course, was the economic well-being of the American people. Since the resumption of the European war in 1803, United States exports and imports had increased every year through 1807.[15] The British and French maritime controls, however irritating to American pride, had not stopped this profitable trade. What did stop it was the United States government under the Republican party. France could not prevent American trade with British areas, and Britain licensed much trade with the Continent. The fact is that the United States had prospered under the British system. Practical considerations of dollars and cents pointed to accepting a state of affairs that brought booming trade, and most merchants and Federalists urged that this be done. But what suited prosperity did not suit American ideology as championed by the Republican party. One stood in the way of the other. James Monroe thought that even republicanism was imperiled. Where would submission to British regulation, he asked, "have left the U States? & what effect would it have had on the character—, & destiny of our republican system of govt? My idea was that such a step would have put it in great danger if it had not subverted it eventually."[16]

---

[15] The figures for exports in millions of dollars are: 1803–56, 1804–78, 1805–96, 1806–102, 1807–108; for imports: 1803–65, 1804–85, 1805–121, 1806–129, 1807–139. *Historical Statistics*, 538.

[16] Monroe to John Taylor, June 13, 1812, Roger H. Brown, *The Republic in Peril: 1812* (New York and London, 1964), 85.

Furthermore the time soon came when not only was Republican-sponsored ideology at stake, but also the Republican party. Having long insisted upon the inalienable nature of its principles, the party could not have abandoned them without calamitous consequences at the polls. It could not have tolerated British-supervised prosperity. There is much truth in the remark that the War of 1812 was "determined by American party rivalries."[17]

Just before his term expired, Jefferson had experienced the humiliation of seeing a disenchanted Congress repeal his cherished Embargo and Non-Importation Acts. In their place it substituted the Non-Intercourse Act of March 1, 1809. The new measure reopened trade, both exports and imports, with all countries except Great Britain and France and their dependencies, and it provided that if either Britain or France repealed her maritime controls as against the United States, trade would be resumed with that country. It banned American waters to French as well as to British warships. Britain and France were now on the same footing.

With the Madison administration in office, and the anti-British legislation of 1807 discarded, an opportunity existed for a clearing away of the Anglo-American differences. Some weeks before Madison entered the White House, the new Tory Foreign Secretary, George Canning, had instructed his Minister at Washington, David Erskine, to try to reach an agreement. He authorized Erskine to revoke the Orders in Council provided that the United States would open up trade with Britain but not with France, would recognize the Rule of 1756, and would permit the royal navy to help enforce an American ban against trade with France. Madison's Secretary of State, Robert Smith, saw no particular difficulty in the first two stipulations, although he thought it unnecessary to write the second into the record. He rejected the third one. Nevertheless Erskine decided that Canning's conditions had been sufficiently complied with, and he exchanged notes with Smith on April 18, 1809 giving assurances that the

---

[17] Keith G. Feiling, *The Second Tory Party, 1714–1832* (London, 1938). See also Henry Adams, *History of the United States of America . . .* (New York, 1889–1890), VI (1809–1813), 196–97.

Orders would cease applying to the United States on June 10, 1809. He also indicated that Britain would restore the sailors impressed on the *Chesapeake* and provide financial compensation for the relatives of those killed. During the negotiations the prospect was raised that impressment might end altogether. The United States had already prohibited the employment of foreign seamen on public ships and was considering a similar ban applying to merchantmen. Britain would then have no reason to impress on American ships.

Great was the joy in the United States that the Orders were soon to expire and trade with British areas about to reopen, and particularly that the heavy threat of war with Britain had been lifted. Madison hastily announced that the Non-Intercourse Act would no longer apply to Great Britain beginning June 10.[18] Some six hundred ships sailed from America for foreign ports, laden with goods that had been swamping the country. But at the end of July Americans were dismayed to learn that Canning had repudiated the agreement and recalled Erskine for exceeding his instructions. As if this was not enough, Erskine's successor, Francis James Jackson, behaved in such an overbearing way that the administration refused to have any dealings with him and then demanded his recall, a demand London complied with in 1810.

Canning's repudiation of Erskine was a mistake comparable to Jefferson's treatment of Monroe and Pinkney's treaty. The British would have been well advised to take half a loaf for the sake of American good will. Yet this is not the whole story. The main point at which Erskine departed from his instructions concerned the role of the British navy in enforcing an American ban on trade with France. Could not the United States have accepted some kind of enforcement without abandoning the basic principle of freedom of the seas? If both Tory rigidity and doctrinaire republicanism had been eased, the Erskine agreement might have held firm and subsequent events taken a different course. But perhaps no mitigation of these attitudes was possible, given the political and psychological circumstances. In any

---

[18] Madison to Congress, April 19, 1809, Richardson, *Messages and Papers*, I, 457.

case, a chagrined President, whose excessive haste in accepting Erskine's assurances was embarrassingly evident to all, had to back down and reimpose the Non-Intercourse Act.

It soon became obvious that this measure, like the Embargo Act, had failed. Despite a vast amount of smuggling, the ban on exporting to British and French areas worked great hardship on the American economy. The act was repealed on May 1, 1810; in its place was substituted a new measure called Macon's Bill No. 2. It maintained the ban on British and French warships, but reopened trade, both imports and exports, with Britain and France. Like the Non-Intercourse Act, it had a bribe: a provision that if either of the belligerents revoked its measures against the United States before March 3, 1811, nonintercourse would be reinstated against the other belligerent unless it followed suit within three months. The United States was back where she had been before the Embargo Act; once again she could export to and import from any country in the world. Economic pressure had failed to move Britain or France.

The termination of America's restrictive trade measures took the country out of Napoleon's Continental System. Just as Canning had contemplated using the Non-Intercourse Act (through Erskine) to induce the United States to ban commerce with France, so now Napoleon manipulated Macon's Bill to cause the United States to stop trading with Britain. He instructed his Minister of Foreign Affairs, the Duke of Cadore, to write the American Minister in Paris that since Washington had ended the ban on trade with France, "the decrees of Berlin and Milan are revoked, and that after the 1st of November they will cease to have effect; it being understood that, in consequence of this declaration, the English shall revoke their orders in council, and renounce the new principles of blockade, which they have wished to establish; or that the United States, conformably to the [Macon] act you have just communicated, shall cause their rights to be respected by the English." [19]

What did this mean? Were the Decrees revoked? Were they to be revoked only if and when either England revoked her

---

[19] Cadore to John Armstrong, American Minister to France, Aug. 5, 1810, *American State Papers, Foreign Relations*, III, 387.

Orders or the United States "shall cause their rights to be respected by the English" (whatever that might mean)? According to Cadore himself, the revocation was "conditional"; its execution "will depend on the measures which the United States shall take if England persists in her orders of Council and in the principles of blockade which she has tried to establish."[20] But this significant qualification was not made known to the Americans. Washington chose to interpret the French note as meaning actual revocation. Secretary of State Smith contended that "the reservations under the expression 'it being understood' are not condition precedent affecting the operation of repeal"; Madison wrote that Cadore's letter "states an *actual* repeal of the French Decrees,"[21] but if he really believed this he was in error. Probably the President had doubts about revocation but believed that Napoleon's move offered opportunities too great to be risked by questioning the latter's good faith. The French move "promises us, at least, an extrication from the dilemma of a mortifying peace, or war with both the great belligerents," he thought.[22] The word "mortifying" is enlightening. Presumably Madison could not bear the thought of peace at the price of compromising, not American security or well-being, but American ideology as upheld by his Republican party.

On November 2 the President proclaimed that the "edicts of France have been so revoked as that they ceased on the said 1st day of the present month to violate the neutral commerce of the United States,"[23] and that consequently nonintercourse would be reinstated against Britain if she did not withdraw her Orders within three months. This was a crucial declaration that made war difficult to avoid. Yet the decision to issue it was taken when Washington's only news of the French action came from

---

[20] Cadore to Louis Turreau, Minister to the United States, Aug. 23, 1810, quoted in Brown, *Republic in Peril*, 23–24.

[21] Smith to Armstrong, Nov. 2, 1810, *ibid.*, 24; Madison to Pinkney, Oct. 30, 1810, *Letters and Other Writings of James Madison . . .* (New York, 1884), II, 487.

[22] Madison to Attorney-General Caesar A. Rodney, Sept. 30, 1810, quoted in Reginald Horsman, *The Causes of the War of 1812* (Philadelphia, 1962), 188.

[23] Proclamation of Nov. 2, 1810, Richardson, *Messages and Papers*, I, 482.

Pinkney (Monroe's successor as Minister in London) and from British newspapers—a frail foundation indeed.

When Great Britain did not respond in time, the United States on March 2, 1811 renewed against her the sections of the Non-Intercourse Act banning imports. Exports to Britain were still allowed; but since return cargoes were banned, voyages to England were less profitable and exports as well as imports fell off sharply.[24]

From that time the Madison administration persisted in maintaining, against much evidence, that the Berlin and Milan Decrees had been revoked. Imports from Great Britain continued to be prohibited. The official assurance doggedly adhered to—that France, the faithful ally of the Revolution, befriended the United States whereas the archfoe Great Britain was vindictively hostile —could not fail to prejudice public and congressional opinion in favor of war. Some Americans perceived this. The French have baited "a trap to catch us into a war with England," John Quincy Adams warned.[25] "It is my conviction that the great object of their policy is to entangle us in a war with England," Jonathan Russell, American Chargé d'Affaires in France, wrote James Monroe, now Secretary of State.[26] Probably the President understood this, but if he was not to have a "mortifying" peace he had to put pressure on Britain and take the chance that she would repeal the Orders before developments got out of hand.

Another factor, too, was inclining thoughts to war. This was the economic depression, resulting in large measure from the embargo and the subsequent American commercial restrictions. Most Americans, irrationally but understandably, blamed the old enemy, Great Britain, rather than the administration. They supported the Republican party's refusal to conform with the British

---

[24] Exports to Britain had the following values in millions of dollars: 1809–6; 1810–12; 1811–14; 1812–6. *Historical Statistics*, 551. Exports of United Kingdom produce to the United States had the following values: 1805– £11,010,000; 1806–£12,390,000; 1807–£11,850,000; 1808–£5,240,000; 1809– £7,260,000; 1810–£10,920,000; 1811–£1,840,000. Heckscher, *Continental System*, 245.

[25] Samuel E. Morison and Henry S. Commager, *The Growth of the American Republic* (New York, 1962), I, 401.

[26] Russell to Monroe, July 13, 1811, Mahan, *Sea Power, 1812*, I, 268.

maritime system, even though prosperity would have followed from doing so and hard times had come from declining to.

In 1810 and 1811 Congressional elections were held. Did Napoleon time the Cadore letter with an eye to them, and did it affect their outcome? The letter was dated August 5, 1810, the Berlin and Milan Decrees were to cease applying to the United States on November 1, and Madison proclaimed on November 2 that they had done so. Much of the voting occurred not long after one or another of those dates, and it is reasonable to suppose that voters were influenced by the reported French benevolence. Although the elections probably did not reflect an upsurge of belligerent opinion, and the swing to belligerency occurred largely after them, it is a fact that almost half the former members of Congress were defeated and that such war hawks as Henry Clay, John C. Calhoun, and Felix Grundy were newly elected to the House of Representatives. These and other warminded men took the leadership in strong and successful agitation for hostilities.

The twelfth Congress convened on November 4, 1811. Three days later Harrison defeated followers of Tecumseh and the Prophet at Tippecanoe, but at the cost of sixty-one American lives and more than a hundred wounded. The frontier rang with denunciations of the Indians and their supposed British backers; and the battle greatly strengthened the war hawks in Congress. Although impressment of Americans had fallen off, British maritime regulations were still applied rigorously, and the administration's insistence that the French Decrees had been repealed was as unwavering as ever. Early in the session the leading war hawk, Clay, was elected Speaker of the House; and as the days passed, one member of Congress after another, even oldfashioned Jeffersonians, reluctantly became convinced that nothing but fighting could head off national disgrace.[27] A massive change of mood was sweeping through Washington. This was bound to happen, sooner or later, if economic sanctions con-

---

[27] Norman K. Risjord, "1812: Conservatives, War Hawks, and the Nation's Honor," William and Mary Quarterly, XVIII (1961), 196–210. Henry Adams estimated that in early 1812 "Hardly one third of the members of Congress believed war to be their best policy" (History, VI [1809–1813], 170); yet in June the House voted for war 79 to 49.

tinued to fail and Republicans to stand humiliated before an unyielding Great Britain; and the war-hawk pressure only hastened the change.

Sometime in March the President himself swung over to the war party. His realization that 1812 was a presidential election year and that his nomination depended upon a congressional caucus acting in May must have influenced him. Influential too was the arrival of a dispatch on March 21 in which Britain reiterated that the French Decrees had not been repealed and intimated that she would maintain her Orders. On March 31 Monroe told a House committee that Madison wanted war before Congress adjourned in early July; and at the beginning of April the President secretly and urgently asked for an embargo to keep American ships at home where they would be safe in the event of hostilities. Congress complied on the 4th. War was inevitable unless Britain changed her ways.

That she would do so was still possible. Since 1793 she had been almost uninterruptedly at war with the most powerful military force in the world. Since 1807 trade with the United States, her most important market and a major source of supply, had been disrupted. A depression, which had started in 1811, gripped the country. Caused in its inception by matters other than American economic coercion, it was undoubtedly aggravated by the closing of the great trans-Atlantic market. From 1810 to 1811, when Madison reimposed nonimportation against Britain, British exports to the United States fell disastrously from £10,920,000 to £1,840,000.[28] Unemployment was soaring, factories were closing, and riots were breaking out. By the spring of 1812 thousands of manufacturers and workmen were petitioning Parliament to repeal the Orders in Council. A British army in Spain needed American food. Napoleon was about to invade Russia, and the Czar did not want British aid funneled away into an American war. On the other hand, backing down before the United States would not be politically easy, and among the Tories scorn for the former colonials now sabotaging Britain's

---

[28] Heckscher, *Continental System,* 245. In 1810 total exports amounted to £49,980,000; exports to the United States alone were thus almost 25 percent of the total.

struggle to save freedom for mankind, as they saw it, ran deep. To repeal the Orders, moreover, might tip the scales in favor of Napoleon at a moment of supreme crisis. The ministry temporized by issuing a statement on April 21: "if at any time thereafter the Berlin and Milan Decrees should be absolutely and unconditionally repealed, by some authentic act of the French Government, publicly promulgated, then the Orders in Council . . . shall without any further order be, and the same are hereby declared from thenceforth to be, wholly and absolutely revoked." [29] Unfortunately Americans interpreted this, not as a step toward repeal (which it was), but as yet another expression of British obduracy.

For several months the American Minister at Paris had been asking the French government for proof that the Berlin and Milan Decrees had been repealed, and also for compensation for the many American ships that France had seized or destroyed even after the alleged repeal. (As late as March 23, 1812 word reached Washington that a French squadron was sinking American ships on the high seas.) On hearing of the British declaration of April 21 he used it to bolster his demand. At about the same time Paris learned of the American embargo of April 4. Realizing that the United States was close to war and that one more nudge might push her over the edge, and perceiving too that further hedging about repeal would play into the hands of the Federalists and could even cost Madison the election, the French on May 10, 1812 gave Barlow a decree dated April 28, 1811 stating that as of November 1, 1810 the Berlin and Milan Decrees are "considered as not having existed in regard to American vessels." [30] This new decree was bogus; as Jonathan Russell, now Chargé at London, perceived, "There was something so very much like fraud on the face of it. . . ." [31] It had, in fact, been drawn up hastily in 1812 and predated.

News of the French move reached London at a critical time.

[29] Mahan, *Sea Power, 1812*, I, 270.

[30] *Ibid.*, 272.

[31] Jonathan Russell to Monroe, June 30, 1812, *ibid.*, 276. Bradford Perkins calls the decree "obviously fraudulent." *Prologue to War, England and the United States, 1805–1812* (Berkeley and Los Angeles, 1961), 336.

On May 11, the day after the fake decree was released, Prime Minister Spencer Perceval was shot in Parliament by a lunatic; he died on the spot. Shortly before this tragedy the House of Commons had begun to hear testimony for the repeal of the Orders in Council. From all over Britain witnesses gave evidence that industries were being ruined and that thousands of people were close to starvation because of the loss of the American market. Perceval's assassination at a crucial moment threw the government into confusion; not until June 8 could the new Prime Minister, Lord Liverpool, get Parliament's approval for his Cabinet. On the 16th Lord Castlereagh, the new Foreign Secretary, intimating that the French decree of April 28 partially met the British requirement, announced the forthcoming suspension of the Orders in Council; on the 23rd he declared them revoked.[32] The bogus French decree had given a convenient excuse for a step London wanted to take in any case.

The step did not come in time. On June 1 Madison had sent a special message to Congress asserting that Great Britain "presents a series of acts hostile to the United States as an independent and neutral nation." He cited impressment, the Orders in Council, and other maritime difficulties; he also mentioned the Indian warfare, attributing it to British instigation. "We behold, in fine, on the side of Great Britain a state of war against the United States, and on the side of the United States a state of peace toward Great Britain." What should be done he left to Congress to decide, "happy in the assurance that the decision will be worthy the enlightened and patriotic councils of a virtuous, a free, and a powerful nation."[33] The legislators did not disappoint him. The House voted for war 79 to 49; the Senate 19 to 13. The United States declared war on June 18, unaware that two days earlier Great Britain had announced the imminent repeal of the Orders in Council.

---

[32] The Orders were not legally to expire until Aug. 1, by which date it was thought that the United States, being apprised of Britain's move, would be able to reciprocate by ending the ban on British imports. Bradford Perkins, *Castlereagh and Adams, England and the United States, 1812–1823* (Berkeley and Los Angeles, 1964), 12n.

[33] Richardson, *Messages and Papers*, I, 499–505; the quoted passages are on pp. 500, 504, and 505.

If Perceval had not been killed would the British have repealed the Orders sooner, even in time to head off the American declaration? No firm answer can be given. It is conceivable that the removal of the Prime Minister, a strong supporter of the Orders, hastened repeal more than the resulting confusion delayed it. Even on the assumption that repeal would have come earlier without the assassination, impressment and the Indian menace would have remained as causes of rancor. Furthermore, at least by May the Madison administration and many members of Congress had become psychologically conditioned for hostilities; and they could not easily have readjusted their thinking to paths of peace. On the other hand Congress would have found it extremely awkward to declare war if the administration's basic contention of British hostility versus French cooperation had been suddenly undermined; and a change of only four votes in the Senate would have reversed the war vote there. In that event President Madison would appear in a different light. The historian of today would explain that the President's clever juggling with the alleged repeal of the French Decrees would, except for a madman's bullet, have produced a great triumph: the preservation of peace and yet British acceptance of American principles.

We may quickly pass over the history of the fighting. In Europe the war entered upon its climactic phase, now with a North American sideshow. Attempted American invasions of Canada failed disastrously. By 1814 the United States was struggling to defend herself. Britain held a huge area on both sides of Lake Michigan, another in Maine, and had smaller footings in several places along the coast. Napoleon, defeated, was on the island of Elba, and some of the Duke of Wellington's veterans were already in North America. The United States was in a desperate plight.

Meanwhile moves looking to peace had been taking place. The first occurred just a few days after the outbreak of war when the British Minister called on Madison to say goodbye. The President, perhaps regretting the plunge he had taken, talked of peace: Britain had only to revoke the Orders in Council (news that she had already done so had not reached Washington) and agree to negotiate about impressment. Nothing came of this informal offer; certainly Madison himself did not view it hopefully. In March 1813 Russia proposed mediation. Eagerly

Madison accepted. He appointed Secretary of the Treasury Albert Gallatin; James Bayard, a Federalist Senator; and John Quincy Adams, Minister to Russia, as American peace commissioners. But Britain, with events breaking rapidly in her favor, declined the Russian offer. In November 1813, in response to another move by St. Petersburg, she suggested direct negotiations. The United States accepted with alacrity. Madison appointed two more peace commissioners, Henry Clay and Jonathan Russell, thereby completing an exceptionally able delegation. The British negotiators were less distinguished: Vice-Admiral Lord Gambier; Henry Goulburn, an Undersecretary of the Colonial Office; and William Adams, an Admiralty lawyer. Formal negotiations commenced in Ghent in August 1814.

The Treaty of Ghent, signed December 24, 1814, restored all occupied territory and provided for several boundary commissions to settle the ownership of disputed areas. Although there would have been no British-occupied land to be restored if the United States had not embarked upon hostilities, and although the war's outcome contrasted sharply with earlier boasting about conquering Canada, this second British confirmation of American borders may have established American independence somewhat more securely than before. But the same result would have been achieved, tacitly if not formally, without the fighting.

The end of the war saw no corresponding confirmation of American principles. Most notably the treaty was silent on the vexed question of neutral rights, nor did it touch upon impressment. In 1813 Monroe had admonished the American commissioners with regard to impressment: "If the encroachment of Great Britain is not provided against, the United States have appealed to arms in vain. If your efforts to accomplish it should fail, all further negotiations will cease, and you will return home without delay."[34] Yet so low were American fortunes driven that the following year the Secretary of State had to tell the commissioners to drop this *sine qua non*, if necessary to end the fighting.[35]

As the future was to show, however, impressment had in fact

[34] Monroe to Gallatin, Adams, and Bayard, April 15, 1813, Perkins, *Castlereagh*, 50–51.

[35] Monroe to commissioners, June 27, 1814, *ibid.*, 54.

come to an end. Not because of the War of 1812, but because of changing needs and legal opinions on the part of Great Britain and other great powers in the coming decades, Britain never again impressed an American. In time, too, she formally recognized the rights of expatriation and naturalization. And although future Anglo-American disputes were to occur over neutral rights, developing views of international law during the nineteenth century caused Great Britain to accept an interpretation of freedom of the seas close to the American one. But again this cannot be attributed to the War of 1812.

The commercial articles of the Jay-Grenville Treaty had expired in 1807. After peace was concluded, some of the negotiators stayed on at Ghent to make a new commercial treaty, signed in 1815. Limited to four years, it basically revived the provisions of the earlier treaty.[36] But no more than that treaty did it open up the West Indian commerce, attainment of which was to be a future objective of American policy.

The boundary commissions established at Ghent had varying success. One commission divided the Passamaquoddy Islands between Britain and America; another set the line from the St. Lawrence River to the western shore of Lake Huron but could not agree on the line from there to the northwest corner of the Lake of the Woods (west of Lake Superior); a third failed to determine the boundary from the source of the St. Croix River to the St. Lawrence. Despite the failures, these commissions, like those under the Jay-Grenville Treaty, set precedents for several major Anglo-American arbitrations during the rest of the century.

In one matter the war did produce an immediate victory for the United States, although the same result would have come in due course in any event. At the outset of the peace negotiations, Great Britain had made the establishment of a large Indian buffer zone in the northwest a *sine qua non* of peace. She did not long persist in the demand, and her restoration of the area to the United States disillusioned the red man. Tecumseh was killed in 1813. At varying dates in 1814 and 1815 the Indian

---

[36] The American negotiators were Gallatin and Clay; the British, Goulburn, Adams, and Frederick J. Robinson, vice-president of the Board of Trade.

tribes signed treaties with Washington renouncing the British tie and accepting American rule. Some treaties provided for the sale of land, and in general, just as the Jay-Grenville Treaty caused the Indians to realize that they must leave Ohio, so the Treaty of Ghent had the effect of persuading them to retreat still farther west. For the United States this represented another release from British entanglements.

Two other agreements should be mentioned. The end of the war found both countries building warships on the Great Lakes. Washington believed, mistakenly, that Britain intended to push ahead to naval supremacy there. Since the United States was in a typical postwar mood of economy and would be able to construct ships on the lakes faster than Britain in the event of a future crisis, the administration hoped to make an agreement with London to stop the building. The British were willing to go along. They too were tired of heavy expenditures, which they had been incurring for many more war years than had the Americans. The folly of a naval race was so apparent (except to the Canadians) that a sort of standstill arrangement was easily negotiated, paradoxical though this might seem after the years of controversy and war. By the Rush-Bagot Convention, concluded in Washington in April 1817, each country was to maintain not more than one small armed ship on Lake Champlain, another on Lake Ontario, and two on all the upper lakes.[37] Construction of additional ships was to stop. Since the convention said nothing about armies or land fortification, its overall military significance was slight. For many years to come the boundary remained fortified, the scene of occasional minor fighting.

The second postwar agreement, the Convention of 1818, signed in London in October, tidied up other loose ends left over from Ghent. One of the world's great natural resources was the fisheries off Newfoundland, Nova Scotia, and New Brunswick. In colonial days Americans had fished within territorial waters in those areas and had dried their catches on the coasts. The "liberty" to do these things, conferred by the treaty of 1783, had terminated, so Britain contended correctly, with the

---

[37] Richard Rush was the Acting Secretary of State, Charles Bagot the British Minister at Washington.

War of 1812. The United States denied the contention. British cruisers began to arrest American fishermen in the northern waters. An early phase of what was to become a frequently dangerous Anglo-American dispute took shape. The Convention of 1818 gave American fishermen "for ever" the "liberty" to fish in specified waters and also the "liberty for ever" to cure on specified coasts; it stated further that on all other portions of the coast they would be allowed to land in order to obtain wood, water, shelter, and repairs, but "for no other purpose whatever."

Three other matters the Convention dealt with. The northern boundary of the Louisiana Purchase of 1803 had not been clearly defined. The Convention set the line at the forty-ninth parallel from the Lake of the Woods to the Rocky Mountains; as for the area west of the mountains (as regards which the negotiators could not agree upon a definitive settlement), the Convention provided that for ten years it should be "free and open" to both countries. The Convention renewed the commercial agreement of 1815 for ten years. Finally, it provided that a dispute as to whether Britain should pay compensation for slaves taken away by her troops during the War of 1812 was to be referred to some friendly state or sovereign (the Czar of Russia was selected) for decision; the Czar decided that Britain should pay compensation for some of these slaves.[38]

Largely because of the strengthening of her government and economy the United States had achieved a somewhat more equal relationship with Great Britain, though she had failed, it is true, to win recognition from London of the doctrines she so ardently espoused and to gain trading rights with the West Indies. The two conventions of 1817 and 1818, like the Ghent agreements, reflected and to a limited extent contributed to America's stronger position. The young republic could now more confidently encounter Britain in other places than the high seas.

---

[38] Hunter Miller, ed., *Treaties and Other International Acts of the United States of America* (Washington, 1931–1943), II, 658–61. The American negotiators were Rush (now Minister to Great Britain) and Gallatin (now Minister to France); the British, Goulburn and Robinson.

CHAPTER III

Setting the Stage for Expansion:
The Monroe Doctrine and West Indian Commerce

B Y ABOUT 1815 America's population and economy had be- come large enough and her political system well established enough so that her future as a strong country could not be doubted. She had come through the war, if not unscathed, at least unconquered. For the time being a mood of confident nationalism replaced the earlier divisions.

Beyond the settled areas along the coast stretched thousands of miles of territory unoccupied save by infrequent bands of Indians, far fewer in number than the terrible foe sharing the continent with them. Undistracted by war, Americans could devote more energy to moving south and west. They thronged into the still empty spaces east of the Mississippi, they began to occupy the enormous expanses of the Louisiana Purchase, before long they went still farther afield: toward Spanish colonies to the south and British colonies to the north, into the Mexican states of Texas and California, and into the Oregon country, whose ownership as between Great Britain and the United States had been left to future decision by the Convention of 1818.

Just as America's continuing struggle for independence and her championing of American ideology had led time after time to crises with Great Britain, so her territorial expansion led to clashes with that same archfoe. War did not come again, but frequently it seemed close. The new focus of Anglo-American discord was not on the high seas, dominated by the British navy; and it might be thought that the United States, moving west away from Britain, would not have encountered British power. Such was not the case. The only country that could hope to contain the expanding republic was Great Britain. Most of

Spain's once great strength in the New World was soon to collapse, and France had no adequate North American base with which to threaten the United States. Britain alone had the power and the bases.

She had also the will. The stronger the republic, the greater the menace to the British North American and West Indian colonies; even the Central and South American colonies might be endangered. Britain too was an expanding country; she did not want Americans to preempt bases at San Francisco, Puget Sound, Honolulu, and Central America that some day she might need herself. Furthermore an expanding United States could be expected to develop formidable economic strength, and therefore to be an unwelcome commercial rival at a time when Britain's rapid industrialization made foreign trade increasingly vital to her. Then too a dramatically successful republic might seduce Britons away from their customary allegiance to Lord and King, and set in motion a slide toward democracy in Great Britain herself. Nor should one overlook the deep-rooted dislike of colonials who had been so impertinent as not only to rebel but to hold their own in two wars against their former rulers.

These were the principal reasons why Britain sought to thwart American expansion. For many years during the nineteenth century she tried to bolster up areas around the periphery of the republic. One must not suppose, however, that this was her major foreign policy aim. Much more than on the United States her attention was centered on Europe; even her new empire rising in Asia and Africa was more important to her. Consequently she was seldom willing to engage much of her strength in order to contain American expansion, however unwelcome it may have been.

But if Britain's policy toward the United States was low on the former's scale of priorities, it was very high on the American scale. In its foreign policy calculations Washington almost always had to consider, before anything else, the probable British reaction. The State Department kept its attention riveted on London to a much greater extent than on any other capital.

The various agreements and arbitrations that followed the Treaty of Ghent improved British-American relations somewhat. So did the final severance of the British tie with the Indians, who consequently were never again an important cause of discord. More basic was the gradual erosion over the years of revolutionary fervor in the United States; and on the other hand the slow growth in Great Britain of a less condescending attitude toward the upstart republic. Time was bound to bring these developments, but for many years the changes were minimal. Although trans-Atlantic hostility was less intense than it had been before the War of 1812, it was still strong. Little liking was lost in either country for the other.

Tempting areas for acquisition lay close at hand in Spanish Florida and Cuba, and before the United States faced west she faced south. In Florida, indeed over almost all Latin America, Spanish power was rotting. Few developments in international affairs are more conducive to friction than the appearance of a power vacuum consequent upon the dissolution of a great political structure; and British-American rivalry over the spoils of Spanish empire led to much stress. Great Britain preferred Spanish to American rule in the Caribbean because a weak Spain would pose less of a threat to her own colonies than would the rising republic.

Even before peace was restored in 1814 the United States had started pushing against Florida. Spain was in no hurry to get out, and Washington suspected that Great Britain was behind her recalcitrance. In March 1818 a spectacular affair precipitated matters. General Andrew Jackson with a small army burst into Florida, ostensibly to rout out border-raiding Indians. He took some Spanish posts; and, as though to make as much trouble as possible, he seized two Britons who had been associating with the tribes, Robert Ambrister and Alexander Arbuthnot, and executed them. All this he did without definite orders from Washington. But John Quincy Adams, Secretary of State under President James Monroe, defended the incursions as justified in self-defense.

Spain protested angrily. More worrying to Washington was what Britain would do. Her press reacted with violent denunciations of a Yankee atrocity. But fortunately Ambrister and Arbuthnot were not government agents and Whitehall decided that their activities among the Indians did not justify a protest. Convinced that she could not count on British help, Spain ceded Florida to the United States by a treaty signed in 1819. The treaty, which was transcontinental in scope, had another important provision. It set the northwestern boundary of Spain's North American possessions at the forty-second parallel; thereby it strengthened American claims to the Oregon country that, it will be recalled, had just been declared "free and open" to British and American settlers by the Convention of 1818. Not many years later Washington began to push these claims vigorously.

With Florida gone, Spanish Cuba lay exposed. London feared that the momentum of American expansion would propel the United States into the nearby island. Cuban opponents of Spanish rule were already asking Washington for assurances that their island would be annexed if they rebelled against Spain. "I hope I may not have to tell you," the new British Foreign Secretary, George Canning (he succeeded Castlereagh, who committed suicide in 1822), wrote the Duke of Wellington in November 1822, "that the Yankees have occupied Cuba, a blow which I do not know how we can prevent. . . ."[1] The United States, however, did not want another war with Britain, and was also afraid of stirring up agitation over slavery so soon after the Missouri Compromise of 1820 had calmed it down for the moment. But Americans were no less apprehensive than the British. They feared that Britain, having lost the buffer of Florida, would annex Cuba to acquire another; and the appearance in late 1822 of a British squadron off the island heightened their alarm. With each country eyeing the other warily, neither took the fatal step into Cuba. No rebellion against Spain occurred for many years to come. For the time being Cuban dangers diminished.

By early 1823 most of the other Spanish colonies in the New World had practically secured their independence, and the United States—but not Great Britain or the Continental countries—had recognized several of them. Their recovery by Spain, acting alone, was hopeless, the more so because Spain herself was in a disturbed state as a result of a rebellion that had forced the King, Ferdinand VII, to agree to a liberal constitution.

---

[1] Bradford Perkins, *Castlereagh and Adams, England and the United States, 1812–1813* (Berkeley and Los Angeles, 1964), 308.

This attack on the principle of monarchy alarmed the great Continental powers, which were joined together in the Holy Alliance; at the Congress of Verona in 1822 they denounced the constitution despite vehement British protests. France, as their deputy, now prepared to invade Spain to suppress the constitution. The British people could not passively accept such an expansion either of French power or of absolutism. Canning warned France not to provoke Britain to war. Nevertheless a French army crossed the Pyrenees in April 1823 and quickly suppressed the liberals. Rumors now spread that the Holy Alliance would convene a congress on Latin America, and even that France, perhaps aided by the Continental powers, would send troops all the way to Latin America to check the revolutionary tide there.

To the United States the developments in Latin America were thrilling vindications of her own republicanism and liberty. She anticipated profitable trade with the new countries now that the Spanish colonial monopoly was broken, and she reacted with horror at the defeat of liberalism in Spain, and with dread at the prospect of European invasion of the New World. For once, Britain's policy elicited her approval. "The course which you have taken in the great politics of Europe," the British Minister at Washington wrote the Foreign Secretary in May 1823, "has had the effect of making the English almost popular in the United States. The improved tone of public feeling is very perceptible, and even [Secretary of State John Quincy] Adams has caught a something of the soft infection."[2]

With British and American interests apparently running parallel, Canning made a bold move. Conversing in mid-August 1823 with the American Minister, Richard Rush, he asked bluntly whether the United States would go "hand in hand" with Britain to deal with the gathering storm. On August 20 he proposed that the two countries publicly declare the principles they supported as regards the Spanish-American colonies.

For ourselves [he said] we have no disguise.
1. We conceive the recovery of the Colonies by Spain to be hopeless.

---

[2] Stratford Canning to George Canning, May 8, 1823, Dexter Perkins, *The Monroe Doctrine, 1823–1826* (Cambridge, Mass., 1927), 60.

2. We conceive the question of the Recognition of them, as Independent States, to be one of time and circumstances.
3. We are, however, by no means disposed to throw any impediment in the way of an arrangement between them, and the mother country by amicable negotiation.
4. We aim not at the possession of any portion of them ourselves.
5. We could not see any portion of them transferred to any other Power, with indifference.[3]

After so many years of friction and two outright wars, did Canning really believe that Great Britain and the United States could cooperate together to the extent he was suggesting? In a famous speech in Liverpool at this time he declared hopefully, "The force of blood again prevails, and the daughter and the mother stand together against the world."[4] Canning did not want a permanent ideological division between the Old World and the New; he intended his Liverpool statement to be a reply to a July 4 address by John Quincy Adams in which the latter stressed the differences between Europe and the United States. No doubt he did sincerely desire a measure of cooperation with Washington and thought it not impossible.

Yet Canning was too perspicacious to expect a sudden reversal of relations with the trans-Atlantic republic. He called his démarche a "flirtation." A flirtation it was, never even approaching a marriage. Although he did have a faint hope for some sort of British-American reconciliation, he had much stronger hopes of achieving other goals. For one thing, the Tories could not endure another such humiliation as had been administered when France, flouting British warnings, invaded Spain. Furthermore British manufacturers, like American, relished the prospect of an enormous market opening up to their products, after some three centuries of near monopoly by Spain. Although Britain hoped strongly that the new Latin American countries would turn to monarchical forms of government, she would accept them as republics rather than see them conquered by the Holy

---

[3] Canning to Rush, Aug. 20, 1823, William R. Manning, ed., *Diplomatic Correspondence of the United States Concerning the Independence of the Latin-American Nations* (New York, 1925), III, 1478.
[4] Speech of Aug. 25, 1823, Perkins, *Castlereagh*, 319.

Alliance. Acting alone, she might not be able to frighten the allies into calling off an invasion of Latin America, any more than she had been able to dissuade France from attacking Spain. And if France, helped or not by other Continental monarchies, did attack across the ocean, Britain could scarcely avoid going to war. Canning must have read with interest the report of the "soft infection" in the United States. Perhaps a dramatic stand in concert with that country would give the Continental monarchies pause. At any rate the United States was the only country that could conceivably be cajoled to Britain's side.

Besides these considerations Canning could not have been oblivious of another possible benefit. "We aim not at the possession of any portion of them ourselves" was the fourth point of his proposed declaration. No doubt he was thinking of Cuba. An American renunciation of intent to take that island would be a major achievement; it would strengthen both the Tory party and British security in the Caribbean Sea. Probably the Foreign Secretary's thoughts embraced other former and present Spanish lands as well, notably Texas, which was already casting an enticing spell over not a few Americans. But it was Cuba that seemed to stand next on the American list, and Canning's concern is shown by the fact that two years later he made another attempt to tie Washington's hands. In August 1825 he proposed that the United States, Great Britain, and France each sign a disclaimer of intent to take the island.[5] But nothing came of this move.

Canning's suggestion of 1823 came as a surprise to Rush. He responded cautiously that before any joint action could be taken, Britain would have to put herself on the same footing as the United States by recognizing the new Latin American countries. In subsequent interviews he stuck to this demand, whereas the Foreign Secretary insisted on his second point—that recognition was a matter of "time and circumstances." With negotiations deadlocked, Rush asked Washington for instructions. Canning, apparently dropping hope of assistance from the

---

[5] Canning to Rufus King (American Minister at London), Aug. 7 and 21, 1825, Manning, *Diplomatic Correspondence*, III, 1557–60, 1562–63.

United States, turned to the French Ambassador, Prince Jules de Polignac. He wrote the main points of several conversations with him in a memorandum, the so-called Polignac memorandum, which Polignac virtually accepted on October 9, 1823, under what amounted to a British threat. The memorandum stated that no country except Spain should have favorable commercial treatment in Latin America, that England would be forced to recognize the rebels if a European power intervened in the Spanish-colonial dispute, and that England did not want a congress on Latin American affairs and would not participate unless the United States was invited. This step made the British position so clear that it ended any possibility of European intervention in Latin America. Canning sent a copy of the memorandum to Rush, telling him that he would have been glad to act with the United States but had been unable to wait any longer. "You will see," he concluded rather condescendingly, "that we were not unmindful of your claim to be heard: but I flatter myself that neither you nor we shall now have to lift our voice against any of the designs which were apprehended a few months ago."[6]

The Foreign Secretary, it is clear, was well pleased with himself. He would have been less pleased had he known what had happened across the Atlantic three weeks earlier. Rush's account of his talks with the Foreign Secretary reached Washington in early October. The startling British offer caused tremendous excitement and intense discussion within the administration. President Monroe also consulted the two elder statesmen of his Republican party, Thomas Jefferson and James Madison. Both advised him to accept the offer. Jefferson's reply, however, laid down a charter of two worlds, just such a charter as Canning proscribed: the question raised, he wrote, "is the most momentous which has ever been offered to my contemplation since that of Independence. . . . America, North and South, has a set of interests distinct from those of Europe, and peculiarly her own. . . . While the last is laboring to become the domicile of

---

[6] Canning to Rush, Dec. 13, 1823, *ibid.*, 1506–1507.

despotism, our endeavor should surely be, to make our hemisphere that of freedom."[7]

But the Cabinet was cautious. The members' distrust of Britain was vigorously fanned by a dispatch from Rush dated October 10 and received November 16, 1823, saying that Canning seemed to have backed away from his offer.[8] In particular Secretary Adams, a confirmed Anglophobe whose dislike of Canning stemmed in part from the latter's hostility during the years before the War of 1812, suspected that the Foreign Secretary's main purpose was to keep the United States out of Cuba and Texas. He perceived, too, that the joint declaration would tend to unite the Atlantic world, precisely what he wanted to avoid. Adams argued for separate action: the United States should not "come in as a cock-boat in the wake of the British man-of-war."[9] His colleagues agreed; and the President, with considerable help from the Secretary, drew up a statement that in time came to be called the Monroe Doctrine. Washington did not then know that London had abandoned the proposed Anglo-American cooperation (any more than Canning knew that the

---

[7] Jefferson to Monroe, Oct. 24, 1823, Andrew A. Lipscomb and Albert E. Bergh, eds., *The Writings of Thomas Jefferson* (Washington, 1903–1904), XV, 477. Theodore R. Schellenberg, "Jeffersonian Origins of the Monroe Doctrine," *Hispanic American Historical Review*, XIV (1934), 1–31. See also Madison to Monroe, Oct. 30, 1823, *Letters and Other Writings of James Madison . . . Published by Order of Congress* (New York, 1884), III, 339: "It is particularly fortunate that the policy of Great Britain, though guided by calculations different from ours, has presented a co-operation for an object the same with ours. With that co-operation we have nothing to fear from the rest of Europe, and with it the best assurance of success to our laudable views. There ought not, therefore, to be any backwardness, I think, in meeting her in the way she has proposed; keeping in mind, of course, the spirit and forms of the Constitution in every step taken in the road to war, which must be the last step if those short of war should be without avail."

[8] Arthur P. Whitaker, *The United States and the Independence of Latin America, 1800–1830* (Baltimore, 1941), 494–502; for the effect of the dispatch on the Cabinet see *ibid.*, 494–502. See also Charles Francis Adams, ed., *Memoirs of John Quincy Adams, Comprising Portions of His Diary from 1795 to 1848* (Philadelphia, 1874–1877), VI, 188.

[9] Perkins, *Monroe Doctrine, 1823–1826*, 74.

United States was shortly to move unilaterally when he had the discussions with Polignac in October), so that it is barely possible that the President did not view his remarks as closing the door to the British. A few days after the message was written, but before it was delivered, Adams instructed Rush that if Britain would recognize the new governments, and if an emergency should arise in which a joint statement would influence the Continental powers, then the Minister should notify Washington, and the United States would "cheerfully join in any act by which we may contribute to support the cause of human freedom, and the Independence of the South American Nations."[10] To that limited extent, at least, Washington did envisage the possibility of concerted action with Great Britain.

In his annual message to Congress, December 2, 1823, Monroe made three points that have come to be known collectively as the Monroe Doctrine. First, he declared that "the American continents . . . are henceforth not to be considered as subjects for future colonization by any European powers."[11] Russia had recently been making claims relating to the American northwest, but the noncolonization section of the doctrine was directed at Great Britain, the only European country then considering the acquisition of colonies in the New World—Cuba possibly, parts of the Oregon country very probably. The President went on to assert that "The political system of the allied powers is essentially different . . . from that of America," and that therefore "we should consider any attempt on their part to extend their system to any portion of this hemisphere as dangerous to our peace and safety."[12] This was a general principle. As for the particular issue of the moment, that is, Latin America, Monroe declared:

With the existing colonies or dependencies of any European power we have not interfered and shall not interfere. But with the Governments who have declared their independence and maintained it, and

---

[10] Adams to Rush, Nov. 29, 1823, Manning, *Diplomatic Correspondence*, I, 212.

[11] James D. Richardson, ed., *A Compilation of the Messages and Papers of the Presidents, 1789–1897* (Washington, 1899), II, 209.

[12] *Ibid.*, 218; he repeated this warning in a later passage. *Ibid.*, 219.

whose independence we have, on great consideration and on just principles, acknowledged, we could not view any interposition for the purpose of oppressing them, or controlling in any other manner their destiny, by any European power in any other light than as the manifestation of an unfriendly disposition toward the United States.

Finally, the President reiterated the traditional American policy, "adopted at an early stage . . . not to interfere in the internal concerns" of Europe.[13]

Whether deliberately or not, Monroe had committed the United States only as regards the small number of "existing colonies or dependencies" (Canning's proposed disclaimer had been much broader, relating to former as well as present colonies); at the same time he was warning Europe to keep hands off the much larger number of countries which had declared independence, off, in fact, "any portion of either continent."[14] As far as President Monroe was concerned, the United States was free to expand over this large area.

The immediate practical consequences of these statements were slight; it was the Polignac memorandum, not Monroe's declaration, that warned off the Holy Alliance. Nor did the statements become a "doctrine" basic to United States foreign policy until much later. In 1823 Canning's overture prompted the Americans to make a move that almost certainly they would not have made otherwise. Cleverly they seized the opportunity and blew a loud republican bugle call. Monroe's "lecture" to Europe, as Adams called it, was about all the famous doctrine amounted to at the outset, though it did earn the United States a little easy credit in Latin America.

The President's pronouncements exposed Canning to taunts of having been tricked by Washington. To counter them and to bolster Britain's standing in Latin America, the Foreign Secretary published a paraphrase of the Polignac memorandum in February 1824. He was anxious to prevent the United States from arranging a New World association closed to Britain and the Continent. "The avowed pretension of the United States to put themselves at the head of the confederacy of all the Americans

13 *Ibid.*, 218–19.
14 *Ibid.*, 219.

and to sway that Confederacy against Europe is *not* a pretension identified with our interests, or one that we can countenance or tolerate," he asserted firmly. More irksome was the noncolonization principle, and this Canning rejected "in the most unequivocal manner. . . ."[15] By that time he must have realized that he had made a mistake by approaching Rush before Britain was ready to recognize the new Latin American countries. But Canning tried to put the best face possible on the affair, and boasted, "I called the New World into existence to redress the balance of the Old."[16] His boast was justified. Monroe's lecture notwithstanding, the Latin American countries realized that they owed much more to Great Britain than to the United States.

But Canning's accomplishments did not include an improvement in Anglo-American relations. His incautious flirtation, like many others, served mainly to increase mutual suspicions. In 1824 each of the two English-speaking countries viewed the other with deep distrust.

The Monroe Doctrine set the stage for United States expansion in the indirect sense that Washington avoided a commitment not to expand, and also in the sense that the warning against European colonization reserved the New World, on paper at least, to the United States. During the 1820s Washington was also occupied with commercial expansion; most notably it was striving to reopen trade with the British West Indies.

It will be recalled that the Convention of 1815, renewed in 1818 (and indefinitely extended in 1827), provided for trade between the United States and British possessions in Europe, and between the United States and the British East Indies, on a nondiscriminatory basis. American ships were still banned from British West Indian and North American ports; however, goods went back and forth across the international boundary by land.

---

[15] Canning to Sir Charles R. Vaughan (British Minister to the United States), Feb. 18, 1826, Harold W. V. Temperley, *The Foreign Policy of Canning, 1822–1827; England, the Neo-Holy Alliance, and the New World* (London, 1925), 158; Canning to Stratford Canning, May 31, 1824, Perkins, *Castlereagh,* 341. See also Temperley, *Canning,* 127, and "The Later American Policy of George Canning," *American Historical Review,* XI (1906), 779–97.

[16] Temperley, *Canning,* 154; the remark was made on Dec. 12, 1826.

Although the United States and the West Indies constituted a natural trading area within which a considerable commerce had flourished before the Revolution, mercantilistic thinking favored a colonial monopoly. Besides, Great Britain saw every reason to bar Americans, who had rebelled in 1776 and attacked her in 1812, from empire privileges. However, since the West Indies did need American goods, she permitted American ships to carry certain articles to Bermuda, and British ships to trade between the United States and the British West Indies and North American colonies.

This was a situation most unwelcome to that intense nationalist, Secretary of State Adams. Under his prodding, Congress passed progressively stiffer measures retaliating against Britain. These culminated in an act of 1820 closing American ports to British ships coming from any British possession in the New World, and also to British West Indian goods not coming directly from the place of origin. As a result, commerce ceased altogether between America and the West Indies. This pleased British North American exporters of lumber and fish, now free of American competitors; but it greatly displeased West Indians who wanted American goods, and Americans whose products no longer had a West Indian market.

Under pressure from the influential West Indian planters and British manufacturers, worried about losing the profitable American market, Great Britain in 1822 opened certain ports in the West Indies to United States ships carrying enumerated goods. These ships were permitted to carry back to America most West Indian products. Thereupon the United States reopened her ports to British ships with produce of the British West Indian and North American colonies, but she did not abolish the higher tonnage dues and tariff rates imposed on foreign ships and produce. She attempted to justify the discriminations by pointing to British imperial preference, as a result of which American products imported into the West Indies were taxed more heavily than British products. Washington insisted that if the American discriminations were to end, so should the British. This was an untenable position since the United States had no more right to dictate conditions of inter-British commerce than Britain did as regards conditions of interstate commerce. Personal factors made the argument sharper, for George Canning—that "implacable and rancorous enemy of the United States," John Quincy Adams harshly called him[17]—was still Foreign Secretary, and in 1825 the redoubtable Adams entered the White House.

In 1825 Britain made a new offer. She considerably expanded the 1822 list of enumerated articles that American ships could carry to her colonies, but made the continued admission of these ships conditional upon the removal of the American discriminations. But Adams refused to abandon measures that were mainly his own handiwork.

Several years of fruitless argument ensued. Trade continued; so did the American discriminations against British ships and goods, and the British preferences on goods coming from British lands. In 1826 and 1827 Great Britain, exasperated with Adams's uncompromising stand, reclosed her West Indian and North American ports to American ships. In return the United States prohibited imports of colonial products in British ships. Once again all commerce within this natural trading area came to a stop. Adams did make some gestures toward a settlement, but they came to nothing.

Not until Andrew Jackson became President in 1829 was progress made. Adams no longer controlled foreign policy; Canning had died in 1827. Notwithstanding his anti-British record, particularly evident in his hasty execution of the two British subjects in Florida, Jackson showed greater flexibility than his predecessor had. He simply abandoned part of the American position and proposed agreement on the basis of the British offer of 1825: the United States would admit British ships from the West Indian and North American colonies without discrimination, provided that Britain would open her ports on the terms proposed in 1825. Without much ado Britain agreed.

Jackson's "Reciprocity of 1830," as it was called, represented a fair compromise. The United States no longer insisted that her products must be taxed at the same rates as products traded within the British empire; and Great Britain abandoned her original insistence that American commerce with the West Indies

---

[17] Samuel F. Bemis, *John Quincy Adams and the Foundations of American Foreign Policy* (New York, 1949), 445.

must be limited to a small number of enumerated products carried in British ships. In a way, however, it was a considerable achievement for the United States to have pushed herself back into a British trading preserve. By preparing the ground for commercial expansion with the West Indies she realized a major objective of her foreign policy.

CHAPTER IV

Border Disputes

B Y THE MID-1820s the danger of European intervention in Latin America had vanished for the time being. The danger, which never had been great, had been dissipated by Foreign Secretary Canning's firm stand, slightly assisted by President Monroe's embryonic doctrine. Thereafter the United States, no longer on the defensive, was in a stronger position to undertake the main business at hand: expansion over an almost unoccupied continent and into a few strategic places outside North America. The prospects for commercial expansion also became brighter in consequence of Andrew Jackson's Reciprocity of 1830.

The new expansion, occurring mainly in the 1840s, took a westward course, though before 1842 it seemed about to go north and in the 1850s the pressure was on Central America. Southern expansion, as we have seen, was opposed by Great Britain. No less did she seek to curb America's westward expansion across the continent, and also America's moves against British North America and Central America.

The British-American confrontation took the form of three sharp clashes, each threatening the peace: the first arising over minor Canadian rebellions in 1837, and complicated by the aftermath of the Texan revolution of 1836; the second over the Oregon country in the far northwest, and entangled with events leading to the Mexican War; the third over Central America. The first two were ended by major Anglo-American treaties. The settlement of the third was more complex, but it represented a turning point. Relations between the two countries improved and perhaps a serious threat of war would never have arisen again had not the Civil War broken out. That tragic event revived

49

British hopes of containing the United States, because nothing less than a North American balance of power appeared on the verge of being realized, produced by the disruption of the union itself. The present chapter will deal mainly with the problems occasioned by the Canadian rebellions; the following two chapters with the Oregon and Mexican questions and the complications in Central America.

In 1836 Sam Houston's Texan forces rebelled successfully against Mexico; in 1837 rebellions, quickly suppressed, occurred in Upper and Lower Canada. The Texans immediately declared independence and then petitioned Washington for annexation. American expansion to the southwest appeared imminent. Not only that, but the disturbances in Canada seemed to presage the crumbling of British power in North America. These thrilling events sent a fever of expansion coursing through American veins. An intoxicating vision of American institutions and rule spreading irresistibly gripped people's imagination. Within a few years Manifest Destiny would be at its height—the feeling that destiny itself manifestly ordained the United States to expand at least to the Pacific Ocean, perhaps over all North America, perhaps even farther.

Britain's main concern was for her North American colonies but she was worried too by the decay in Mexico that threatened to remove that country as a barrier to the United States. She tried to repair the breach by propping up Texas. A stronger Texas could check an American advance to the southwest, and someday might even serve to balance the United States in classic European style. Furthermore Texas could provide an alternative source of supply for cotton, a commodity essential to Britain's vitally important textile industry. A low-tariff Texas could become a large British market and, by example, stimulate the southern states to press more strongly for United States tariff reduction. Finally Texas, if pushed hard, might abolish slavery. Having freed the slaves in her own empire, Britain wanted them freed everywhere, partly for humanitarian reasons, partly to be rid of slave-labor competition. As a minimum, she wanted to suppress the infamous African slave trade. Most of these hopes would vanish should Washington heed Texan pleas and annex the shaky new republic.

To Britain's relief President Andrew Jackson thought it both prudent and good politics to spurn the Texan suit. Not until the end of his administration, in 1837, did he venture even to extend recognition. His successor, Martin Van Buren, likewise refused to annex. Northerners wanted no extension of slavery, and annexation might have precipitated another national crisis like the one settled by the Missouri Compromise. Thus Great Britain was granted a period of grace within which to work for Texan independence.

Meanwhile she confronted more urgent matters to the north, where by 1837 a backlog of altercations had developed. Several sections of the long boundary were in dispute. It will be recalled that one of the commissions set up under the Treaty of Ghent had failed to determine the line from Lake Huron to the northwest corner of the Lake of the Woods, and that another commission had been unable to agree on the line from the source of the St. Croix River in Maine to the St. Lawrence River. Under a treaty of 1827 the northeastern boundary had been referred to the arbitration of the King of the Netherlands; the United States had rejected his recommendation of 1831. Other difficulties related to identifying "the Northwestern-most Head of Connecticut River" (as designated in the peace treaty of 1783), and to the discovery that the boundary along the forty-fifth latitude had been inaccurately surveyed. Above Lake Champlain, at Rouses Point, the United States had built an important fort; it was just north of the true line. Moreover the Oregon country was still open to joint occupation, with all the perils of that indecisive situation.

On both sides of the Atlantic memories of the Revolution and the War of 1812 were vivid. Although republican fervor was less intense in the United States than formerly, the dislike of lordly, overbearing Britain was sharp; on the other hand, British scorn for democratic, uncultured, aggressive, slave-owning America was no less intense. Americans were furious over the supercilious attitudes expressed in magazines and books by a stream of British visitors; Britons were indignant over America's failure to protect their writers by a copyright law, and over the repudiation by several states of their debts to Englishmen in consequence of the panic of 1837. Large numbers of unemployed Americans, whom anti-British agitators could hope to incite, added to the latent perils. It was not a time when the two countries could safely indulge in rivalry over Texas and in controversies along the northern border.

Fortunately that perennial British-American safety valve, the intertwining of their economies, was becoming increasingly effective. By 1830 British-American commercial relations were "something unique between two sovereign States."[1] In 1836 the United States exported $58,000,000 worth of goods to the United Kingdom out of an export total of $124,000,000—almost half of all American exports going to that one country. In 1839 the comparable figures were $57,000,000 and $112,000,000, over half American exports going to the United Kingdom; in 1840, $55,000,000 and $124,000,000. As for imports, the United States in 1836 imported $76,000,000 worth of goods from the United Kingdom, as against total imports of $177,000,000, between half and a third of the total thus coming from that one country; in 1839, $65,000,000 against $156,000,000; in 1840, $33,000,000 against $98,000,000.[2] Britain's trade with the United States constituted a smaller proportion of her total trade, but it was highly important for her economy. Eighteen percent of total British exports went to the United States in 1825, ten percent in 1840. In those two years Britain imported 13 percent and 27 percent of her total imports from the United States.[3] Among the imports were cotton, on which her enormous textile industry depended. Countries so dependent on each other would be hesitant to resort to hostilities.

The Canadian revolts led to a series of incidents straining British-American peace. Altercations continued during the next five years; not until 1842 did the Webster-Ashburton Treaty

[1] Frank Thistlethwaite, "The United States and the Old World, 1794–1828," C. W. Crawley, ed., The New Cambridge Modern History, War and Peace in an Age of Upheaval (Cambridge, 1965), IX, 597; see also Thistlethwaite, The Anglo-American Connection in the Early Nineteenth Century (Philadelphia, 1959), ch. 1.

[2] U.S. Bureau of the Census, Historical Statistics of the United States, Colonial Times to 1957 (Washington, 1960), 551, 553.

[3] Harry C. Allen, Great Britain and the United States, A History of Anglo-American Relations (1783–1952) (New York, 1955), 58–59.

bring tranquillity to the border. The causes of the rebellions were complex. Here we need mention only the inspiration of the democratic, republican institutions south of the border; this led to some sentiment for annexation to the United States faintly comparable to the one entertained in Texas. Aware of these currents, Americans greatly exaggerated their significance. The tide of Manifest Destiny ran northward as well as westward, and the feeling was strong that a British presence in North America was outmoded and doomed. Viewing much of British North America as ripe for incorporation in the union, Americans hoped for rebel success.

But hardly had the little uprisings occurred in late 1837 when they virtually collapsed. The leader, William L. Mackenzie, escaped to Buffalo, where he organized a so-called Patriot army. Canadian refugees and some Americans occupied Navy Island, a Canadian island in the Niagara River. Mackenzie appointed Rensselaer Van Rensselaer, the dissipated son of an American general, to command this motley array. Devoid of military talent, the young Van Rensselaer envisaged himself as a Sam Houston of the north, charged with liberating another great area from unwanted rule. On December 29, 1837 Canadian soldiers swept down upon Navy Island looking for a rebel supply ship called the *Caroline*. Not seeing her there, they crossed to American territory, found the *Caroline*, and set her afire. She sank in the river. Some fighting took place during which an American, one Amos Durfee, was killed.

Violent anger gripped Americans all along the border at this pollution of their soil by the ancient foe. Durfee's body was displayed on the porch of the Buffalo City Hall, his funeral was advertised by placards depicting a coffin. Northern states were in an uproar, much as a year earlier the southwest had been aroused over Texas. Sympathy for the rebels flared up; excited speakers demanded war with England. The *Buffalo Daily Star* reported that "the whole frontier from Buffalo to Lake Ontario now bristles with bayonets."[4] Canadians responded in kind. In a public address the Lieutenant-Governor of Upper Canada made

---

[4] Issue of Jan. 7, 1838, James M. Callahan, *American Foreign Policy in Canadian Relations* (New York, 1937), 165.

matters worse by declaring: "The People of Upper Canada detest Democracy. . . . They are perfectly aware that there exist in the Lower Province one or two individuals who inculcate the Idea that *this* Province is about to be disturbed by the Interference of Foreigners [i.e., Americans], whose Power and whose Numbers will prove invincible. In the name of every Regiment of militia in Upper Canada I publicly promulgate—Let them come if they dare."[5]

Washington reacted more calmly. It warned Americans not to help the rebels and sent Major-General Winfield Scott to the border to quiet things down. Not until May 1838 did it protest the British attack on the *Caroline* and ask for a disavowal and redress.[6]

The rebel stand on Navy Island did not last long. The island was far from being a pleasant winter resort. Cold and wind swept, unable to get reinforcements, and bombarded from the Canadian shore, the rebels fled to the United States in January 1838. Van Rensselaer and Mackenzie were arrested. The rebellion collapsed.

But refugee Canadians and American sympathizers did not give up. In May 1838 they destroyed a Canadian steamer, the *Sir Robert Peel,* thus avenging the *Caroline.* They joined a secret organization known as the Hunters, whose members vowed "until death [to] attack, combat, and help to destroy, by all means that my superior may think proper, every power, or authority, of Royal origin, upon this continent; and especially never to rest till all tyrants of Britain cease to have any dominion or footing whatever in North America."[7] The number of Hunters is unknown; estimates run as high as 200,000, but probably a figure of 40,000 to 50,000 is closer to the truth. In November 1838 some two hundred of them seized a windmill in Prescott, Upper Canada, and held it for several days, until overcome by

---

[5] Ephraim D. Adams, *The Power of Ideals in American History* (New Haven, 1913), 77.

[6] Andrew Stevenson (American Minister at London) to Palmerston, May 22, 1838, *House Executive Document* 183, 25 Cong., 3 Sess. (Serial 347), 9.

[7] Albert B. Corey, *The Crisis of 1830–1842 in Canadian-American Relations* (New Haven, 1941), 76.

Canadian militia. Some of them were tried, convicted, and hanged. In December a Hunter band marched through Detroit shouting "Remember the *Caroline*." Carried away by excitement, they crossed the border to Windsor and set a schooner on fire. Four of them were killed on the spot, others were executed later. Night after night refugees and others raided across the line, burning houses and stealing cattle. Retaliatory raids from Canada followed. Throughout 1838 the border was in turmoil.

Then, in 1839, a new crisis broke out along the undetermined Maine boundary. The so-called Aroostook War was touched off when Maine and New Brunswick lumberjacks clashed in the disputed zone in February 1839. Excitement ran high. Maine sent her militia into the area; Congress appropriated $10,000,000. New Brunswick and Nova Scotia also took warlike steps. In itself this was a trivial, even comic affair, but also one with explosive potentialities. Fortunately it was brought under control. Major-General Scott rushed off to this new danger spot to preserve peace; and on February 27 the British Minister in Washington, Henry S. Fox, and Secretary of State John Forsyth signed an agreement for a temporary settlement.

But Anglophobia was growing; enormous stretches of the boundary continued to be disputed; Britain continued to encourage Texan independence. And the *Caroline* case still rankled. Every year Buffalo commemorated the anniversary of her destruction, and orators denounced all things British. Hopes that the affair would soon be forgotten were dashed when in November 1840 a certain Alexander McLeod was arrested in New York state, charged with arson and murdering Amos Durfee. He was imprisoned in Lockport.

The British Minister, Fox, asked for his immediate release; he argued that since the destruction of the *Caroline* was a public act an individual acting under orders was not responsible. Forsyth rejected the contention; in any event, he said, Washington could not interfere with the New York courts. Irritably he reminded Fox that Britain still had not answered the American note of May 1838 demanding redress for the *Caroline*.

It was fortunate that McLeod's apprehension occurred almost coincidentally with the election to the presidency of the Whig candidate, William Henry Harrison, the victor at Tippecanoe. He and his Secretary of State, Daniel Webster, took office on March 4, 1841. Harrison died a month later and was succeeded by John Tyler of Virginia. Webster, for many years a Senator from Massachusetts, was one of the country's leading statesmen and something of an Anglophile. He reversed Forsyth's position regarding responsibility when carrying out orders, but agreed that the federal government had no authority over a state court. To protect McLeod he sent Attorney-General John J. Crittenden to Lockport. Less auspicious was Britain's tardy reply to the American demand regarding the *Caroline*. She acknowledged responsibility, but refused redress, for the vessel's loss.[8]

The McLeod case aroused enormous interest in Britain, Canada, and the United States. Members of Congress denounced Webster as pro-British and made venomous attacks on Great Britain. The House Committee on Foreign Affairs issued a report severely critical of Britain's position regarding the *Caroline* and McLeod, and warning solemnly of an awesome technological development: "Steam-power has recently brought us so near together, that, in event of any further conflict, *war, with its effects*, will be precipitated upon us with much more rapidity than formerly."[9]

As the date of the trial approached, fears mounted that McLeod, whether innocent or not, would be condemned. Unfamiliar with the American system, Englishmen suspected Washington of ulterior motives in denying federal jurisdiction in state courts. Foreign Secretary Lord Palmerston's warning is well known: "McLeod's execution would produce war, war immediate and frightful in its character, because it would be a war of retali-

---

[8] Palmerston to Stevenson, Aug. 27, 1841, Alastair Watt, "The Case of Alexander McLeod," *Canadian Historical Review*, XII (1931), 150. Palmerston implied that he had delayed replying in order to avoid reopening a delicate matter not taken seriously by Washington. He had acknowledged the note of May 1838 on June 6, 1838. *House Executive Document* 183, 25 Cong., 3 Sess., 9–10. See also *Senate Document* 1, 27 Cong., 1 Sess. (Serial 390), 13–26.

[9] *Congressional Globe*, 27 Cong., 1 Sess., 121–24 (June 25, 1841), 173–75 (July 9, 1841); *House Report* 162, 26 Cong., 2 Sess. (Serial 388), 6. The report was dated Feb. 13, 1841.

ation and vengeance." The American Minister in London, Andrew Stevenson, agreed: "One thing is certain, if McLeod is executed, there will be *immediate war!*"[10]

Reports reached Washington that the Hunters and Patriots would try to precipitate hostilities. They would invade Canada again; they would release McLeod and lynch him. Both the federal government and New York took precautionary measures. The New York Governor, William H. Seward, sent additional guards to the jail and gave detailed instructions to the local sheriff. "There is much reason," he cautioned him, "to apprehend that the country would be involved in war if any injury should befall Alexander McLeod while he remains in the custody of the law." President Tyler warned Hunters and Patriots, "evil-minded persons . . . , that if in any lawless incursion into Canada they fall into the hands of the British authorities they will not be reclaimed as American citizens nor any interference made by this Government in their behalf."[11]

At the trial McLeod produced a persuasive alibi indicating that he had not participated in the *Caroline* raid. He was acquitted on October 12, 1841. Even had he been convicted, Seward would probably have pardoned him. Altogether the case was not so dangerous as the ominous atmosphere had suggested. But Washington had passed through an anxious time, and the next year the government enacted a law giving the federal courts jurisdiction in cases of persons accused of committing crimes by order of a foreign government.

Mention has been made of the African slave trade. British people had very strong feelings about the nefarious traffic, and this put pressure on London to take effective action to stop it. Since the United States was much the world's largest importer of slaves, British efforts to suppress the traffic inevitably led to conflict with that country. It is true that American law prohibited

---

[10] Palmerston to Fox, Feb. 9, 1841, quoted in Thomas A. Bailey, *A Diplomatic History of the American People* (New York, 1969), 209; Stevenson to President Tyler, Feb. 9, 1841, Corey, *Crisis of 1830–1842*, 137.

[11] Seward to David Moulton, Sept. 24, 1841, Corey, *Crisis of 1830–1842*, 143–44; Tyler's proclamation, Sept. 25, 1841, James D. Richardson, ed., *A Compilation of the Messages and Papers of the Presidents, 1789–1897* (Washington, 1899), IV, 72–73.

the slave trade, but it was ineffective. For a moment in 1824 the United States had seemed to be moving toward cooperation when she signed a convention with Britain for a reciprocal right to search slave ships flying the American or British flag. However, the Senate refused to approve without attaching amendments intended to be unacceptable to London as, in fact, they were.

By agreements with other nations Britain had the right to search their vessels suspected of carrying slaves. Only the United States, mindful of the southern states and remembering the outcry over impressment prior to the War of 1812, refused to permit her ships to be searched. The result was that slavers, about to be boarded, hoisted the Stars and Stripes. Britain did not insist on the right to search vessels flying the American flag, but only on the right to visit them in order to ascertain their nationality.[12] But Washington would not allow even this. If British sailors boarded a ship suspected of unwarrantably flying the American flag and discovered that she was in fact American, Great Britain ran the risk of incurring a protest and demand for reparations. Consequently the international movement to stop the traffic foundered on American intransigence. To the British people Uncle Sam appeared not only crude, uncultured, aggressive, but also the immoral, brutal defender of the inhumane slave trade.

In November 1841, a month after McLeod's acquittal, a cargo of slaves mutinied and seized control of an American ship, the *Creole*, carrying them from Hampton Roads, Virginia, to New Orleans. A white man was killed. The Negroes took the ship to Nassau in the Bahamas, where the British liberated all except the actual murderers. This was the latest of several similar incidents, and the outcry among Southerners against tampering with private American property reached a high, insistent pitch. Washington protested and demanded reparations on the ground that if a vessel was driven by necessity into a foreign port, local law could not overturn property rights.

The *Creole*, the slave trade, the northeastern boundary, the still explosive case of the *Caroline*, the Patriots and Hunters—here was a collection of controversies demanding early resolution

---

[12] Aberdeen to Minister Edward Everett, Dec. 20, 1841, *House Document* 192, 27 Cong., 3 Sess. (Serial 422), 8.

if British-American affairs were not to get out of hand. To them should be added the unknown boundary of the Oregon country, still open to joint occupation under the Convention of 1818. Although in 1841 this was not yet a pressing matter, Americans were beginning to move to that distant place in increasing numbers. British settlers, mainly associated with the Hudson's Bay Company, were already there. It behooved statesmen to draw the line before trouble occurred. In addition, British intrigues in Texas alarmed expansionists. The southwestern frontier, like the northern and the northwestern, boded ill for the future.

In September 1841 Sir Robert Peel became Prime Minister of Great Britain. Lord Aberdeen, a conciliatory man and a lover of peace, replaced Palmerston in the Foreign Office. Determined to reach a general settlement, the new Tory government appointed Lord Ashburton as special envoy to Washington, much as many years earlier John Jay had gone to London during another crisis. Ashburton was an unusual choice in that he was not a professional diplomat but a retired banker of the famous house of Baring Brothers (he was himself a Baring). Married to an American, he knew the United States well. He showed himself a capable, fair-minded negotiator.

His counterpart, Secretary of State Daniel Webster, was also a conciliatory man, anxious to reach an agreement. His talks with Ashburton proceeded informally and smoothly. The two men signed the Webster-Ashburton Treaty on August 9, 1842. The Senate quickly approved it.

The Maine boundary, as drawn by the treaty, represented a compromise. It was far enough to the south not to block a military road that Britain wanted to build from Montreal and Quebec to St. John and Halifax. On the other hand it was north of Britain's maximum claim, and inhabitants of Maine and New Brunswick living along the St. John River were granted free navigation of the river to its mouth. The United States got some 7000 of the 12,000 square miles under dispute, 893 square miles less than she would have had under the King of the Netherlands' award of 1831.

Farther west the United States got most of the controverted area near the head of the Connecticut River, and the line was arched slightly north of the true forty-fifth latitude so as to leave her in possession of the fort at Rouses Point. The United States also got a favorable boundary between Lake Superior and the Lake of the Woods; an unanticipated outcome was that she acquired the mainly unsuspected but tremendously valuable iron ore in the Mesabi Range.[13]

The treaty took a small step toward suppressing the slave trade. Each country promised to maintain enough warships off the African coast to deal with suspected slavers flying its flag; in case of need the squadrons could act jointly. Unfortunately, the traffic continued to flourish, mainly because the United States failed to provide an adequate force.

In view of the recent raids across the border, the negotiators tried to tighten up some inadequate provisions for extradition in the Jay-Grenville Treaty of 1794. The new treaty added to the number of extraditable offenses, all non-political, but most crimes remained unextraditable until many years later.

The *Creole* and *Caroline* cases were dealt with in exchanges of notes accompanying but not actually part of the treaty. The *Creole* proved to be a thorny matter. Southerners were determined to plug the drain on their slave property, but no British diplomat would restore the Negroes freed in Nassau or give assurances against liberation in future such cases. The most Ashburton would do was to promise "that instructions shall be given to the Governors of Her Majesty's Colonies on the Southern borders of the United States to execute their own laws with careful attention to the wish of their Government to maintain good neighbourhood; and that there shall be no officious interference with American vessels driven by accident or by violence into those [colonial] ports."[14] A mixed commission, set up under a convention of 1853 to examine the *Creole* and other

---

[13] At least one British critic of the treaty denounced the government for giving up "beyond Lake Superior" millions of acres "which contain a rich mineral field that must hereafter prove of the greatest value to America." Hansard's *Parliamentary Debates*, Third Series, LXVIII, 650 (April 7, 1843).
[14] Ashburton to Webster, Aug. 6, 1842, Hunter Miller, *Treaties and Other International Acts of the United States of America* (Washington, 1931–1943), IV, 468. Wilbur D. Jones, "The Influence of Slavery on the Webster-Ashburton Negotiations," *Journal of Southern History*, XXII (1956), 48–58.

such cases, returned a judgment against Britain in 1855 for the *Creole* of $110,330.[15]

Lord Ashburton stoutly defended the destruction of the *Caroline*. "I would appeal to you, Sir," he wrote Webster, using much the same argument that John Quincy Adams had employed when defending Jackson's foray into Florida in 1818, "to say whether the facts which you say would alone justify this act, viz: 'a necessity of self defence, instant, overwhelming, leaving no choice of means and no moment for deliberation', were not applicable to this case in as high a degree as they ever were to any case of a similar description in the history of nations." He denied that monetary redress was due. But he did soften his position, and thereby help Webster politically, by a semi-apology: "Looking back to what passed at this distance of time, what is perhaps most to be regretted is that some explanation and apology for this occurrence was not immediately made: this with a frank explanation of the necessity of the case might and probably would have prevented much of the exasperation and of the subsequent complaints and recriminations to which it gave rise."[16] Accepting this as satisfactory, Webster closed the matter.

Finally, the two men exchanged letters regarding impressment. The letters did little more than restate each country's familiar position, though Ashburton did hold out the hope that Britain might in time make a change.

More difficult than Webster's negotiations with Ashburton were those he had to undertake with Maine and Massachusetts. Maine had formerly been joined to Massachusetts, and the latter had retained a half ownership in Maine's public lands after Maine became a separate state in 1820. Accordingly Webster had to persuade both states to accept his new boundary. The tangle of conflicting interests among the federal government and the two state governments could have shipwrecked the treaty.

---

[15] *Senate Executive Document* 103, 34 Cong., 1 Sess. (Serial 824), 241–45, 52. The commission rejected a claim for damages by Alexander McLeod., *ibid.*, 327.

[16] Ashburton to Webster, July 28, 1842, Miller, *Treaties*, IV, 453, 454. Webster to Ashburton, Aug. 6, 1842 *ibid.*, 455. Regarding his statement Ashburton wrote Aberdeen, Aug. 13, 1842: "I hope you will not think it too apologetic." Jones, "Influence of Slavery," 49*n*.

Luckily Webster had two maps of dubious authenticity, one of them marking the Maine boundary with a strong red line such as Benjamin Franklin was supposed to have drawn on a map during the peace negotiations in Paris at the end of the Revolution. Both maps supported the British claim. Webster sent Jared Sparks, a well known historian and the discoverer of the red-line map in the French archives, to Maine and Massachusetts to show the local officials the incriminating evidence. They saw the point of accepting a compromise quickly before Britain learned about the maps. But Washington had to agree to give each of the states $150,000.

When the Whig opposition in England learned about the strong red line, it denounced Ashburton for his "capitulation." Lord Palmerston waxed particularly indignant.[17] Could he have forgotten that, when Foreign Secretary not long before, he had had in his possession a map certainly dating from the Paris negotiations that demonstrated the validity of the extreme American claim? Did Lord Aberdeen on taking office learn about this map? Probably he did not; the chances are that in 1842 only Daniel Webster held what he believed, erroneously, to be evidence of the other side's contention. In any case, the present-day Maine boundary is considerably to the south of where the diplomats of 1783 probably intended it to be.

The Webster-Ashburton Treaty was a monument to British-American good sense; it was concluded at a time when many ugly passions made it difficult to be sensible. The treaty settled a long list of disputes, and thereby greatly alleviated tension. Apart from impressment, still in theory a bone of contention but never to arise in the future as an actual issue, only two matters of disagreement remained: the boundary of the Oregon country and Britain's role in the new republic of Texas. Unfortunately, each of these was dangerous.

---

[17] *Parliamentary Debates*, Third Series, LXVII, 1162–1218 (March 21, 1843).

CHAPTER V

Westward Expansion:
Texas, California, and Oregon

W E HAVE ALREADY NOTED the various reasons why Great Britain attempted to bolster up that ramshackle new country —the Republic of Texas. As we have seen, Texas achieved a precarious independence in 1836 and was recognized by Andrew Jackson the next year. Just as Britain had endeavored successfully to contain United States expansion in the northeast, so she now tried to contain it in the southwest. To that end she signed treaties with Texas in 1840, but because that country did not promptly implement one of them (for the suppression of the slave trade), delayed ratification until 1842. With the treaties concluded, she formally recognized Texas and sent a diplomatic envoy there.

In 1843 the Whig President, John Tyler, decided to revive the politically explosive matter of annexation. He needed some dramatic success to have any chance of being elected in 1844; he was a southern supporter of slavery and an expansionist. Moreover he was worried about British intrigues in Texas, real and imaginary. Most disturbing was a remark regarding Texas made by Lord Aberdeen (Foreign Secretary in Prime Minister Sir Robert Peel's Tory Ministry), that Great Britain "desires, and is constantly exerting herself to procure, the general abolition of slavery throughout the world. . . ." Even though the Foreign Secretary tried to be reassuring by adding that "Her objects are purely commercial, and she has no thought or intention of seeking to act, directly or indirectly, in a political sense, on the United States through Texas,"[1] this did not lull Tyler's fears.

---

[1] Aberdeen to Sir Richard Pakenham (Minister at Washington), Dec. 26, 1843, *House Executive Document* 271, 28 Cong., 1 Sess. (Serial 444), 49.

If Texas, under British pressure, freed her slaves, she would be a haven for runaway American slaves that Southerners could not tolerate. Everything consequently pointed to annexation. A Texan-American treaty providing for this was signed on April 12, 1844 and sent to the Senate for its approval.

London reacted to these fast-moving developments in somewhat the same way it had when the pressure was on Cuba earlier. In late May 1844 Aberdeen contemplated an international arrangement whereby Mexico would recognize Texas and, in return, Britain and France—and also the United States, if she wished—would guarantee the Lone Star republic's independence and the territorial limits of both Texas and Mexico. Foolishly Mexico was still not prepared to face the fact that Texas existed, and the European powers dropped their scheme.

Luckily for Great Britain the annexation treaty met rough waters in the Senate. The debate on approval took place as the national conventions were deciding whom to nominate for President in 1844. It was not the moment for dispassionate consideration of the most delicate issue in American politics. After the treaty was signed, Secretary of State John C. Calhoun, replying to Aberdeen, had boasted to the British Minister, Sir Richard Pakenham (Fox's successor), that annexation was "the most effectual, if not the only means of guarding against the threatened danger" of abolition in Texas induced by Great Britain.[2] This injudicious utterance, which the government rashly published, tied the treaty to the preservation of slavery and thereby strengthened opponents of annexation. The Senate rejected the treaty decisively, June 8, 1844.

During the election the Democratic candidate, James K. Polk, boldly insisted on annexing Texas as soon as practicable. His victory over the better-known Whig candidate, Henry Clay, presaged urgent steps in that direction. Still in the White House during the lame-duck session, Tyler wanted for himself the glory of getting Texas. He turned to the device of a joint resolution, requiring a simple majority of both houses instead of a two-thirds majority of the Senate. The House passed an annexation resolution in January 1845; the Senate (having seen the popular mood

---

[2] Calhoun to Pakenham, April 18, 1844, *ibid.*, 51.

during the election) reversed its earlier vote and followed suit a month later.

Texas still had to go through the formalities of accepting annexation. This gave Britain a last, but forlorn, chance to keep that republic alive. In May 1845, cooperating with France, she at length induced Mexico to offer to recognize Texas on the condition that Texas would never join another country. It was too late. The Texans rejected the offer in June and voted in October to join the United States. In December the Lone Star republic passed out of existence, becoming an American state. Polk publicly reprimanded Britain and France for having interfered.[3]

After the joint resolution of annexation was passed, the Mexican Minister demanded his passports and, before long, Mexico and the United States severed diplomatic relations. Mexico had made it plain that annexation would mean war; and by the autumn of 1845 the United States consequently had to consider the strong possibility of imminent hostilities. At that very time she also faced a crisis with Great Britain over Oregon.

It will be recalled that the Convention of 1818 set the international boundary at the forty-ninth parallel from the Lake of the Woods to the Rocky Mountains; west of the mountains the Oregon country was to be "free and open" to British and American settlers for ten years. By the treaty of 1819 ceding Florida, Spain renounced claims north of the forty-second parallel, and by an American-Russian treaty of 1824 Russia renounced claims south of 54° 40'. An Anglo-American convention of 1827 renewed the terms of 1818 indefinitely, subject to a year's notice of termination.

By the end of 1845 some five thousand Americans lived in Oregon south of the Columbia River, considerably south therefore of the forty-ninth parallel. Congress had been agitating for some years for the abrogation of joint occupation and a permanent delineation of the boundary. The feeling was strong that the United States should expand in the northwest. During the election of 1844 Polk and the Democrats came out not only for "the

---

[3] Annual Message, Dec. 2, 1845, James D. Richardson, ed., *A Compilation of the Messages and Papers of the Presidents, 1789–1897* (Washington, 1899), IV, 387–88.

re-annexation of Texas" but also—as if searching for the ultimate of recklessness—for "the re-occupation of Oregon," American title to which was asserted to be "clear and unquestionable." It was the heyday of Manifest Destiny. In his inaugural address on March 4, 1845 the new President, Polk, reiterated that "Our title to the country of the Oregon is 'clear and unquestionable'. . . . "[4] This assertion disturbed London, for it could not be excused as campaign oratory.

However, President Polk's first formal approach to Great Britain was conciliatory. Probably he had Texas somewhat in mind; later in the year the Texans would be voting on whether or not to join the United States, and the prospect of war with Great Britain might deter them. On July 12, 1845 Secretary of State James Buchanan proposed to London that the boundary along the forty-ninth parallel be extended from the Rockies all the way to the Pacific Ocean; and that, since this line would cut off the southern tip of Vancouver Island, Britain should have any free ports she might desire on that tip. He excused Polk for retreating from 54° 40' on the ground that the President "found himself embarrassed, if not committed, by the acts of his predecessors."[5] The Secretary refrained, however, from offering Britain the free navigation of the Columbia River, as some previous administrations had done.

Altogether this proposal was a reasonable one; according to Prime Minister Peel, it "might probably have been the foundation of some future and final settlement";[6] and one may speculate that Polk was prepared to bargain and even to accept, if necessary, a boundary close to the one eventually agreed upon (which went through Juan de Fuca Strait). Unfortunately Minister Pakenham, without even consulting London, refused to accept the proposal. The President reacted angrily. On August 30, 1845, against the advice of his Secretary of State, who wanted to temporize because of the deteriorating situation with Mexico, he

---

[4] *Ibid.*, 381. For attacks on Polk's assertion see Hansard's *Parliamentary Debates*, Third Series, LXXIX, 115–24, 178–201 (April 4, 1845).

[5] Buchanan to Pakenham, July 12, 1845, *Senate Document* 1, 29 Cong., 1 Sess. (Serial 470), 169.

[6] *Parliamentary Debates*, Third Series, LXXXIII, 154 (Jan. 23, 1846).

reasserted the American claim to all Oregon up to 54° 40′ and formally withdrew the compromise offer.[7] Perhaps in his indignation he had overlooked the coming Texas vote; possibly he thought that by then it was too late for the Texans to draw back from annexation.

About two weeks after Polk revived his demand for 54° 40′ he and the Cabinet, as though they were bent on risking the country's destruction in a frenzy of expansion, decided to take advantage of the crisis with Mexico in order to acquire California with its fine port of San Francisco, and also all the territory between there and Texas. California was then a remote Mexican border area, scantily populated, insecurely held. As in Oregon, the number of Americans was growing, and little insight was needed to foresee another Texan-style revolt. Great Britain herself did not want the place, though some Englishmen viewed it longingly, but she did want the grasping Yankees to slow down. Local British agents urged London to take a strong line— but in vain. The most that Aberdeen would say—and this only to a British Consul in Mexico—was that Britain would "view with much dissatisfaction" any other country taking over California.[8] Certainly this mild remark did not deter so resolute a man as Polk, if indeed he ever heard about it, which is unlikely.

Suspecting American intentions, the Mexican Minister in London asked the Foreign Secretary whether Britain, aided by France, would help defend California. Aberdeen sounded out Paris, but turned down the Mexican. After abandoning Texas, Great Britain had no intention of fighting for California. Oregon was enough of a problem.

However ineffectual these British gestures—and the fact is that Britain did almost nothing to save California—they worried the President. To some extent his desire to annex California, as Texas, was prompted by apprehension lest Britain get there first. Having already rebuked Britain and France for backing Texas,

---

[7] Buchanan to Pakenham, Aug. 30, 1845, *Senate Document* 1, 29 Cong., 1 Sess., 192. Milo M. Quaife, ed., *The Diary of James K. Polk During His Presidency, 1845 to 1849* . . . (Chicago, 1910), I, 11–12, Aug. 30, 1845.

[8] Aberdeen to Barron (Consul at Tepic, Mexico), Dec. 31, 1844, George L. Rives, *The United States and Mexico, 1821–1848* . . . (New York, 1913), II, 51.

he warned them publicly against trying to contain America anywhere on the continent:

The rapid extension of our settlements over our territories heretofore unoccupied, the addition of new States to our Confederacy, the expansion of free principles, and our rising greatness as a nation are attracting the attention of the powers of Europe, and lately the doctrine has been broached in some of them of a "balance of power" on this continent to check our advancement. The United States, sincerely desirous of preserving relations of good understanding with all nations, can not in silence permit any European interference on the North American continent, and should any such interference be attempted will be ready to resist it at any and all hazards.[9]

Ever since withdrawing his compromise offer and reviving his demand for 54° 40', the President's public statements about Oregon had been harsh and unyielding. After having offered to retreat far below 54° 40' only to be rebuffed, he was in no mood to run afoul of die-hard expansionists by appearing overly conciliatory. In his annual message of 1845 he referred to Great Britain's "extraordinary and wholly inadmissible demands" and the impossibility of making a compromise with her; he recommended giving the year's notice needed to terminate the Convention of 1827.[10] Presumably American occupation of the whole Oregon country would follow. That would lead to war with Great Britain, and this at a time when, with Texas just annexed and the resolve made to take California and the entire southwest, war with Mexico could be expected. Twice London offered to arbitrate (December 27, 1845 and January 16, 1846); twice the United States refused. In the face of these rebuffs, it would not be easy for Britain to make another offer.

But running alongside Polk's hard public stand was a series of secret proposals that demonstrate that his attitude was, in reality, much softer than it appeared on the surface. During the six months after the President reverted to his demand for all of Oregon, Secretary Buchanan several times informed the British that if they made a new boundary proposition, Polk would con-

---

[9] Annual Message Dec. 2, 1845, Richardson, *Messages and Papers*, IV, 398.
[10] *Ibid.*, 395.

sider it carefully. Plainly the President was prepared to compromise no matter what he said openly; and this manifest disposition not to insist on 54° 40' was of the utmost significance in preparing the way to the coming agreement. However, not until the end of February 1846 did Buchanan indicate what terms would be acceptable. His silence undoubtedly made London hesitate about making an offer that might be snubbed.

Yet Britain did want an accord. Relations with France were disturbing, a terrible potato famine devastated Ireland and, at home, a first-rate political crisis over repealing the corn laws was near its peak. Convinced that Oregon could be defended only at exorbitant cost, the government needed a quick settlement with the United States on almost any reasonable basis. It could not, however, afford to give the impression of yielding to Yankee braggadocio. The Whig opposition would be sure to make capital out of that, and the British public had responded indignantly to Polk's violent language during the campaign of 1844 and to his bluster as President. One way to gain greater freedom of maneuver was to persuade the British people that Oregon, especially north of the Columbia River, was not worth so much as they thought and that the American case was worth more. Accordingly Foreign Secretary Aberdeen secretly inspired press propaganda that might pave the way to concessions. Some knowledge of this came to Washington. Doubtless it made the administration more confident of an eventual British retreat.

But Aberdeen accompanied these pacific moves with warnings to Washington not to push him too far; he well knew that neither the Cabinet nor the public, even if it should come to attach less importance to Oregon, would sanction a humiliating retreat, and he may have thought that a show of strength would induce Polk to accept arbitration. On December 30, 1845 he warned Louis McLane, the American Minister, of the perils that might come from refusing to arbitrate. He said that Britain was already making war preparations, though denying that they were connected with Oregon. Alarmed, McLane wrote Buchanan: "it is perfectly obvious that they [the preparations] are in a great degree, and especially so far as they consist of an augmentation in the number of steam vessels, and of the naval marine generally, precisely of the character to be the most appropriate and the most useful

in a war with our country."[11] About three weeks later the Foreign Secretary heard of Washington's rejection of the December
arbitration offer. Summoning McLane to another, much more
serious interview on January 29, 1846, he this time threatened
war. McLane reported on February 3 that the Foreign Secretary
had declared that he would no longer oppose "preparations
which might be deemed necessary, not only for the defence and
protection of the Canadas, but for offensive operations. . . . these
would consist, independent of military armaments, of the immediate equipment of thirty sail of the line, besides steamers and
other vessels of war. . . ."[12]

The ominous report reached Washington late Saturday night,
February 21. Some controversy has developed among historians
as to whether Polk backed down because of it. There is no doubt
that the administration was shaken. The news, the President
wrote in his diary, "was not altogether of so pacific a character
as the accounts given in the English newspapers had led me to
believe."[13] Several times during the next few days he met urgently with political leaders and the Cabinet. Their concern is
evident from the fact that a long, major dispatch went off to
McLane on February 26, only three or four working days after
the report arrived. For the first time since July 1845 the United
States proposed specific terms instead of merely saying that she
would consider a British suggestion. Polk now agreed that if
Britain made a proposition "extending the boundary to the
Pacific by the forty-ninth parallel and the strait of Fuca," he
would submit it to the Senate, "though with reluctance."[14] In
July he had proposed that the line cut across Vancouver Island.

---

[11] McLane to Buchanan, Jan. 3, 1846, *Senate Document* 117, 29 Cong., 1
Sess. (Serial 473), 3–4. This report may have persuaded Polk to suggest,
at a Cabinet meeting on January 24, tariff concessions as a means of persuading Britain to give way in Oregon. Quaife, *Diary of Polk*, I, 191–92.
Nothing came of this.

[12] McLane to Buchanan, Feb. 3, 1846, Hunter Miller, *Treaties and Other
International Acts of the United States of America* (Washington, 1931–
1943), V, 58.

[13] Quaife, *Diary of Polk*, I, 241, Feb. 21, 1846.

[14] Buchanan to McLane, Feb. 26, 1846, *Senate Document* 489, 29 Cong., 1
Sess. (Serial 478), 44.

If the boundary went to the ocean by way of Juan de Fuca Strait, the entire island would be British, and Britain would control one side of the entrance to the inland waters. These two changes— naming specific terms and renouncing all Vancouver Island— represented a large concession, and it is reasonable to suppose that Aberdeen's threats helped persuade Polk to make it.

The changes did not, however, represent anything like a head-long retreat by Polk. As a matter of fact Secretary Buchanan had asked the President in December 1845, long before Aberdeen's chilling interview with McLane, whether he would accept an offer to extend the forty-ninth parallel, not across Vancouver Island but through Juan de Fuca Strait; and instead of spurning this as unthinkable, Polk had mildly replied that if the United States was granted free ports north of the parallel, he "might submit it [such an offer] to the Senate for their previous advice" after consulting three or four Senators. We have speculated that as early as July 1845 the President may have been ready to bargain for the Fuca Strait line. Moreover Polk was not willing, even after reading McLane's alarming news, to concede the free navigation of the Columbia River: ". . . I repeated . . . ," he wrote firmly in February 1846, "that I would not yield it."[15] In short, Aberdeen's strong words caused the President to shift his position significantly but they did not cause him to abandon 54° 40'; he had been prepared to do that for many months.

But however limited these changes of February, they had great importance. Once they had occurred, it became much easier for Britain to make a boundary offer, as Washington had repeatedly suggested. For now that she knew what terms the United States would accept, she was relieved of the fear that a third offer might be rebuffed. Before long she made such an offer, and an agreement was then close at hand.

In April Congress passed a joint resolution authorizing the year's notice for abrogation of the Convention of 1827, as Polk had proposed in his annual message. Polk approved the resolution on the 27th. Notice of it went to London the 28th. On the face of it abrogation was preparatory to occupying all of Oregon up to 54° 40'. Texas had been annexed. The administra-

---

[15] Quaife, *Diary of Polk*, I, 135, Dec. 23, 1845; 252, Feb. 25, 1846.

tion had determined to get California and the southwest. War
with Mexico was imminent. Was it not inexcusably reckless to
choose this moment to challenge the greatest power in the world?

That there was an element of risk cannot be denied. But
McLane had recently predicted that Britain would probably
agree to the forty-ninth parallel to Juan de Fuca Strait, together
with the free navigation of the Columbia "at least for such
period as may be necessary for the trade of the Hudson's Bay
Company."[16] Thus when giving the abrogation notice Washington had reason to believe that the British were likely to accept
the main terms it had already proposed on February 26; and in
fact Buchanan, when transmitting the notice, reminded London
of the proposal. The one remaining point of difference, that is,
the navigation of the river, need not be insuperable in view of
London's apparent readiness not to insist on permanent free
navigation.

Soon after receiving the notice Great Britain responded as
McLane had foreseen. Aberdeen sent a draft treaty to Pakenham
running the boundary through Juan de Fuca Strait and providing
that the Columbia "shall be free and open to the Hudson's Bay
Company and to the Subjects of Great Britain trading with the
said Company. . . ."[17] Polk had asserted that he would never
grant free navigation, but doubtless he had meant general navigation for British subjects. Navigation restricted to the Hudson's
Bay Company and its trade was a different matter. At any rate,
it was not the moment to argue. The United States had declared
war on Mexico on May 13. Pakenham gave the draft to Buchanan on June 6. Without delay the President sent it to the Senate.
Buchanan and Pakenham signed the treaty on June 15. The
Senate promptly approved it, word for word as written in
London.

Although she could have struck the United States a devastating blow by allying herself with Mexico, Britain did not seriously consider doing so. After the Oregon agreement she had no
justification for war. The Peel government was about to fall. The

---

[16] McLane to Buchanan, March 3, 1846, Miller *Treaties*, V, 64. McLane
wrote this before receiving the instruction of Feb. 26.

[17] Aberdeen to Pakenham, May 18, 1846, *ibid.*, 77–78.

catastrophic potato famine was raging in Ireland. Britain merely offered mediation in 1847, which Polk politely declined.

In March 1848 a defeated Mexico signed the Treaty of Guadalupe Hidalgo. It confirmed American possession of Texas; it also gave the United States not only California, but also New Mexico, Arizona, Nevada, Utah, and parts of Colorado and Wyoming. In the whole southwest Great Britain's rather half-hearted efforts to contain American expansion had failed utterly. In Oregon, however, as earlier in the northeast, in both of which areas she had important interests and took a strong stand, she had persuaded Washington to compromise.

Never again after 1846 was the United States to move aggressively against British North America. With the virtual abandonment of American moves to expand to the north and of British opposition to westward expansion, the major cause of Anglo-American friction had disappeared. But a new danger was arising as the United States again turned southward, toward Central America.

CHAPTER VI

Crisis and Détente: Central America

GREAT BRITAIN'S halfhearted attempts to save Texas, California, and the southwest had come to nought, though she had had greater success in the northeast and Oregon. In 1848 the now colossal republic stretched from sea to sea. Moreover the expansionist fever was but little abated. Mexico, having lost so much, seemed about to lose more. Hardly was the Treaty of Guadalupe Hidalgo concluded when President Polk made the ominous request to Congress to prevent Yucatán from becoming a European colony. In response Senator Edward A. Hannegan presented a bill for the temporary military occupation of Yucatán; he argued that England, "a most formidable Power," was threatening American interests there, and that once she had Yucatán she would soon take Cuba.[1] Although debated for nine days, the bill was not passed. More endangered were the northern Mexican states, where filibustering raids contributed to turmoil along the border; most of Mexico, in fact, was close to anarchy. In two annual messages (1858 and 1859) President James Buchanan asked for authority to occupy temporarily parts of Sonora and Chihuahua.[2] But neither Yucatán, Sonora, nor Chihuahua was to go the way of Texas and California. Mexico

---

[1] Message of April 29, 1848, James D. Richardson, ed., *A Compilation of the Messages and Papers of the Presidents, 1789–1897* (Washington, 1899), IV, 583; *Congressional Globe*, 30 Cong., 1 Sess., Appendix, 591 (May 5, 1848), 596–97 (May 5, 1848).

[2] Annual messages of Dec. 6, 1858, and Dec. 19, 1859, Richardson, *Messages and Papers*, V, 514, 567–68.

succeeded in preserving a shaky territorial integrity until the American Civil War relieved the pressure on her.

Lord Palmerston, again Foreign Secretary in 1846, predicted that Americans would be less interested in getting Canada now they had got so much in the southwest. Less interested perhaps they were than in the days of the Hunters and Patriots, but Americans did not forget Canada. If they had done so, their memories would have been jogged when in 1849 some prominent Canadians, whose political power was threatened by recent domestic developments and who were alarmed by the seriously depressed economy (mainly the result of the loss of privileged access to the British market in consequence of the repeal of the corn laws in 1846), went so far as to issue a manifesto calling for annexation to the United States. The annexation movement soon petered out. Most Canadians looked, instead, to commercial reciprocity. In 1849 they enacted legislation providing for the duty-free admission of American imports whenever the United States passed an equivalent measure. Congress considered reciprocity bills over several years, but too much opposition existed for any to be adopted.

However, it was not toward Mexico or Canada that America's efforts to expand were mainly directed during the thirteen years between the Mexican War and the Civil War, but toward Central America, to a less extent toward the Caribbean Sea, and to a still less extent toward the Pacific Ocean. Several converging factors pointed to Central America. Soon after the acquisition of California in 1848, gold was discovered there. Fortune seekers flocked to the west coast, so many that in 1850 California entered the union as a state. East of the Mississippi River the United States had a considerable population; along the Pacific Ocean she had a smaller but rapidly growing one. In between lay hundreds and hundreds of miles of inhospitable land lacking adequate water and shelter, occupied by rattlesnakes, dangerous animals, and more dangerous Indians. It was hazardous to travel across this barrier between the two settled coasts. Thousands preferred to sail to Central America, cross the narrow isthmus by land, and continue by another ship. Soon after the Mexican War Cornelius Vanderbilt developed a fleet of steamers going to Central America, and a land transit across Nicaragua; a rival company sponsored a route across Panama (then a state of New Granada, as Colombia was called), where a new railway speeded the transit.

Consequently American money was invested in Central America, many Americans acquired firsthand experience with Nicaragua and Panama, and the federal government began to interest itself in this vital area. For decades visionaries had dreamed about an interoceanic canal; but after the Mexican War and the settlement of the west coast a canal became, for a while, pressing business.

The ships sailing between eastern United States and Central America often stopped at Cuba. Interest in that long island, athwart vital lines of communication, revived during the 1850s; and partly for this reason and because a base there would be important for the defense of a future canal, Cuba again tempted annexationists, who during the 1840s had been preoccupied with Canada, Texas, Oregon, and California.

West coast settlement had another effect: residents there became more conscious of the opportunities and dangers of the Pacific Ocean. Especially did the Hawaiian Islands come into public awareness, as did Cuba on the other side of the continent. Commerce developed with them, and their significance for defending California and a canal became evident.

California gold provided capital for the rising New England textile industry and other industries. At the same time large-scale immigration from Ireland, after the potato famine of the mid-1840s, furnished cheap labor. For various reasons the textile industry hoped to find large markets among the teeming multitudes of China and Japan. The significance of a canal, and hence of Cuba and Hawaii, for their exports to the Far East was obvious.

The increasingly virulent sectional struggle also influenced American expansion. During the years between the Mexican War and the Civil War the Old Northwest threw in its lot with the Northeast instead of with the South; millions of Irish and German immigrants swelled the northern but not the southern population; California and then Minnesota and Oregon came into the union as free-soil states, tipping the federal balance against the South. Such developments put the slave states on the defensive. Many southern leaders concluded that the balance must be redressed; and the most likely areas for new slave states were Central America and the Caribbean, notably Cuba.

Central America especially, but also Cuba, Hawaii, and the Far East (for exports), preoccupied American diplomats after the Oregon settlement, the Mexican War, and the gold rush brought thousands of Americans to the west coast, and sectional lines were drawn ever more sharply. They were the main targets of the expansionist drive from 1848 to 1861, and it was over them (except in the Far East) that a new phase of Anglo-American friction arose as Great Britain continued her efforts to contain America's outward thrusts.

During those thirteen years between the two wars the White House was occupied by Polk during his final year in office, by the Whigs for four years, and then by the Democrats for eight. The Mexican War hero, Zachary Taylor, was President from 1849 until his death in 1850; he was succeeded by Millard Fillmore; neither was an enthusiastic expansionist. In 1853 the Democrats took power under Franklin Pierce. James Buchanan succeeded him in 1857. Pierce and Buchanan, themselves northerners, were under the domination of southerners who, believing that the South's increasing weakness in Washington endangered the union, pushed for territorial expansion. In his inaugural address Pierce said plainly that "certain possessions" should be taken and that he would "not be controlled by any timid forebodings of evil from expansion."[3]

The Secretaries of State reflected these attitudes: the prudent, capable rather than brilliant John M. Clayton, under Taylor; his successor, the great Whig leader and former Secretary of State, Daniel Webster, whose famous treaty of 1842 we have described, still rather Anglophile but now an old man who died in 1852. Then came the more adventurous Democratic Secretaries: William Marcy, who well served his expansionist-minded chief, President Pierce, but tried not to tarnish the good name of the United States by unscrupulous action; and Buchanan's aggressive but aged Secretary, Lewis Cass, of whose selection the *Manchester Guardian* wrote too pessimistically that it "augurs ill for the future policy of the new President, and for the maintenance

---

[3] *Ibid.*, 198.

of peace and good feeling between England and the United States."[4]

On the British side, the dominating figure was Henry John Temple, Viscount Palmerston, Foreign Secretary under Lord John Russell from 1846 to 1852; Home Secretary from late 1852 to early 1855 in the coalition ministry of Lord Aberdeen, who led Britain into the Crimean War against Russia; Prime Minister from 1855 to 1858 and again from 1859 to late 1865. Britain was at the height of her power and no governmental leader ever made her weight felt more strongly than did Lord "Pumicestone." A man who called Americans "most disagreeable Fellows . . . totally unscrupulous and dishonest" could not be thought of as befriending the United States, nor could one who said "that if all the other crimes which the human race has committed, from the creation down to the present day, were added together in one vast aggregate, they would scarcely equal . . . the amount of guilt which has been incurred by mankind, in connexion with this diabolical Slave Trade," feel sympathy for the world's main bulwark of slavery.[5] But Palmerston recognized facts, and he deserves much of the credit for bringing the two English-speaking countries closer together in the late 1850s.

Apart from Palmerston, the principal Foreign Secretary was the Earl of Clarendon, a member of a famous family who held office from 1853 to early 1858 and again after the Civil War. Like his fiery chief, he was no lover of America but he too was a realist who knew when to yield gracefully.

In Central America Great Britain was already well ensconced in 1848. She was strong in Belize (the later British Honduras) and the Bay Islands, and had a protectorate over Nicaragua's Mosquito Coast. From her base in nearby Jamaica her ships could quickly reach the mainland. The United States, flushed with her sweep across the continent, was determined to move into this British preserve. As early as 1846 an opportunity had arisen when

---

[4] *Manchester Guardian*, March 9, 1857, reprinted in *ibid.*, March 14, 1957.
[5] Palmerston to Foreign Secretary Clarendon, Dec. 31, 1857, Kenneth Bourne, *The Foreign Policy of Victorian England, 1830–1902* (Oxford, 1970), 334; Hansard's *Parliamentary Debates*, Third Series, LXXVI, 931 (July 16, 1844).

New Granada, apprehensive over British moves in the neighborhood, offered to give America equal rights with those enjoyed by her own citizens in any canal that might be built across Panama, provided the United States would guarantee the neutrality of the isthmus and New Granada's sovereignty over it. On his own initiative the American Minister at Bogotá signed a treaty incorporating these terms, and President Polk submitted it to the Senate. It is significant that that body delayed approval until after the Treaty of Guadalupe Hidalgo had given the United States the California coastline. By then the need of a canal was too obvious for the Senate not to seize the opportunity before it. It approved the treaty in June 1848.

Another envisaged canal route, for many years the favorite route, lay through Nicaragua: up the San Juan River that separated that country from Costa Rica, on through Lake Nicaragua, and (by a prospective canal) across the narrow land barrier between the lake and the Pacific Ocean. Shortly before the Senate approved the New Granada treaty, Great Britain seized Greytown (or San Juan del Norte), an impoverished village at the mouth of the river, claiming it as part of her Mosquito protectorate. Thereby she established herself at the Caribbean end of any future Nicaragua canal. When Nicaragua appealed to Washington, President Polk sent off an envoy, Elijah Hise, to see what was afoot. Hise signed a treaty with Nicaragua giving the United States the exclusive right to construct and fortify a canal; by the treaty the United States also acquired a protectorate over Nicaragua, and guaranteed that country's sovereignty and neutrality. About the same time Cornelius Vanderbilt got canal construction rights from Nicaragua.

By the time Polk's Nicaraguan treaty was signed, President Zachary Taylor and the Whigs were in power. Instead of submitting the treaty to the Senate they held it in reserve. They sent their own emissary, Ephraim G. Squier, to Central America; he signed a treaty in September 1849 with Honduras giving the United States the right to establish a naval base on Tigre Island, which would enable her to dominate the Pacific end of the prospective waterway. This treaty too the Whigs held in reserve. Like Polk's treaty and Vanderbilt's private endeavors, it threatened to offset British strength at Greytown.

The British Consul-General to Central America, Frederick Chatfield, countered in October 1849 by ordering a British naval squadron to seize Tigre Island. He then signed a treaty with Costa Rica supporting that country's claim to the north bank of the San Juan River. If Costa Rica owned the river, she could block a Nicaragua canal. Although Britain some weeks later disavowed the taking of the island, anyone could see that she and America were headed for a showdown if their power struggle continued much longer.

In these circumstances Lord Palmerston had recourse to what had already become a time-honored British-American device: he dispatched a special envoy to Washington in late 1849. Sir Henry Lytton Bulwer, who replaced Sir Richard Pakenham as British Minister, was charged with the assignment of heading off a clash in Central America (and also of settling Canadian issues discussed below). Both the Whig administration of President Zachary Taylor and the Liberal ministry headed by Lord John Russell wanted an accord. Nevertheless the differences between the two countries were serious, and Bulwer and Secretary of State Clayton seem to have decided to write a treaty in obscure language as the only way of getting any agreement at all. The Clayton-Bulwer Treaty, signed April 19, 1850, provided that neither country would ever maintain exclusive control over a canal in Central America, or fortify a canal; and that neither would "colonize, or assume, or exercise any dominion over . . . any part of Central America. . . ." Both countries agreed to guarantee the canal's neutrality.[6] In binding herself not to colonize in Central America, the United States was for the first time accepting the sort of commitment that Britain had urged with respect to Cuba and Texas.

The treaty's immediate effect was to ease the tension but, unfortunately, a serious controversy soon developed over its meaning. After the treaty was signed Bulwer notified Clayton that Britain did not understand it as applying to her "settlement at Honduras or to its Dependencies." Clayton answered on July 4 that the treaty did not "include the British settlement in Hon-

---

[6] Hunter Miller, ed., *Treaties and Other International Acts of the United States of America* (Washington, 1931–1943), V, 672.

duras, (commonly called British Honduras, as distinct from the State of Honduras,) nor the small islands in the neighborhood of that settlement, which may be known as its dependencies."[7] Both these communications were made before the exchange of ratifications on July 4, 1850. Bulwer sent another note—some conjecture has been raised as to whether it was, in fact, surreptitiously inserted in the American archives without Clayton's knowledge—that did not reach Clayton or the State Department before July 5 at the earliest, though it was dated July 4.[8] In it he wrote that he interpreted Clayton's letter of the 4th to mean that the Secretary did not think it necessary to define the exact limits of British Honduras nor to define its dependencies, and that the Secretary recognized that the negotiators did not intend the treaty to include "whatever is Her Majesty's settlement at Honduras, nor whatever are the Dependencies of that settlement. . . ."[9] After these various obscure statements it was impossible to be sure what the two countries considered as falling within the treaty's scope.

In 1852 Great Britain declared the Bay Islands to be a crown colony. Were they included among "the small islands in the neighborhood" of British Honduras which Clayton had agreed were not embraced by the treaty? If so, the United States had no cause to protest. But protest she did, arguing strenuously that the treaty did embrace the Bay Islands and that Britain consequently had violated it.

Furthermore Britain did not abandon the potectorate over the Mosquito Coast. The United States contended that the treaty obligated Britain not to have any dominion anywhere in Central America, except in Belize properly defined. But in the British view the treaty was prospective only; its intent was to prevent either country from acquiring any *new* territory.[10] Whatever the

---

[7] Bulwer Declaration, June 29, 1850, *ibid.*, V, 681; Clayton to Bulwer, July 4, 1850, *ibid.*, 682.

[8] *Ibid.*, 691–703; J. D. Ward, "Sir Henry Bulwer and the United States Archives," *Cambridge Historical Journal*, III (1929), 304–13.

[9] Bulwer to Clayton, July 4, 1850, Miller, *Treaties*, V, 684–85.

[10] James Buchanan (American Minister at London) to Clarendon, Sept. 11, 1855, *Senate Executive Document 1*, 34 Cong., 1 Sess. (Serial 810), 73–75; Clarendon to Buchanan, Sept. 28, 1855, *ibid.*, 76–78.

merits of these arguments, the fact is that Britain and America were at loggerheads. Instead of ending the clash in Central America, the treaty had added new fuel. Congress debated the situation in a bad temper, with Clayton defending his role in the negotiations and Senator Stephen A. Douglas assailing him.

In March 1853 the more expansionist-minded Democrats under President Franklin Pierce took office in Washington. One year later England and France declared the Crimean War on Russia, and the United States' principal adversaries found themselves occupied far away. However, for the time being American attention shifted from Central America to other areas of Anglo-American tension: to Cuba, Santo Domingo, Hawaii, and Canada, in all of which places disturbing events occurred in 1854 as the Crimean War got under way. These events were important not only in themselves, but because by adding to the British-American tension they made a Central American accord considerably more difficult of attainment.

Since the Mexican War several filibustering expeditions against Cuba had sailed from American ports. So alarmed was Great Britain that in September 1851 she, together with France, had dispatched a squadron to patrol Cuban waters. Daniel Webster, then Secretary of State, had protested, saying that the United States could not tolerate this monitoring of her behavior on the high seas. Britain had replied with the familiar proposal that the United States join her and France in an agreement never to take Cuba. Partly, it may be, because of the current disenchantment with the similar commitment it had made toward Central America in the Clayton-Bulwer Treaty, Washington had refused.[11]

With Pierce in the White House and the Crimea preoccupying Britain and France, the United States offered Spain $130,000,000 to sell the island. Madrid declined. The administration then gave some passing thought to taking it by force—as had been suggested in the so-called Ostend Manifesto drawn up by the American Ministers to Spain, France, and Great Britain. But the Democrats were badly divided by a crisis in Kansas and

---

[11] *Senate Executive Document* 1, 32 Cong., 1 Sess. (Serial 611), 74–83, and *ibid.* 13, 32 Cong., 2 Sess. (Serial 660).

Nebraska, which Secretary Marcy sorrowfully admitted had deprived them of strength that "could have been much more profitably used for the acquisition of Cuba. . . ."[12] Perhaps, too, they were swayed by a British warning that despite Britain and France's involvement in the Crimea, "on the question of policy there is no part of the world in either hemisphere with regard to which we are not entirely in accord."[13] But the United States did not forget about the rich island so temptingly near, and in his annual messages of 1858, 1859, and 1860 President Buchanan recommended buying it—just as he was also urging expansion into Mexico.

Like Cuba, both Santo Domingo and Hawaii were strategically located for the protection of a future canal, and Hawaii had an important commerce with the west coast. In 1854 a Pierce agent made a treaty with Santo Domingo for the cession of Samaná Bay, an excellent naval base. But Britain and France successfully put pressure on the little country to repudiate the agreement. Developments regarding Hawaii were more complicated, but their outcome was similar. In 1843 Great Britain and France had made the characteristic suggestion that the United States join them in a hands-off agreement regarding these Pacific islands, and Washington had returned the characteristic refusal. After the Mexican War the Hawaiian King offered his country to the United States. The Whigs refused to accept but made it plain (as they had just done with Central America in the Clayton-Bulwer Treaty, and as was also their policy toward Cuba) that Hawaii must never go to any other power. Then in 1854, that year when the Democrats took the steps we have noted in Cuba and Santo Domingo, Secretary of State Marcy signed a treaty of annexation. But since Hawaii (possibly at British instigation)

---

[12] For the Ostend Manifesto see Amos A. Ettinger, *The Mission to Spain of Pierre Soulé, 1853–1855, A Study in the Cuban Diplomacy of the United States* (New Haven, 1932). Marcy to John Y. Mason (American Minister to France), July 23, 1854, Ivor D. Spencer, *The Victor and the Spoils: A Life of William L. Marcy* (Providence, 1959), 324.

[13] Foreign Secretary Clarendon in the House of Lords, Feb. 25, 1854, Kenneth Bourne, *Britain and the Balance of Power in North America, 1815–1908* (Berkeley and Los Angeles, 1967), 179. The warning aroused senatorial ire. *Congressional Globe*, 33 Cong., 2 Sess., 826–36 (Feb. 20, 1855).

insisted on a clause making her a state, Marcy did not submit the treaty to the Senate; presumably the administration feared to provoke a storm over the status of slavery in a new state.

At that same time, important developments were occurring over Canada, still disappointed by America's failure to respond to her overture for reciprocity. When Bulwer went to the United States to make the canal treaty, his instructions gave equal stress to the need for a reciprocity treaty. But the opposition in America remained strong, and in any case Washington was disinclined to help Britain solve a colonial problem, especially at a time of friction in Central America. Reciprocity was postponed again.

More alarming was the resurgence of the old fisheries quarrel, which as will be recalled had been temporarily ended by the Convention of 1818. A disagreement had arisen over the meaning of the Convention's ban on American fishing in "bays." Britain contended that Americans had no right to fish even in the very largest bays, and certainly not in inshore waters as they customarily did. Partly under pressure from British North America, partly to get a lever to induce Washington to view reciprocity more favorably, London decided in May 1852 to send a naval squadron to the fisheries to enforce the agreement of 1818. Its arrival angered Americans, just as had the appearance of British and French ships off Cuba a few months before. "The fishermen shall be protected in all their rights of property, and in all their rights of occupation," Secretary Webster threatened in a Massachusetts speech. Commodore Matthew C. Perry was ordered to the fishing grounds on the frigate *Mississippi* to protect Americans, and at Portsmouth, New Hampshire, a small naval force gathered for possible action.[14] Rival warships policed the same waters. Fortunately they did not clash, but one more danger had been added to the long British-American list.

Both countries realized that they already had quite enough problems elsewhere. The United States, only seven years from civil war, wanted no more difficulties with Great Britain than necessary; and Britain, confronting the ominous Near Eastern

---

[14] Speech at Marshfield, July 25, 1852, Charles C. Tansill, *The Canadian Reciprocity Treaty of 1854* (Baltimore, 1922), 44. *Ibid.*, 54–55; *House Executive Document* 21, 33 Cong., 1 Sess. (Serial 717).

questions, was anxious to avoid hostilities in North America. Reciprocity and the fisheries at least offered greater hope of successful resolution than did the interminable argument over the Clayton-Bulwer Treaty. After another futile reciprocity move in Congress and some desultory diplomatic talk, Secretary Marcy drew up a draft treaty in September 1853 and sent it to London. Months passed while Britain sounded out her North American colonies.

Then in late May 1854 Lord Elgin, the Governor-General of Canada, went to Washington, and during a few days of whirlwind negotiations he and Marcy came to terms.[15] The Marcy-Elgin Treaty, signed June 5, gave American fishermen considerably greater privileges than they had enjoyed under the Convention of 1818. Henceforth they were permitted to fish within the three-mile limit along the east coasts of British North America. British subjects could fish in American east-coast waters north of the thirty-sixth parallel, a right of little value and seldom exercised. Americans could navigate the St. Lawrence River and Canadian canals on the same terms as natives; British subjects were granted the free navigation of Lake Michigan. Reciprocity provisions listed a fairly large number of commodities, mainly agricultural but also (of special benefit to British North Americans) fish and fish-oil, to be admitted duty-free into the colonies and the United States.

The treaty, following upon the Webster-Ashburton Treaty and the Oregon Treaty, brought tranquillity to the northern border and the fisheries that was to last several years. But this one accord of 1854 did not dissipate the smouldering British-American hostiliity resulting from conflicting interests in many places. In that same year the moves toward Cuba, Santo Domingo, and Hawaii took place. And only a few weeks after the reciprocity treaty was signed, there erupted at Greytown, that strategic spot at the Caribbean end of the prospective Nicaragua canal, a sensational incident that undid much of the good accomplished by Elgin and Marcy. Because of a minor insult to an American

---

[15] Spencer, *Life of Marcy*, 302–304, shows that the usual account of Elgin's lavish and persuasive entertainment of Senators opposing reciprocity has been greatly exaggerated.

official there, Secretary of State Marcy sent the naval ship *Cyane* to Greytown. The commanding officer demanded reparations of $24,000. Receiving nothing at all, he gave warning of a bombardment and then, despite a protest by a British officer, proceeded to destroy Greytown on July 13, 1854. The callous act, far beyond what Marcy had intended, aroused anger in America and still more in Britain.[16] The bombardment took place just after news of the American pushes in Santo Domingo and Hawaii. "We are fast 'drifting' into a War with the U. States . . . ," the First Lord of the Admiralty said, and Palmerston foresaw the British navy "burning all their [American] Sea Coast Towns."[17]

It was natural for Britain to suspect that the *Cyane* affair heralded a more determined American effort to oust her from Central America. In the summer of 1855 an American filibuster landed at Greytown—"acting under secret instruction" from Washington, Foreign Secretary Clarendon concluded.[18] He was soon defeated. Much more successful and more worrying to London was another filibuster, William Walker, "the grey-eyed man of destiny," who seized Nicaragua in late 1855 and ruled it into 1857. The British assumed—incorrectly, however—that the United States was using Walker to circumvent the anticolonization provisions of the Clayton-Bulwer Treaty; they feared that Nicaragua would be following the road taken by Texas. Despite the burden of the Crimean War, Britain and France strengthened their naval forces off Central America, and when Costa Rica declared war on Walker in 1856, Britain supplied her with munitions.

Even though the American moves in Cuba, Santo Domingo, and Hawaii had failed, they seemed to indicate an intolerably

---

[16] *House Executive Document* 126, 33 Cong., 1 Sess. (Serial 734); Allan Nevins, *Ordeal of the Union,* II, *A House Dividing, 1852–1857* (New York, 1947), 365–67.

[17] Graham to Clarendon, Oct. 24, 1854, Richard W. Van Alstyne, "Anglo-American Relations, 1853–1857, British Statesmen on the Clayton-Bulwer Treaty and American Expansion," *American Historical Review,* XLII (1937), 497; Palmerston memorandum on a draft dispatch dated Sept. 10, 1854, Bourne, *Balance of Power,* 182.

[18] Clarendon to Palmerston, Oct. 25, 1855, Bourne, *Balance of Power,* 187.

reckless and aggressive spirit. And the Clayton-Bulwer Treaty notwithstanding, Central America appeared in terrible danger of falling. Obviously another Anglo-American crisis, more serious than the one supposedly alleviated in 1850, was at hand. In 1856 Great Britain was holding fast in Belize, the Bay Islands, and the Mosquito Coast; and Washington was continuing to insist that she was violating the Clayton-Bulwer Treaty. Costa Rica attacked Walker in February; the United States gave him diplomatic recognition in May. It was a presidential election year. At the Democratic nominating convention in June speakers praised Walker and excoriated the British. For the first time the Irish, after massive emigration since the potato famine, were playing a major role in American politics. The Crimean War was ending, leaving Britain freer to make a stand in the New World.

For almost a year another controversy had been developing. The United States had charged that the British Minister, John F. T. Crampton, and some Consuls were secretly and illegally recruiting Americans for service in the British army. London disclaimed any intention of violating American laws. But suddenly it became known that Crampton was in danger of being dismissed. Palmerston and Clarendon, at least, did not want to take such an insult without retaliation.[19] On May 28, 1856, three days before the Democratic convention met, the Minister was handed his passports.

The news reached London on June 11. Over the rest of the month and into July the House of Commons debated relations with the United States. The emphasis was on Crampton and Central America. Surprisingly enough, speaker after speaker spoke sympathetically about America and insisted that hostilities must be avoided. At no cost, Lord John Russell said, should Britain and America allow "the miserable States in Central America . . . to commit these two great nations to hostilities with each other." Benjamin Disraeli thought that if Britain "is to regard every expansion of the United States as an act detrimental to her

---

[19] Richard W. Van Alstyne, "John F. Crampton, Conspirator or Dupe?" *American Historical Review*, XLI (1936), 492–502; *Senate Executive Document 35*, 34 Cong., 1 Sess. (Serial 819), 1–243; Bourne, *Balance of Power*, 195.

interests and hostile to her power, we shall be pursuing a course which . . . will involve this country in struggles that may prove of a disastrous character."[20] Britain and America had reached a turning point. If events were allowed to drift much longer, war would result. Crampton's dismissal had awakened the members of Parliament to the critical state of affairs. In alarm, they drew back. An all-important Central American settlement began to take shape.

The truth is that by 1856 or 1857 the British people had become convinced that the United States was destined sooner or later to overrun Central America. William Walker had persuaded many that the Clayton-Bulwer Treaty could not stop American expansion. So why keep arguing about a useless treaty? This outlook was strongly reinforced by the new realization that a canal could not soon be built after all. Resistance to American expansion perhaps made sense when control of a great interoceanic waterway was thought to be at stake, as it was in 1850. To many it made no sense when this was seen to be no longer the case. The thinking of commercial circles went even further. They were beginning to look with relish upon early American annexation of the decadent Central American countries, in the belief that this would introduce stability and prosperity and consequently a thriving commerce beneficial to Great Britain. Rather disgustedly, Foreign Secretary Clarendon observed that the British people "don't care two straws about Central America. . . ."[21]

But the British people did not view the United States only in a Central American context. There is reason to think that many of them, especially those not in the upper class, felt positively well disposed toward her, and that the *Manchester Guardian* was expressing a widespread view when it said in 1857:

---

[20] *Parliamentary Debates*, Third Series, CXLII, 1505, 1512 (June 16, 1856). See also *ibid.*, CXLIII, 14–109 (June 30, 1856), 120–206 (July 1, 1856), 1456–57 (July 25, 1856).

[21] Clarendon to Palmerston, Dec. 30, 1857, Kenneth Bourne, "The Clayton-Bulwer Treaty and the Decline of British Opposition to the Territorial Expansion of the United States, 1857–60," *Journal of Modern History*, XXXIII (1961), 289.

Of all foreign powers, there is none with whom we are so anxious to keep on good terms as our transatlantic cousins. Their language, their race, their institutions should render them our natural allies. Our commercial relations with them are of such incalculable importance that the least sign of a seriously hostile spirit on either side must overcloud the peace and endanger the comfort of millions of our countrymen. There is perhaps no nation on earth with whom we would not rather quarrel than with America.[22]

As for the Ministry, even such enthusiastic brandishers of British power as Palmerston and Clarendon certainly did not want war. The Prime Minister did believe that Britain should strive to slow down United States expansion, and Clarendon would have welcomed the dispatch of a large fleet to Central America in 1856—if the government had had public support. But he realized, as no doubt did Palmerston, that what he called "the cowardly feeling" about the United States would prevent such a move.[23]

Thus strange as it may seem, at first, in the case of a government under Palmerston, Britain decided to accept the inevitable and taper off her opposition to American expansion in Central America. This change of front was made easier when Costa Rica, aided by British guns, defeated William Walker in 1857. Subsequently he twice sailed for Nicaragua from the United States, but a British warship seized the filibuster in 1860 and handed him over to Honduras, where he was executed.

It remained to do something about the trouble-making Clayton-Bulwer Treaty. Coincidentally with informing London of Crampton's ouster, Washington had asked for negotiations on Central America. Clarendon and the American Minister, George M. Dallas, signed a treaty in October 1856 that would have reconciled the two countries' differences, but Senate amendments were unacceptable to London.[24] Nevertheless the British had

---

[22] *Manchester Guardian*, March 9, 1857, reprinted in *ibid.*, March 14, 1957.
[23] Palmerston to Clarendon, July 4, 1857, Van Alstyne, "Anglo-American Relations, 1853–1857," 499, and Dec. 31, 1857, Bourne, *Victorian England*, 335; Clarendon to Palmerston, June 4, 1856, Bourne, *Balance of Power*, 197.
[24] Marcy to Dallas, May 24, 1856, *Senate Document* 161, 56 Cong., 1 Sess. (Serial 3853), 2–10.

shown a willingness to retreat, and once the crisis of 1856 had passed, the trend was toward a settlement. At one point in 1857 President Buchanan recommended abrogating the treaty "by mutual consent," and Britain would probably have been agreeable.[25] But in fact she found a simpler procedure. Instead of negotiating with the United States, she approached Honduras and Nicaragua. In late 1859 the British Consul in Central America, Sir Charles L. Wyke, concluded a treaty with the former country recognizing Honduras's title to the Bay Islands; and early the next year he signed a treaty with Nicaragua providing that the Mosquito Coast was under Nicaragua's sovereignty and that Britain would terminate her protectorate three months after the treaty's ratification. By these concessions Great Britain in effect abandoned the interpretation of the Clayton-Bulwer Treaty that she had been insisting upon since 1850. Referring to the Wyke treaties, President Buchanan said as much: "The discordant constructions of the Clayton and Bulwer treaty between the two Governments, which at different periods of the discussion bore a threatening aspect, have resulted in a final settlement entirely satisfactory to this Government."[26]

It was these two treaties, not the Clayton-Bulwer Treaty, which brought a British-American accord in Central America. The Clayton-Bulwer Treaty could now assume the role originally envisaged for it. Although several times before the treaty's termination in 1901, Washington pressed Britain to agree to its abrogation, it furnished a generally beneficial although at times controversial framework for British-American affairs in Central America over the years to come.

A number of diverse incidents also testified to the better relations. The first concerned the slave trade, always a delicate matter for a slave-owning country. It will be recalled that in the Webster-Ashburton Treaty the United States agreed to maintain off the African coast a large enough squadron to enforce her

---

[25] Annual message, Dec. 8, 1857, Richardson, *Messages and Papers*, V, 444; Palmerston to Clarendon, Dec. 31, 1857, Bourne "Clayton-Bulwer Treaty," 290.

[26] Annual message, Dec. 3, 1860, Richardson, *Messages and Papers*, V, 639.

laws against slavers flying the American flag. She had failed to
do so. Britain was as determined as ever to suppress the horrible
traffic in "black ivory." In 1858 her warships searched American
merchantmen near Cuba and in the Gulf of Mexico suspected of
being slavers fraudulently flying the Stars and Stripes. A minor
crisis flared up when United States warships hurried to the Gulf.
It subsided when Britain, in June of that year, made substantial
concessions. As his term in the White House neared its end,
Buchanan proudly told Congress: "Our relations with Great
Britain are of the most friendly character. Since the commence-
ment of my Administration the . . . dangerous questions arising
from the . . . right of search claimed by the British Government
have been amicably and honorably adjusted."[27] The President,
however, was overly optimistic. Further difficulties were to occur,
and a final settlement was reached only when the secession of
the Confederacy left the North free to make a treaty with Britain
in 1862 granting a mutual right of search.

In 1858 the Atlantic cable was laid (although it soon went
out of action until 1866), and Queen Victoria and President
Buchanan exchanged congratulatory messages. Two years later
the Prince of Wales, the future Edward VII, made a successful
visit to the United States, a visit that could not have been under-
taken at an earlier time.

Off the shores of distant China, a country where British and
American interests were usually to run parallel, a symbolic event
took place. We have noted how Britain and France sometimes
collaborated against American expansion. In the Far East, however, the United States collaborated with these nations in opening that area to western trade. In two little wars against China
between 1857 and 1860 Britain and France extracted commercial concessions which Washington promptly demanded, and
received. During the second round of hostilities some British
ships found themselves endangered by Chinese gunfire. An
American Commodore, Josiah Tatnall, happened to be close by,
escorting the American Minister to China. With the Minister's
consent, he and some of his crew boarded the British flagship
and helped with the fighting. "Blood is thicker than water," the

---

[27] *Ibid.*

Commodore is supposed to have explained as the cannonballs flew by.[28]

It would be difficult to exaggerate the significance of the Central American accord. It signalized the end of Britain's long-sustained efforts to contain the United States. Despite British resistance—never very strong, it must be admitted—the United States had taken Texas and swept on across the continent. She had pushed tentatively but firmly against Cuba, Santo Domingo, and Hawaii; and few people doubted that those places would some day be American. She had pushed much harder in Central America, that strategic area where an interoceanic canal would sooner or later be built. In the late 1850s Great Britain had given up her efforts to hold firm there. She had concluded that the struggle was not worth the price; indeed many Englishmen were beginning to welcome American penetration of the area as a step toward greater commerce for all. It is true that Britain could not have tolerated American aggression north of the international line, but after the Oregon settlement little danger remained of any major forceful move in that direction.

If, within reason, the United States could expand as she wished, free of British opposition, the chief cause of Anglo-American clashes would be removed. Although slavery, the Irish, and other difficulties remained, some such rapprochement as the one occurring at the end of the century might well have come years sooner. But history traverses a rough and winding road, and events seldom unfold as prophets expect. What prevented Anglo-American affairs from following a predictable pattern of growing friendship was, of course, the Civil War. When the Confederacy seceded in 1860 and early 1861, British hopes of containing America, which had dwindled three or four years earlier, suddenly soared with a vengeance. All at once it appeared that, not only was containment feasible, but a real North American balance of power was establishing itself. Disraeli's prediction had come true. He had remarked that American expansion into sparsely populated territory "is not injurious to England . . .—(let me say this in a whisper lest it

---

[28] Warren I. Cohen, *America's Response to China, An Interpretative History of Sino-American Relations* (New York, 1971), 25–26.

cross the Atlantic)—more than that—it diminishes the power of the United States."[29] In 1860, it was plain, America's expansion had not only diminished her power, it had destroyed her unity.

We must now turn to developments during the Civil War. That conflict was to undo the British-American reconciliation of the late 1850s, produce a serious war-scare and several periods of great tension, and leave a legacy of deep hatred in the victorious North.

---

[29] *Parliamentary Debates*, Third Series, CXLIII, 1456–1457 (July 25, 1856).

CHAPTER VII

Regrowth of Animosity: The Civil War Years

THE UNITED STATES, teetering on the brink of sectional disaster ever since the Mexican War, finally collapsed when several southern states seceded in 1860. Outright civil war erupted in April 1861. Great Britain and the United States had already fought two wars, and had experienced many serious controversies as well as several war scares. For a long time, America's aggressiveness and her republican, democratic institutions had alarmed Englishmen; Yankee boorishness had disgusted them. No wonder that by and large the British ruling class felt a thrill of satisfaction as the ungainly republic split in two. Americans, they thought vindictively, were at last getting their just deserts; American political institutions were revealing their hollowness.

In addition to this almost automatic reaction, there was a dangerous change in commercial relations. We have observed the effect of trans-Atlantic trade in mitigating disputes. But during the Civil War the trade connection, instead of being a potent deterrent of war, threatened for several months to become just the opposite. Britain's principal import from North America was cotton, needed for the cotton-textile industry of the Midlands on which some four million Britons depended for their livelihood. During the years 1851–1860 over 80 percent of the cotton used in Britain came from the United States.[1] Cotton seemed indeed to be King. Early in the war imports of cotton from America declined sharply, from 2,580,700 bales in 1860 to 72,000 bales in 1862.[2] The expectation was general that Brit-

---

[1] Emerson D. Fite, "The Agricultural Development of the West During the Civil War," *Quarterly Journal of Economics*, XX (1906), 263.
[2] *Ibid.*

ain would be forced to intervene in order to regain a vital raw material, although in fact she had an unusually large stockpile of it. The British Minister at Washington, Lord Lyons, told President Abraham Lincoln's Secretary of State, William H. Seward, that if cotton rose in price and if Southern ports were blockaded, "an immense pressure would be put upon H. M.'s Government to use all the means in their power to open those Ports."[3] Prices did rise, and the ports were blockaded. Economic distress in the cotton textile areas of Britain became severe.

It might be thought that Britain's long crusade against slavery would have precluded sympathy for the Confederacy. Beyond doubt the British people were violently opposed to slavery. Prime Minister Palmerston himself shared this attitude, as we have seen; his biographer has called his efforts to end the slave trade "the great humanitarian enterprise of his life." However, President Lincoln, in his inaugural address, had emphasized that he had "no purpose, directly or indirectly, to interfere with the institution of slavery in the States where it exists."[4] Many a conservative, upper-class Englishman must have welcomed this affirmation, which justified morally a position he would have taken anyway. John L. Motley, then American Minister to Austria-Hungary and a future Minister to Great Britain, thought as late as the autumn of 1862 that only emancipation of the slaves would save the North from a war with both Great Britain and France. As for more liberally inclined Englishmen, most of them did not at first realize the extent to which the Civil War was a social as well as a political conflict, nor did they grasp that Lincoln's disclaimer was in large measure tactical. Having just welcomed Lombardy's secession from Austria-Hungary, they saw the South as exercising a similar right of self-determination. Washington seemed no less tyrannical than Vienna.

Why, then, did Britain not intervene militarily? She could have insured Southern victory, established a North American

---

[3] Lyons to Lord John Russell, March 26, 1861, Thomas W. L. Newton, second baron, *Lord Lyons, a Record of British Diplomacy* (London, 1913), I, 31.

[4] Herbert C. F. Bell, *Lord Palmerston* (London, 1936), I, 231; address of March 4, 1861, James D. Richardson, ed., *A Compilation of the Messages and Papers of the Presidents, 1789–1897* (Washington, 1899), VI, 5.

balance of power, tarnished the lure of democracy, and made safe her cotton supply. The danger of intervention, military or diplomatic, was great until early 1863, when conditions changed. Indeed, one may conjecture that Britain would have acted decisively had it not seemed certain for many months that the South could not be defeated. "There is an all but unanimous belief that you *cannot* subject the South to the Union," Richard Cobden, the great British exponent of free trade, wrote the chairman of the Senate Foreign Relations Committee, Senator Charles Sumner, in July 1862. And when the Chancellor of the Exchequer, William E. Gladstone, said later in the year that "there is no doubt that Jefferson Davis and other leaders of the South have made . . . a nation," he was not contradicting Cabinet opinion.[5] So why run any risk when the Confederacy appeared to be in no danger?

Even so, had she anticipated an easy victory over the North, Britain might have gone to war. Good grounds there were for expecting that she would win. But in fact the struggle would be grim, as she well knew. Could the North American colonies be defended? What dreadful losses would swarms of Yankee privateers inflict upon the British merchant marine? Cobden thought that intervention would have been "easy, and indeed popular, if you had been a weaker naval power."[6] And what untoward move might not be made by some watchful European rival? Lord Clarendon, the former Foreign Secretary, expressed the typical hesitation: "The [Northern] villains seem to be desirous of picking a quarrel with us, wh. as it wd. complete their everlasting and irretrievable ruin I shd. be glad of if I did not feel sure that N[apoleon III, Emperor of France] wd. instantly leave us in the lurch and do something in Europe wh. we can't stand."[7]

The Ministry had also to consider pro-Northern sentiment in

[5] Cobden to Sumner, July 11, 1862, John Morley, *The Life of Richard Cobden* (London, 1908), II, 402; speech in Newcastle, Oct. 7, 1862, John Morley, *The Life of William Ewart Gladstone* (New York, 1903), I, 713.
[6] Cobden to Sumner, Feb. 13, 1863, Morley, *Cobden*, II, 403.
[7] Clarendon to Lord Granville, Sept. 14, 1861, Kenneth Bourne, "British Preparations for War with the North, 1861–1862," *English Historical Review*, LXXVI (1961), 629.

Great Britain. In contrast to those who, in the words of John Bright (Cobden's close associate), "form what is called 'society' at the 'West End' of London," many people in Britain admired republicanism and democracy and considered American institutions superior to their own.[8] They strongly favored the North as against the more conservative, hierarchical South; and despite Lincoln's inaugural statement, believed that the conflict would decide the fate of slavery. These people were apt to be nonconformists living in the Midlands and connected with the cotton-textile industry. Their spokesmen were John Bright and Richard Cobden. Many British intellectuals also favored the North—such persons as Sir Charles Lyell, Thomas Huxley, Algernon Swinburne, Leslie Stephen, Dante Gabriel Rossetti, John Stuart Mill, Anthony Trollope, George Meredith, and Elizabeth and Robert Browning. British opinion was sufficiently divided to make the government think twice before rushing into war.

Finally, not even Prime Minister Palmerston, however disapproving of the United States, wanted hostilities. If he sometimes talked belligerently, he was nevertheless a statesman who did not lightly commit British power in circumstances as hazardous as those sure to follow a break with the North. Nor was his political position strong enough to support an adventurous North American policy. His Foreign Secretary, Lord John (Earl, in May 1861) Russell, was also a vigorous defender of British interests and yet a prudent diplomat. Other members of the Cabinet, especially the Duke of Argyll, were more friendly to the North.

Although Palmerston and his ministry did not want to start a war, they almost had one in late 1861. On November 8 a Northern warship, the *San Jacinto*, Captain Charles Wilkes commanding, stopped the British mail steamer *Trent* in the Bahama Channel and seized two Confederate envoys going to Europe, John Slidell and James M. Mason. They were taken to

---

[8] Bright to Motley, Jan. 9, 1862, George W. Curtis, ed., *The Complete Works of John L. Motley* (New York, 1889), XVI, 226; Frank Thistlethwaite, *The Anglo-American Connection in the Early Nineteenth Century* (Philadelphia, 1959).

Massachusetts and imprisoned. Mason and Slidell were well known; Northerners detested them and considered them diplomats of great skill. Rejoicing in their arrest and desperately needing a success after inconclusive fighting and a humiliating defeat at Bull Run, the North erupted with a sustained chorus of acclaim for Wilkes. The Governor of Massachusetts gave him a banquet, the Secretary of the Navy wrote him a congratulatory letter, the House of Representatives gave him a vote of thanks, and Congress voted him a gold medal.

It was particularly sweet that Wilkes had stopped a British ship. Northerners deeply resented the ruling class's sympathy for the Confederacy and scorn for democracy. In April 1861 Britain had proclaimed her neutrality. Though this step was justified by Lincoln's previous announcement of a blockade, she would have shown more tact by acting less quickly. To Northerners neutrality seemed an inexcusably cold-blooded attitude toward an antislavery crusade and proof of Britain's malevolence. The old hatred for the English, momentarily lulled in the late 1850s, surged up again. Motley was a good prophet when he said in 1861, "there will never in our generation be the cordial . . . sentiment toward England which existed a year ago."[9]

If Americans looked with dark suspicion on Britain, Britons responded in kind. The government was convinced that Secretary of State Seward was anti-British and temperamentally unfit for his position; Foreign Secretary Russell hoped he "could be turned out, and a rational man put in his place." Seward was reported to have told the Duke of Newcastle in 1860 that if he became Secretary of State he would insult Great Britain, and on another occasion he had spoken of a foreign war as the best means of uniting the country.[10] For several months not only Secretary Seward but President Lincoln and his administration were inexperienced and conducted themselves awkwardly. So alarmed was Lyons by the Cabinet's attitude that he cautioned Ottawa that

---

[9] Motley to his wife, July 7, 1861, Curtis, *Works of Motley*, XVI, 165.
[10] Russell to Lyons, Dec. 1, 1861, Newton, *Lyons*, I, 63; Charles Francis Adams, *Charles Francis Adams* (Boston and New York, 1900), 165; Samuel F. Bemis, *A Diplomatic History of the United States* (New York, 1955), 367. It was not publicly known that Seward actually proposed a foreign war to Lincoln. *Ibid.*

though it sounded preposterous he was afraid the United States might provoke hostilities with Great Britain.[11]

The boarding of the *Trent* aroused British fears that Seward was trying to foment his foreign war. Advised by the government's legal experts that Wilkes had violated international law, Russell sent off an ultimatum on November 30 demanding that the United States apologize, release the prisoners, and allow them to proceed to Europe. Seven days were granted for compliance. These terms, though stiff, were expressed moderatly, in part because of the intervention of Albert, the Prince Consort, who was then close to death; moreover Russell wrote Lyons privately that the Cabinet would be "rather easy about the apology" so long as the commissioners were freed. But he warned that "The feeling here is very quiet but very decided. There is no party about it: all are unanimous."[12]

Not only was the government unanimous but the British people were practically so. Thurlow Weed (Seward's political associate in New York), then in England, discovered "but one voice here. All are for war. . . ." The press exploded with denunciations of America's insult to the Union Jack. War was inevitable; such was the general belief.[13]

Speedily, reinforcements were sent to Canada. By early January 1862 over 11,000 officers and men fully equipped for fighting had left for that colony. The fleet was readied for hostilities; several ships hurried off to join the North American squadron. An embargo was placed on a large quantity of saltpeter just purchased by the United States and desperately needed by her

---

[11] Lyons to Sir Edmund Head (Governor-General of Canada), May 22, 1861, Newton, *Lyons*, I, 39.

[12] Russell to Lyons, Nov. 30, 1861, *Senate Executive Document* 8, 37 Cong., 2 Sess. (Serial 1129), 3–4; Russell to Lyons, Dec. 1, 1861, Newton, *Lyons*, I, 63; see also *ibid.*, 62. Regarding Albert's role see Norman B. Ferris, "The Prince Consort, 'The Times,' and the 'Trent' Affair," *Civil War History*, VI (1960), 152–56. See Law Officers to Russell, Nov. 28, 1861, James P. Baxter, 3rd, "Papers relating to Belligerent and Neutral Rights, 1861–1865," *American Historical Review*, XXXIV (1928), 86–87.

[13] Weed to Zachariah Chandler, Dec. 7, 1861, Lester B. Shippee, *Canadian-American Relations, 1849–1874* (New Haven, 1939), 126; see also Cobden to Sumner, Dec. 19, 1861, Morley, *Cobden*, II, 389.

army. These and other moves were made on the assumption that war was coming, for few believed that Washington could back down in the face of the public jubilation. The Prime Minister assured Queen Victoria that "Great Britain is in a better state than at any former time to inflict a severe blow upon and to read a lesson to the United States which will not soon be forgotten."[14]

With emotions high in both countries, it was fortunate that trans-Atlantic communications were slow. Two months elapsed between the *Trent's* boarding and the final settlement. Tempers could not remain at fever pitch so long. After the first two or three weeks the excitement dwindled somewhat.

The initial opinion in Washington was to stand firm. Some members of the Cabinet and even President Lincoln opposed surrendering Mason and Slidell. But gradually cooler views prevailed; the most hot-headed realized the madness of fighting Great Britain when the Confederacy alone seemed quite enough. Lyons told Seward the British demands on December 19 and gave him a copy of Russell's note four days later. The Secretary immediately got to work drafting a reply. In session most of Christmas Day, the Cabinet accepted it with minor changes; it went to Lyons on the 26th.

Wilkes's action, the reply said, was unauthorized, though he had captured the "contraband persons . . . in what seems to be a perfectly lawful manner." But Seward admitted that Wilkes had made one mistake: he had not taken the *Trent* into port for trial by a prize court. Therefore, the Secretary promised, the prisoners "will be cheerfully liberated." The note was directed not only at London but in large part at the American public. Seward depicted the United States, not as yielding to Britain, but as "really defending and maintaining . . . an old, honored, and cherished American cause. . . ." He implied that Britain, in protesting the arrest of the commissioners, had swung over to the American view about impressment, so that "a question is finally and rightly settled . . . which heretofore exhausting not only all forms of peaceful discussion, but also the arbitrament of war itself, for more than half a century alienated the two coun-

---

[14] Palmerston to the Queen, Dec. 5, 1861, Bell, *Palmerston*, II, 295.

tries from each other, and perplexed with fears and apprehensions all other nations."[15]

The reply substantially met the British demands because the prisoners were released, and if there was no formal apology there was an explanation. Mason and Slidell resumed their interrupted trip. So ended the gravest threat of the Civil War to British-American peace.

But for Northerners it was a bitter pill to free the two envoys and to see them calmly sail off to Europe. Few could have believed that the United States had really won a diplomatic triumph; most must have presumed that, as Lyons said, Washing had yielded to Britain's display of force.[16] Altogether the affair greatly increased ill will toward Britain.

The conviction of British hostility was reinforced by another incident occurring around the same time. In October 1861 Great Britain, France, and Spain agreed to use force if necessary to make Mexico pay some defaulted debts. During the excitement over the *Trent* their troops landed at Vera Cruz. But when Mexico did not give in, the British and Spanish withdrew in May 1862; only the French went ahead and took Mexico City. American resentment was thereafter confined to France, but for a time Britain had shared in it. Few Northerners had doubted that she was taking advantage of America's tragic division in order to violate the Monroe Doctrine, expand her New World empire, perhaps even gain a vantage point for supporting the Confederacy.

Months before Mason and Slidell arrived in Europe, another Southern envoy had gone to Great Britain with the mission of getting warships for the Confederacy. Soon the news that ships were being built reached Charles Francis Adams, the American Minister at London; he belabored Russell to have the work stopped. The Foreign Secretary correctly replied that no law was being broken. In March 1862 one of these vessels, the *Florida,* got away. In July another one slipped into the water off Liverpool, supposedly on a trial run. In fact she went to the Azores; there she

---

[15] Seward to Lyons, Dec. 26, 1861, *Senate Executive Document* 8, 37 Cong., 2 Sess., 9–13.

[16] Lyons to Russell, Dec. 31, 1861, Newton, *Lyons,* I, 74.

was armed and given a crew consisting mainly of Englishmen. This was the famous *Alabama*. Sailing under the Confederate flag, she destroyed nearly sixty Northern ships before finally being sunk in 1864. Russell himself confessed that the *Alabama*, "roaming the ocean with English guns and English sailors to burn, sink and destroy the ships of a friendly nation, is a scandal and a reproach."[17] But the British law was defective and the government, despite its anxiety to stop these transactions, could at first do little.

In the United States nothing else aroused so violent a fury as the *Alabama* and the other cruisers built in Britain. The conviction was widespread that the British government was conniving in their building in order to help the South break up the union. These ships did not give rise to a sudden surge of anger that fell off as time passed. On the contrary, they engendered a smouldering rage that kept rising with every new loss of a Northern vessel and that was sharpened by the frustration over the inability to strike back at Great Britain.

From early in the war Napoleon III had wanted to intervene to stop the fighting and bring about Southern independence. He had hoped for joint intervention with his country's recent ally, Great Britain. London had been uninterested. But as the months of 1862 passed, with terrible slaughter and the South apparently invincible, diplomatic intervention became more attractive to the British. In mid-September it seemed likely to take place. At that time Prime Minister Palmerston suggested that in certain circumstances it might be advisable for Britain and France to urge the North and South to separate for good. The Foreign Secretary was ready to make a stronger move. He thought that the time had already come to offer mediation, and that if Washington refused to recognize Southern independence, then Great Britain should do so.

If Britain, with perhaps France and other countries, had recognized Southern independence, would Northern defeatism and Southern morale have been so bolstered that the union would

---

[17] Russell to Lyons, March 28, 1863, *ibid.*, 99. For Palmerston's defense of British policy see Hansard's *Parliamentary Debates*, Third Series, CLXX, 90–94 (March 27, 1863).

have split up for good? Would a desperate North have declared war on Britain? No one can say for certain. One can only be sure that mediation would have been attended by a period of great danger. Palmerston and Russell, when discussing the move, envisaged strengthening Canadian defenses and attacking the American coast. Perhaps British-American hostilities would have been avoided, but it was just as well that no mediation offer was made to put the matter to the test.

Two episodes nipped the move in the bud. First, there came the news of a great battle at Antietam. It seemed prudent to await its outcome. Then Lord Granville, the Lord President of the Council, made a strong plea not to change a successful policy that "has met with such general approval from Parliament, the Press, and the public."[18] When the Cabinet met on October 23 the mood had turned against mediation. The South had not prevailed at Antietam. Indeed it began to seem possible, perhaps probable, that the war would not soon be over, in which case the North's superior resources would tell. The Cabinet dropped the matter.

The decision against mediation heralded a change in British-American relations that took place during the first months of 1863; and the danger of a serious clash diminished sharply. Several developments were responsible for this. For one thing, the tide of battle continued to move, slowly but inexorably, in favor of the North. No matter how gallantly the Confederacy fought, she could not win a protracted struggle. By mid-1863 this was becoming plainer all the time.

But the most crucial development of early 1863 was President Lincoln's Emancipation Proclamation. For some time the President had been waiting for the time when such a proclamation would not be interpreted as a desperate attempt to stir up a slave insurrection. Antietam seemed enough of a victory to justify the move. Lincoln issued a preliminary proclamation on September 23, 1862 and the final proclamation on January 1,

---

[18] Palmerston to Russell, Sept. 23, 1862, Spencer Walpole, *The Life of Lord John Russell* (London, 1889), II, 350; Granville to Russell, Sept. 29, 1862, Kenneth Bourne, *The Foreign Policy of Victorian England, 1830–1902* (Oxford, 1970), 361–63.

1863. As a matter of fact, the anti-slave-trade treaty of April 1862, mentioned in an earlier chapter, had already given pause to Englishmen pretending that the conflict had nothing to do with slavery.[19] Emancipation convinced all but the inveterate scoffers. "It is creating an almost convulsive reaction in our favor all over this country," thought Henry Adams, who was in England with his father, the Minister. Pro-Northern sympathy grew by leaps and bounds. Cobden described the change to Sumner: "This state of feeling [in favor of intervention] existed up to the announcement of the President's Emancipation Policy. From that moment our old anti-slavery feeling began to arouse itself, and it has been gathering strength ever since. . . . And I now write to assure you that any unfriendly act on the part of our Government . . . towards your case, is not to be apprehended."[20] No British government would have dared adopt a policy leading to war once it became clear that this would mean fighting for slavery.

By early 1863, furthermore, the difficulties of the British cotton-textile industry were easing. Other sources of supply were being developed in Egypt, India, and elsewhere. In 1860 Britain had imported 785,000 bales of cotton from non-American sources; in 1863 she imported 1,932,000 bales from them. This figure rose to 2,755,000 bales in 1865; it compares with imports of 2,580,700 bales from the United States in 1860.[21] Then, too, as Northern armies advanced, some cotton areas began to open up again to international trade. Whereas only 72,000 bales had been exported from America to Britain in 1862, the figures for the next three years were 132,000 bales, 198,000 bales, and

---

[19] Conway W. Henderson, "The Anglo-American Treaty of 1862 in Civil War Diplomacy," *Civil War History*, XV (1969), 308–19.

[20] Henry Adams to Charles Francis Adams, Jr., Jan. 23, 1863, Worthington C. Ford, ed., *A Cycle of Adams Letters, 1861–1865* (Boston and New York, 1920), I, 243; Cobden to Sumner, Feb. 13, 1863, Morley, *Cobden*, II, 403–404.

[21] Louis B. Schmidt, "The Influence of Wheat and Cotton on Anglo-American Relations During the Civil War," *Iowa Journal of History and Politics*, XVI (1918), 419. See also Fite, "Agricultural Development of the West," 263; Frenise A. Logan, "India–Britain's Substitute for American Cotton, 1861–1865," *Journal of Southern History*, XXIV (1958), 472–80; *Parliamentary Debates*, Third Series CLXIII 350–73 (May 31, 1861).

462,000 bales, respectively.[22] Even though laborers in the Midlands still suffered terrible hardships, they were enthusiastic supporters of the North; no pressure for intervention came from them. On the contrary, at a large public meeting in Manchester on New Year's Eve, 1862, a resolution of sympathy for the North was unanimously adopted after one speaker declared: "Hitherto the people of the cotton districts have been drawing their livelihood in a co-operative system of slavery. He hoped they would draw out of it that night (hear, hear)." A letter expressing strong backing was sent to President Lincoln.[23]

Not only did Great Britain become less dependent on the South, she became more dependent on the North. For three consecutive years, from 1860 through 1862, the wheat crop in Great Britain fell off markedly. Only the United States could make up the deficiency. Exports to Britain rose from 99,000 quarters of wheat and flour in 1859, to 2,143,000 in 1860, 3,602,000 in 1861, and 5,022,000 in 1862.[24] At the very time when the cotton shortage was most acute, British dependence on American wheat was greatest. As Richard Cobden told the Manchester Chamber of Commerce, "You get an article even more important than your cotton from America—your food."[25]

Then, too, the European scene was darkening. Russia invaded Poland in 1863 to suppress a rebellion. Her troops' ruthless behavior aroused anger throughout Europe. France even appealed to the United States to put pressure on the Tsar to deal more leniently with the rebels, but met with a refusal. Concern was felt, too, over the ominously growing strength of Prussia. Otto von Bismarck's "blood and iron" policy was already leading to the crisis that would erupt in a war with Denmark in 1864. Facing trouble in Europe, England had to be more circumspect in North America.

---

[22] Schmidt, "Influence of Wheat and Cotton," 419.

[23] *Manchester Guardian*, Jan. 1, 1863. For Lincoln's reply, dated Jan. 19, 1863, see *ibid.*, Feb. 11, 1863. I am indebted to Mr. Fadlo Hourani for calling my attention to these references.

[24] Fite, "Agricultural Development of the West," 264; Schmidt, "Influence of Wheat and Cotton," 430.

[25] Speech of Oct. 25, 1862, Schmidt, "Influence of Wheat and Cotton," 434; see also *Parliamentary Debates*, Third Series, CLXXI, 1795 (June 30, 1863).

All these developments of 1863—the growing Northern strength, the Emancipation Proclamation, the weakening of King Cotton, Britain's need for wheat, and problems in Europe— meant that Great Britain was far less inclined to risk war than she had been during the *Trent* crisis. But was there not the possibility that an angry United States would provoke hostilities? In 1863 the *Alabama* was still sinking Northern ships; Confederate warships were still under construction in British shipyards. In April, Minister Lyons found "the state of things here, as far as peace with us is concerned, more alarming than it has been since the *Trent* affair."[26] Nevertheless the atmosphere in Washington was considerably better than it had been in 1861. Since then the administration had gained poise and experience. No longer was there any chance, as there had once seemed to be, that the United States would embark upon a suicidal war with Britain. Further trans-Atlantic disputes were to arise, even talk of war. But in the changed circumstances of 1863 and later these disputes presented little danger. We may pass over them quickly.

On February 25, 1863, a few days after Cobden had assured Senator Sumner that hostile action by Great Britain was no longer to be feared, a United States warship captured the British merchant ship *Peterhoff* near the island of St. Thomas, Danish West Indies. Her seizure was ordered by Charles Wilkes, now an Acting Rear-Admiral. The outcry in Britain was loud and angry, surpassed only by that over the *Trent*; and the involvement of the notorious Wilkes added to the excitement. British stock prices fell and the exchanges shut down as war again appeared possible. Although the steamer had been proceeding from London to the neutral Mexican port of Matamoras, she and her cargo were condemned by the United States District Court, Southern District of New York. The doctrine of continuous voyage, applied in the *Essex* case of 1805, will be recalled. The New York court invoked this doctrine in reaching its decision to condemn both ship and cargo, a decision that the Law Officers of the Crown advised was in harmony with British judgments. Consequently London merely advised the owners to appeal to the United States Supreme Court, and this they did.

---

[26] Lyons to Russell, April 13, 1863, Newton, *Lyons*, I, 101.

After the war, in 1867, the Supreme Court altered the earlier verdict: the ship, it declared, was subject to restoration, but the absolute contraband, since ultimately destined to enemy territory, had been rightly condemned.

Another danger of 1863 was the revival of the movement to recognize Southern independence. In the summer two pro-Southern members of Parliament conferred with Napoleon, who assured them of his support. One of them, John A. Roebuck, introduced on June 30 a motion in Parliament for recognition. But the likelihood of recognition in 1863 was enormously less than in 1862. For a while in that earlier year, as we have seen, both the Prime Minister and the Foreign Secretary had favored it; now they opposed it. Roebuck's motion, although debated at length, never had a chance of adoption, and in July he withdrew it.[27] At the end of the month news arrived that Ulysses S. Grant had captured Vicksburg and that Robert E. Lee had failed at Gettysburg. The most inveterate Southern sympathizers knew that any chance of British intervention had virtually ended.

Perhaps they still attached hopes to the Confederate warships, some sailing the high seas, others under construction in Great Britain. On April 3, 1863 the *Georgia* had escaped from the Clyde. Two days later Foreign Secretary Russell ordered the *Alexandra*, about ready to sail, to be seized. In a court test, however, the jury found against the government. Though the government appealed, months would pass before a verdict could be reached. Meanwhile no law existed that could even restrain construction. Seward was so infuriated that he threatened to allow privateers (none existed, but they had just been authorized by Congress) to chase Confederate ships right into British ports—a guaranteed means of creating an explosive situation with Britain. But privateers were never used, and the *Alexandra*, although released in England, was seized again at Nassau and held until the end of the war.

For about a year two sinister ironclad vessels, each equipped with a formidable battering ram, had been under construction by the British firm, William Laird and Sons. The Laird rams, as

---

[27] Russell to Lyons, March 14, 1863, *ibid.*, 99; *Parliamentary Debates*, Third Series, CLXXI, 1771–80 (June 30, 1863); *ibid.*, CLXXII, 662 (July 13, 1863).

they were called, were evidently though not avowedly destined for the Confederacy. They would be ready to sail in August or September 1863, and reports were rife of how they would destroy the Northern navy and raise the blockade. Adams warned that the rams must not sail. But doubts persisted that the courts would sanction their detention, any more than they had that of the *Alexandra.*

Russell, who had shown his concern over the *Alexandra,* started in mid-August to search for a legal means of detaining the ironclads. He could find none; the Solicitor-General stated flatly on September 2 that no such means existed because proof was lacking that the ships were destined for the Confederacy. But the very next day the Foreign Secretary wisely ordered the rams to be held, and Palmerston backed him. In so doing, the two men risked a court reversal and political attack, and they demonstrated their great anxiety not to affront the United States. Unaware of what had happened, an apprehensive Adams wrote threateningly to Russell on the 5th that if the rams sailed "It would be superfluous in me to point out to your Lordship that this is war."[28]

In practice, Russell had ended the danger. Legally, the matter remained undecided for another month. Warned by the Law Officers that detention was illegal, the government evaded a court battle by purchasing the rams for its own use.

This was the last major incident during the Civil War arousing British-American tension. A few smaller matters involved British North American provinces, and through them Great Britain. In late 1863 some Southern sympathizers seized a Northern coasting vessel, the *Chesapeake,* on her regular run between New York and Portland, Maine. A Northern warship illegally recaptured the ship in Nova Scotian waters, and then under orders from Washington turned her over to the provincial authorities. These later restored her to her owners. Further excitement occurred in the autumn of 1864 when Confederate agents seized and plundered an American steamer on Lake Erie, the *Philo Parsons,* and scuttled another vessel, the *Island Queen,* all

[28] Martin B. Duberman, *Charles Francis Adams, 1807–1886* (Boston, 1961), 311.

this as part of an abortive plot to free Southern prisoners held on Johnson's Island, off Sandusky, Ohio. A much more serious incident came a month later, in October, when a band of Southerners based in Canada attacked St. Albans, Vermont, and escaped back across the border. A storm of anger erupted in the North; and it was not appeased when a Canadian court released the raiders.

Far and away more important than these affairs were the Southern warships, busily sinking ships throughout the conflict (and one of them, the *Shenandoah*, even after fighting ended on land). It would be difficult to exaggerate the anger they aroused. Principally because of the *Alabama* and her sister ships, a sullen, bitter, vindictive mood toward Great Britain gripped the North. Minister Lyons believed in 1864 that "three-fourths of the American people are eagerly longing for a safe opportunity of making war with England. . . ."[29] That opportunity seemed to be in sight when General Lee surrendered at Appomattox in April 1865.

---

[29] Lyons to Russell, April 19, 1864, Newton, *Lyons*, I, 128–29.

CHAPTER VIII

Daggers Across the Sea

W HEN THE CIVIL WAR at length ended in 1865, anger against Great Britain was intense throughout the victorious North. Without Britain's support and sympathy the South could not have resisted so long; tens of thousands of soldiers would yet be alive; the country would not be burdened with colossal debts pressing down even on future generations. So it was widely believed in the United States.

Northern anger centered upon the *Alabama* and the other Southern cruisers built in Britain. By allowing these warships to be constructed the British, it was thought, had revealed their burning desire for Southern victory and the destruction of the sacred union. Moreover the cruisers had wreaked such havoc upon Northern commerce that at the end of the conflict the American merchant marine was less than a third of its size at the beginning. Ship owners and insurance companies were quick to blame Great Britain and to present claims for damages. All these claims, whether directed at the *Alabama* or some other cruiser, came to be loosely called the *Alabama* claims.

In the emotional mood consequent upon the years of carnage many a Northerner would have relished an opportunity to strike down the arch-foe. Their anger, however exaggerated, was comprehensible even to an upperclass Englishman like Lord Granville, who was to become Prime Minister Gladstone's Foreign Secretary in 1870.

Never since the world began [he wrote] has there been conduct more irritating than ours to the U.S. during their civil war.

Our delight at the prospect of their break-up, our insulting language when the Northerners were in distress, our scant praise when

111

they succeeded, all our affronts in a language common to both, our bungling about the Alabama which resulted in the destruction of their whole mercantile marine. They would have been angels instead of being exaggerated Britishers if they had not felt sore.[1]

Besides these grievances there were several disputes not so directly related to the Civil War. The Marcy-Elgin reciprocity treaty of 1854 expired in 1866 after the United States denounced it, mainly in order to increase the tariff rates, but also as a spiteful means of punishing Canada for her alleged animosity during the war. It will be recalled that the treaty gave Americans fishing privileges in Canadian and Newfoundland waters. When the treaty ended, so did the privileges. Long accustomed to frequent the inshore waters, American fishermen reacted violently when Canada in 1866 began to enforce the Convention of 1818, by the terms of which, according to the British view, the inshore waters were banned to Americans for general fishing purposes. After experimenting with a licensing system, Canada in 1870 closed the inshore waters to Americans. Her warships patrolled the fishing grounds; American fishermen armed themselves and refused to obey regulations they considered unjustified. The situation was dangerous.

Dangerous, too, were the activities of the Fenian Brotherhood. This was a secret Irish organization founded in the United States to win Ireland her independence. To this end it sought to foment a British-American war. In 1866 and again in 1870 and 1871 Fenian "armies" invaded Canada, as earlier the Hunters had done. Though forced to retreat precipitously, they alarmed border inhabitants. Britain and Canada were indignant over Washington's rather casual attitude toward these scandalous proceedings. But in the tense postwar years no American government could take the political risk of alienating Irish-Americans. Although by no means all of them were Fenians, they naturally sympathized with these crusaders for the old country's freedom. The influence of Irish-Americans in Americal political life was already great, greater than their numbers would suggest. They quickly displayed a remarkable political talent that was all the

---

[1] Granville to Sir F. Rogers, Oct. 22, 1870, Lord Granville Papers, Public Record Office (London), Public Record Office 30/29/77.

more effective in a period when presidential elections frequently hung by a hairbreadth. They were concentrated in northeastern cities, bastions of political power. In New York City the Irish were soon to get control of Tammany Hall; thereby they acquired considerable influence throughout the state, and New York was the most important state, politically and financially, in the nation. By virtue of their political strength, Irish-Americans had much influence on Anglo-American relations throughout the last three decades of the century. It was not an influence that fostered trans-Atlantic friendship.

Other dangers also existed. Despite the Oregon Treaty of 1846, the boundary between Vancouver Island and the mainland was disputed, and for over a decade in the 1860s and 1870s one island in the contested area, San Juan Island, was jointly occupied by British and American forces. Problems existed, too, as regards the use of canals and rivers, and as regards bands of Indians who roamed back and forth across the international line. Partly to strengthen themselves against the American peril some of the British North American colonies joined together in 1867 to form the Dominion of Canada, a step much resented in the United States.

Given the vindictive American attitude after the Civil War, even these relatively minor matters assumed large proportions, although they did not, of course, compare in dangerous significance with the clashes engendered by Fenians and fishermen, and above all with the threatening *Alabama* claims. If some sort of clarifying action were not taken, a third Anglo-American war could not be ruled out.

Yet what could be done? Fruitful negotiations depended on easing the *Alabama* dispute. British governments—the Liberals under Earl Russell (after Palmerston's death in 1865) and then the Conservatives under Lord Derby and Benjamin Disraeli—refused to acknowledge Britain's liability, insisting that her policy during the Civil War had been justified in law. The Conservatives did agree in 1866 to a limited arbitration but this was not acceptable to William H. Seward, still Secretary of State.

In November 1868 Ulysses S. Grant was elected President of the United States; the next month William E. Gladstone, who was to show himself remarkably conciliatory toward America, became Prime Minister of Great Britain. A fresh approach soon became possible. But first, Secretary Seward made one more attempt to make a settlement before his now-imminent departure from office. A new American Minister at London, Reverdy Johnson, and the British Foreign Secretary, Lord Clarendon, concluded the Johnson-Clarendon Convention, signed on January 14, 1869. It provided for individual claims to be submitted to a mixed commission of two Britons and two Americans; if they could not reach a decision, an arbitrator would be chosen, by lot if need be.[2]

However reasonable this arrangement might seem, it was altogether out of keeping with America's postwar mood. Unhesitatingly the Senate rejected the convention 54 to 1, for reasons well expressed in a famous speech delivered shortly after Grant entered the White House by Charles Sumner, still the powerful chairman of the Foreign Relations Committee: "The massive grievance under which our country suffered for years is left untouched. . . . there is not one word of regret" on the part of Great Britain. Sumner emphasized Britain's neutrality proclamation as the fount of all her alleged misdemeanors. "That England became an 'arsenal' for the rebels we know, but this could not have been unless the proclamation had prepared the way." Britain, he asserted, owed the United States at least $125,000,000, ascribable to the cost of defense against the cruisers, the increased insurance rates, and the damage done to the merchant marine. But in addition to the direct claims arising from these matters, there were "the national losses caused by the prolongation of the war and traceable directly to England." In stirring words he implied that her moral and material help to the Confederacy had doubled the duration of the war; this, he estimated, had cost the United States not less than $2,000,000,000, and in "simple equity" Britain was also responsible for this immense sum.[3]

By introducing these "national losses"—consequential or indirect claims, they came more commonly to be called, in contrast

---

[2] *Papers Relating to Foreign Affairs, 1868–1869* (Washington, 1869), Pt. I, 401–404.

[3] *Congressional Globe*, 41 Cong., 1 Sess., Appendix, 21–26 (April 13, 1869).

to the direct claims—the Senator complicated the situation im-measurably. The indirect claims proved to be the crucial point on which the whole Anglo-American arrangement very nearly came to grief. Yet it must be said that it was not Charles Sumner who demanded that Britain make payment in order to settle them. On the contrary, he insisted that he never would have made such a demand, and that his motive in bringing up the indirect claims was only to strengthen the direct claims by demonstrating how much the United States had suffered from Britain's conduct.[4] No doubt he was sincere; nevertheless, by calling attention to the indirect claims, Sumner aroused such a clamor for their payment that the government may have had no option but to present a bill.

It has been surmised that the Senator was hoping to induce Britain to cede Canada in exchange for extinguishing her debt of $2,125,000,000. That he did want the Dominion is certain, but only if it was willing to be annexed. He believed, mistakenly, that the Canadians were agreeable to being annexed, and that Britain was ready to let them go; so that if Washington did not rush into a settlement, London would in time make the cession in order to escape from an unbearable American pressure. Con-sequently the chairman of the Foreign Relations Committee resolutely opposed an early accord.

London, Ottawa, and Washington, on the other hand, were eager to get rid of the smouldering hostility. But they had to move slowly. The emotions aroused by Civil War memories and deepened by Sumner's evocation of the indirect claims limited what diplomats could do. The United States could not lightly dismiss the indirect claims. Great Britain could not lightly agree to pay them or to have them arbitrated, especially after the affront of the Senate's all-but-unanimous rejection of the arbitration that, from her point of view, she had so generously offered. And even more firmly she refused to go to court over her neutrality proclamation; that, she insisted, was an internal British affair not subject to review by outsiders. Consequently, when negotiations

---

[4] Sir Edward Thornton (British Minister to the United States) to Foreign Secretary Lord Granville, Jan. 10, 1871, and March 26, 1872, Granville Papers, Public Record Office 30/29/80.

were resumed after the repudiation of the Johnson-Clarendon Convention, they were cautious and informal.

John Rose was Canada's Minister of Finance in 1869. He had married an American and was a partner in a New York financial house with Levi P. Morton, a leading banker and later Vice-President of the United States. Rose was a friend of Caleb Cushing, a prominent American diplomat who, with the approval of Grant's Secretary of State, Hamilton Fish, had been working behind the scenes to arrange a meeting between Rose and Fish. Cushing was successful, and from July 8 to 11, 1869 Rose was in Washington conferring with the Secretary of State. His main purpose was to prepare the ground for a new Canadian-American reciprocity treaty. Reciprocity was a perennial theme, but neither in 1869 nor for many years thereafter was a new treaty possible. Nor was another matter discussed by the two men, that is, the fisheries, quickly resolved. On the last day of his visit Rose brought up the *Alabama* claims. He told the Secretary that he would shortly be in England and asked whether he could be of help. Fish was interested, but he said frankly that Britain must realize that Sumner had presented the American contention fairly and that no agreement could be reached unless Britain expressed regret for her wartime offenses and promised to pay an indemnity. Rose did not seem to think these conditions out of the question. He and Fish gave some attention to the desirability of a special British commission coming to Washington to negotiate.[5] In time this was to happen, and an agreement was to be reached along the lines envisaged in these informal talks of 1869.

But formal negotiations could not yet take place. Washington was preoccupied with moves strongly backed by Grant to annex Santo Domingo and with a Cuban revolt against Spain that threatened to involve the United States; furthermore, American emotions were still too intense, and British unwillingness to make new concessions too great, for a compromise to be possible. Time and the pressure of events were needed for attitudes to soften. In 1870 the scene began to shift, and by the end of the year the outlook was more propitious.

It was in 1870 that Canada decided to use force to ban Ameri-

---

[5] Hamilton Fish Diary, Library of Congress (Washington), July 11, 1869.

can fishermen from her waters, and that the Fenians invaded Canada again. An early agreement seemed imperative if events were to be kept under control. Probably more basic was the economic situation. American business men were sick and tired of the long quarrel with Britain that hampered their enterprises. Undoubtedly they made known their view to Washington. The Treasury Department was particularly sympathetic, for in order to finance the heavy Civil War indebtedness it wanted the lower interest rates that a settlement would bring.

Similarly in Great Britain developments pointed to the desirability of an accord. In July 1870 the Franco-Prussian war raised the specter of a general European conflict; in October, when Russia denounced treaty obligations providing for the neutrality of the Black Sea, Anglo-Russian hostilities appeared imminent. Canada lay exposed to attack from the United States if the mother country found herself fighting in Europe. In these perilous circumstances a Foreign Office memorandum to the Cabinet stressed the urgency of an accord with Washington.[6] Thus by late 1870 both countries had strong reasons for wiping the slate clean of the accumulation of controversies, particularly the somber altercation over the *Alabama* claims.

By then over a year and a half had elapsed since Sumner's speech and the defeat of the Johnson-Clarendon Convention; the excitement had had time to die down. Sustained diplomacy, less constrained by public emotionalism, was becoming possible. In talks between Fish and the British Minister at Washington, Sir Edward Thornton, the better feeling was evident; and in November 1870 Sir Edward said plainly that London hoped to settle the *Alabama* claims soon.[7] In that same month the American Minister at London, John L. Motley (he had succeeded Reverdy Johnson in 1869), was recalled. Motley was Sumner's protégé. The Senator had offended Grant by helping to defeat a treaty for the annexation of Santo Domingo. Outraged, the President

---

[6] Memorandum by Lord Tenterden (a senior clerk in the Foreign Office and soon to be Permanent Under Secretary of State), considered by the Cabinet on Nov. 19, 1870, Lucien Wolf, *Life of the First Marquess of Ripon, K.G., P.C., G.C.S.I., D.C.L., Etc.* (London, 1921), I, 238–39.

[7] Allan Nevins, *Hamilton Fish, The Inner History of the Grant Administration* (New York, 1937), 425–26; Fish Diary, Nov. 20 and 24, 1870.

struck at Sumner by dismissing the latter's friend. With Motley no longer at the key British post, Sumner's ability to discourage negotiations was diminished.

Since his meeting with Fish in 1869 Rose (now Sir John) had left Canada and moved to England, where he had continued to work for an Anglo-American understanding. Now that the moment had come to make a fresh start, the Cabinet asked him to return to Washington and explore the possibility of comprehensive negotiations.

Sir John arrived there in early 1871. Again he and Fish conferred informally, this time for nearly two weeks. At the outset the Secretary raised the old point that Canada should be ceded, but in the face of Rose's firm opposition he abandoned the topic for good.[8] He did so despite a blunt written statement from Sumner that a withdrawal by Great Britain from the Dominion was indispensable to a settlement and that she should withdraw from even the entire western hemisphere if the settlement was to be complete. Fish also disregarded Sumner's contention that the neutrality proclamation was the fount of all the trouble. But the Secretary was less complaisant about another matter that he himself raised. This was the insistence that, instead of the claims being submitted to arbitration, Great Britain should admit her liability for the cruisers and pay an amount of money to be determined in direct negotiations with the United States. Sir John of course refused; Great Britain, he retorted, admitted no fault at all and would pay nothing unless found in the wrong at an arbitration. After several days of argument Fish gave in. The way then lay open for an accord paving the way to full-scale negotiations that, they both agreed, would have a greater chance of success if conducted by a joint commission rather than through ordinary diplomatic channels.[9]

But the Washington administration still had to move carefully. Having already spurned one arbitration agreement, the Senate

---

[8] Fish Diary, Jan. 9, 1871; Rose to Granville, Jan. 10, 1871, Public Record Office, Foreign Office 5/1298. Robert C. Clark, "The Diplomatic Mission of Sir John Rose, 1871," *Pacific Northwest Quarterly*, XXVII (1936), 227–42.

[9] Rose to Granville, Jan. 12 and 31, 1872, Foreign Office 5/1298.

was quite capable of spurning another. Accordingly Fish had been scrupulous to keep the Foreign Relations Committee informed of the progress of the talks. Sumner's conditions for a settlement have been mentioned, but all the other committee members (with the possible exception of Senator Carl Schurz) backed the proposed arrangement. The Cabinet, too, gave its approval. It stipulated, however, that any arbitration must embrace the "consequential" as well as the direct claims; that is, it reasserted the validity of the indirect claims.[10] On this point, if not as regards the cession of Canada and the evils flowing from the neutrality proclamation, the administration was still close to Sumner. London, too, sanctioned the agreement. Thereupon Secretary Fish and Sir Edward made it public by an exchange of letters stating that a Joint High Commission would meet in Washington to consider the *Alabama* claims, the fisheries dispute, and "any other questions" affecting Canadian-American relations.[11]

The letters did not mention the indirect claims, nor does Fish appear to have spoken to Sir John about the Cabinet's stipulation. Although almost certainly the Cabinet did not then have the exaggerated estimation of these claims that the United States was later to adopt, Fish's silence was probably unwise. Had Great Britain known at the end of 1870 that Washington still considered the indirect claims very much alive, the likelihood of the subsequent misunderstanding would have been diminished. The point, however, is arguable; for if the Secretary had revealed the true situation, Great Britain might have felt obliged to demand a categorical repudiation of the indirect claims, an action impossible for Washington to take. Ambiguity is sometimes the better part of diplomacy.

---

[10] Fish Diary, Jan. 17, 1871.

[11] Thornton to Fish, Jan. 26 and Feb. 1, 1871; Fish to Thornton, Jan. 30, 1871, Foreign Office 5/1304.

CHAPTER IX

A Cloudy Accord

THE JOINT HIGH COMMISSION arranged for by Secretary of State Hamilton Fish and Sir John Rose met for the first time on February 27, 1871; it disbanded about two months later having negotiated the Treaty of Washington. The treaty, though important, was not the definitive Anglo-American settlement that it is often represented to have been. It did settle the minor controversies. But the United States flatly refused even to discuss the Fenian invasions, ostensibly on the ground that the commission had no jurisdiction, really from fear of alienating the Irish vote; and she persisted in this attitude despite the indignant and convincing British rejoinder that the Fenians obviously affected Canadian-American relations and therefore were within the commission's province as defined by Rose and Fish. Eventually Prime Minister Gladstone agreed to waive the matter. The commissioners negotiated what they hoped was a permanent fishery arrangement. But an integral part of it was a projected arbitration at Halifax, Nova Scotia; years of bickering were required before the arbitral commission could be established, and when at last it was, its award so exasperated Americans that the United States abrogated the entire fishery section of the treaty. Thereupon the situation on the fishing grounds deteriorated to a more dangerous state than it had been before the treaty was concluded.

As for the crucial *Alabama* claims, the treaty made what appeared to be a sure provision for arbitration; and this did, in the outcome, represent a major step toward a settlement. Nevertheless, the provision turned out to be not a sure one but an illusory one, so that instead of an accord at Washington there was really an utter misunderstanding. As a result, the arbitration very nearly crashed in ruins—and if it had, the entire treaty would surely have failed too. Had this happened, the recriminations in both countries would have been extreme, and Anglo-American relations would have been far worse than before the Joint High Commission met. Conceivably even war might have resulted. In short, the treaty was so defective that it almost brought not settlement but ruin. It led to success only in the sense that its critical weakness necessitated a rescue operation. This was performed in Geneva in 1872, long after the treaty was signed. Thus Geneva staved off a catastrophe unwittingly prescribed in Washington.

All the same the Treaty of Washington was extraordinarily important. During the century prior to its conclusion Great Britain and the United States had often clashed dangerously. Twice they had gone to war. Although relations improved briefly in the late 1850s, as we have noted, they quickly deteriorated again; and at times during and after the Civil War another Anglo-American conflict seemed possible. Against such a background of hostility it was fortunate that the treaty was negotiated. Even if it was not a final settlement, it did serve as a sort of holding-action that, along with the Geneva arbitration of 1872, may have staved off a third war. Thereby it gave the two countries that invaluable commodity, time—time for the dark Civil War passions to subside and for favorable influences to make themselves felt and bring about better relations at the end of the century.

The American commissioners were headed by Secretary Fish; the other members were Ebenezer Rockwood Hoar, Grant's former Attorney-General; Robert C. Schenck, recently appointed Minister to Great Britain to succeed Motley; Supreme Court Justice Samuel Nelson; and Senator George H. Williams. John C. Bancroft Davis, Assistant Secretary of State, was the delegation's secretary.

Earl de Grey headed the British commission; the other commissioners were Sir Stafford Northcote, formerly Gladstone's private secretary and later a Conservative Chancellor of the Exchequer and Foreign Secretary; Sir John A. Macdonald, Prime Minister of Canada; Montague Bernard, an Oxford professor who had written a book about Britain's neutrality during the Civil War; and Sir Edward Thornton, the British Minister at Washington. Lord Tenterden of the Foreign Office was the secretary.

We may briefly summarize the treaty provisions dealing with Canadian-American affairs. The treaty referred the San Juan Island boundary dispute to the German Emperor as arbiter; his decision of 1872 gave the island to the United States. The treaty also settled a number of disputes regarding the navigation of rivers and lakes and the transport of goods. Many sessions, more than for any other question, were spent on the fishery controversy. In the end Canada gave the United States inshore fishing privileges on the east coast for ten years, and the United States gave Canada corresponding privileges in some of her waters; both countries agreed to admit the other's fish and fish oil duty-free; and either country, after ten years, could give two-years' notice of the termination of these concessions. (The provisions were also to include Newfoundland, so far as applicable.) Since the Canadian fishery concessions were asserted by Great Britain to be greater in value than the United States concessions, an arbitral commission, to be constituted within three months of the treaty's effective date, was to meet at Halifax to determine what sum of money should be awarded the Dominion as compensation.

More attention must be paid to the *Alabama* claims, first to the illusory settlement at Washington, then to the real settlement a year later at Geneva. At the start of the Joint High Commission's meetings, President Grant succeeded in ousting Sumner from his chairmanship of the Foreign Relations Committee. Sir Edward Thornton predicted a reaction in favor of the Senator; "for he is much esteemed by many and is considered to have done good service; above all he is regarded as completely honest, —a quality of which his successor has never been accused."[1] Nevertheless, Sumner's dismissal removed an obstacle to the early conclusion of a treaty.

Secretary Fish presented the American position on the

---

[1] Thornton to Granville, March 14, 1871, Lord Granville Papers, Public Record Office (London), Public Record Office 30/29/80. Sumner's successor as chairman was Simon Cameron.

Alabama claims at a crucial meeting on March 8, 1871. The direct claims amounted at the moment, he said, to about $14,000,000. Regarding the indirect claims, he declared, "that in the hope of an amicable settlement no estimate was made . . . , without prejudice, however, to the right of indemnification on their account in the event of no such settlement being made"; and that this failure to make an estimate should be regarded as a major American concession. Reverting to his suggestion to Sir John Rose the preceding January, he pointed out that if Britain would admit her liability for the cruisers the Joint High Commission itself could decide the amount of money she should pay, and all the claims could be disposed of quickly. Alternatively, he said, Britain's liability or innocence could be determined by arbitration; but in that case the United States would demand that special rules be adopted which would be binding upon the tribunal in reaching its verdict. Finally he insisted that Britain must apologize for the escape of the cruisers.[2]

The apparent waiving of the indirect claims in the event of an "amicable settlement" was of course most gratifying to Great Britain, but to demand that a proud and powerful nation apologize for something it did not admit to be a fault was to ask a great deal. Fish was asking just as much, perhaps even more, when he made the condition that Britain must either confess her liability or else accept an arbitration conducted under rules presumably slanted against her. With little ado the British commissioners rejected the first alternative, as Rose had done.[3] Would they accept the alternative of conditioned arbitration? Stubbornly they resisted. Just as stubbornly Fish argued that the Senate, having already pronounced against the Johnson-Clarendon Convention, would not now reverse itself and accept unrestricted arbitration; only a carefully restricted arbitration, he said, would have any chance of winning its approval.[4]

Gladstone and the Cabinet made the final decision; they yielded, as they had over the Fenians. They agreed that the arbi-

---

[2] Protocol of May 4, 1871, Public Record Office, Foreign Office 5/1304.

[3] Sir Roundell Palmer (one of the British counsel at the Geneva Arbitration) to Granville, March 21, 1871, Granville Papers, Public Record Office 30/29/67.

[4] DeGrey to Granville, March 17, 1871, Foreign Office 5/1308.

trators would be bound by Fish's special rules. The three rules of due diligence, as they were called, specified that a neutral, first, must not permit the arming of a ship for use in war against a country with which the neutral was at peace; second, must not permit a belligerent to use the neutral's ports or waters as a base of naval operations; and, third, must not permit any person within its jurisdiction to violate the foregoing obligations. The treaty provided that the *Alabama* claims were to be submitted to five arbitrators, one each from Great Britain, the United States, Switzerland, Brazil, and Italy, who, meeting in Geneva in June 1872, would return a verdict based on international law and the rules of due diligence. London also gave way as regards an apology; the treaty included a remarkable expression of regret for the escape of the cruisers.

These major British concessions made an agreement possible. The treaty was signed on May 8, 1871. The Senate quickly approved it; Charles Sumner voted with the majority. Great Britain, too, soon approved; but Canada, angry over the fishery articles, delayed a year before following suit.[5] To universal relief, all the many Anglo-American-Canadian grievances seemed to have been disposed of.

London and Washington now set to work preparing their cases for the Geneva tribunal. The American case was officially presented to Great Britain (as prescribed by the treaty) on December 15, 1871, and it was evident at once that the principal dispute—over the *Alabama* claims—had not in fact been disposed of. For to Britain's astonishment the case advanced not only the direct claims but also, and no less strongly, it advanced the indirect claims—the indirect claims that she believed had been abandoned for good at the Joint High Commission's meeting of March 8, 1871. Not only that, but the case raised no less a point than "whether Great Britain ought not, in equity, to reimburse to the United States" all the expenses of the Civil War since the battle

---

[5] *Journal of the Executive Proceedings of the Senate . . .* (Washington, 1901), XVIII, 108–109; *Parliamentary Debates, Dominion of Canada, Fourth Session,* III, 647–48 (May 16, 1872), 868 (May 28, 1872). The United States and Great Britain exchanged ratifications on June 17, 1871. For a British debate on the matter see Hansard's *Parliamentary Debates,* Third Series, CCVI, 1101–1107 (May 22, 1871) and 1823–1901 (June 12, 1871).

of Gettysburg plus interest at 7 percent! It defended this extraordinary contention on the ground that the Confederacy would have collapsed after that battle had it not anticipated a war between the North and Great Britain resulting from the latter's violations of her neutral obligations.[6]

The British people reacted with disgust and anger. They thought the American position grotesquely absurd, but worse—and what really infuriated them—was the conviction that shabby Yankee tricksters were taking advantage of British good faith. Outcry or no, no British government could admit it had been outsmarted. Nor could the government bind itself to accept the verdict of a tribunal, four-fifths foreign, as to whether Britain should pay half the cost of the Civil War. It was therefore to universal applause that Queen Victoria, at the opening of Parliament on February 6, 1872, stated flatly that the indirect claims were not "within the province of the Arbitrators."[7]

But if Great Britain could not arbitrate the indirect claims, the United States, having once presented them, could not withdraw them. In 1872 President Ulysses S. Grant was up for reelection. To have backed down under British pressure would have been psychologically impossible for him and politically impossible for his Republican party. Secretary of State Fish told Sir Edward Thornton sternly that if Britain continued to deny that the tribunal had jurisdiction over the indirect claims, the arbitration would not take place.[8] He did not have to add that the entire Treaty of Washington would then collapse; for the treaty was an

---

[6] The case is in *Senate Executive Document* 31, 42 Cong., 2 Sess. (Serial 1478). A copy of it reached London three or four weeks before the official copy arrived. The copy was forwarded to the Foreign Office by Francis John Pakenham (British Chargé d'Affaires at Washington), who reported that it "has reached me in a rather strange way." Pakenham to Granville, Oct. 31 1871, Granville Papers, Public Record Office 30/29/80; Apparently William M. Evarts (one of the American counsel at the Geneva arbitration) had dropped the copy in a Washington street, and the finder had sold it to the British Legation. Chester L. Barrows, *William M. Evarts, Lawyer, Diplomat, Statesman* (Chapel Hill, 1941), 199–200.

[7] *Parliamentary Debates*, Third Series, CCIX, 4 (Feb. 6, 1872). See Gladstone's similar statement, *ibid.*, 79 (Feb. 6, 1872).

[8] Granville to Thornton, and Thornton to Granville, Feb. 3, 1872, Foreign Office 5/1393.

interdependent whole, no one major section of which could be destroyed without destroying the rest.

Thus Great Britain insisted that during the Joint High Commission's meetings the United States had withdrawn the indirect claims; the United States retorted stoutly that the Treaty of Washington could be searched and searched again without finding the slightest expression of withdrawal. Each country had assumed a position that it could not abandon. The treaty seemed doomed.

How had this extraordinary situation arisen? Fish's statement of March 8, 1871 will be recalled: that whereas he estimated the direct claims at $14,000,000, "in the hope of an amicable settlement" he was not estimating the indirect claims; and that Britain could either pay a sum to be fixed by the Joint High Commission, or submit the question of liability to arbitration. The British commissioners had understood Fish's contrasting attitudes toward the direct and the indirect claims to mean that the latter would be waived if an amicable settlement, that is, a treaty, was made.[9] But now in 1872 Fish argued that only the first suggested alternative, namely, payment of money, could be considered an "amicable settlement," and that since Britain had rejected this in favor of arbitration, the indirect claims had not been waived. Foreign Secretary Granville retorted that the treaty was itself an "amicable settlement" and was so called in its preamble; but Fish countered: "the Treaty is not, of itself, the settlement; it is an agreement between the Governments as to the mode of reaching a settlement...."[10]

It may be wondered why the United States put forward the indirect claims even if she did consider herself legally entitled to do so. Did not Fish foresee that Britain could not arbitrate the claims, and that therefore by advancing them he was endangering a treaty of which he was enormously proud? Fish was an honest, capable man, a fine Secretary of State and the outstanding member of Grant's Cabinet, but imagination was not his strong point. Apparently he did not anticipate that the British

---

[9] Granville to Robert C. Schenck (American Minister to Great Britain), March 20, 1872, *House Executive Document* 294, 42 Cong., 2 Sess. (Serial 1516), 14.

[10] Fish to Schenck, Feb. 27, 1872, *ibid.*, 5–6.

were certain to react violently. What he did fear was that the indirect claims had acquired such popular favor that to pass them over in silence would cause unfavorable repercussions in Congress and harm to Grant in the election of 1872. This fear determined his action.

The merits of the Anglo-American debate over the admissibility of the indirect claims can be argued at length. What is undeniable is that both countries thought they were right and that if they persisted in their attitudes through June, the Treaty of Washington would fail. It was therefore essential to come to terms quickly. In February and March Washington considered several ways of escaping from the deadlock: let Britain pay money instead of arbitrating; let her announce ahead of time that if the tribunal upheld the indirect claims she would pay no award; let her cede Vancouver Island or San Juan Island (not yet awarded by the German Emperor) to settle the indirect claims. Britain rejected them all. Her steadfast position was that she had made a tremendous concession by agreeing to arbitrate, that Washington had caused all the trouble by unjustifiably including the indirect claims in its case, and that consequently it had to find some means of getting rid of them.

Thus matters stood at the end of March, with the tribunal due to convene in little more than two months. In April the United States made two further moves. At President Grant's suggestion, the administration informed Charles Francis Adams, the American Minister at London during the Civil War and one of the arbitrators-designate at Geneva, that the United States, as a probable neutral in future European wars, wanted the tribunal to decide in favor of Great Britain as regards the indirect claims, and thereby set a precedent for the immunity of neutrals under international law from such claims. (This consideration seems to have occurred to the administration only after it presented the indirect claims.) Adams was further told that if he himself agreed that neutrals were immune, it would be helpful if he made his opinion known in London, where he was about to go.[11]

---

[11] Hamilton Fish Diary (Library of Congress, Washington), April 19, 20, and 22, 1872; Adams's diary, April 22, 1872, quoted in George S. Boutwell, *Reminiscences of Sixty Years in Public Affairs* (New York 1902), II, 201. Regarding Fish's ideas about this plan see memorandum by Schenck, April 29, 1872, Foreign Office 5/1397.

The former Minister carried out the suggestion, and doubtless the British leaders were relieved to hear that the American arbitrator would reject the indirect claims. However, this did not persuade them to proceed with the arbitration. For after all the three neutral arbitrators, who constituted the majority, might vote the other way; and in any case the ministry, after having insisted that the tribunal had no jurisdiction over the indirect claims, could not now reverse itself.

The other move of April took the form of a proposed bargain: the United States would not present the indirect claims; in return, Britain—and also the United States—would agree never to advance such claims for acts committed by vessels. The suggestion was clever; if accepted, it would relieve British apprehension about an enormous award, while at the same time it would largely meet the American wish to be protected against indirect claims arising from future wars. Unfortunately a Senate committee, apparently at Fish's instigation, changed the proposal to read that the two countries would not advance indirect claims for violations of "neutral obligations."[12] The committee was trying to protect the United States from claims arising from such lapses as the Fenian raids. But Great Britain, though prepared to accept the principle of neutral immunity in cases related to vessels, would not accept it for *any* breach of neutral obligations. Despite intense negotiations, the two countries could not reach a compromise.

Their failure became evident at the end of May 1872. In two weeks the arbitrators were due to convene at Geneva. Great Britain was still insisting that the tribunal had no jurisdiction over the indirect claims and that therefore she would not submit her summary of argument unless the United States withdrew the claims—yet by the terms of the Treaty of Washington a binding arbitration could not proceed without the summary; just as resolutely the United States was asserting that the tribunal did have jurisdiction and that she would present the claims, and that Britain was solemnly obligated to submit the summary and to arbitrate. Hoping to save the treaty Great Britain made a last-

---

[12] *Papers Relating to the Foreign Relations of the United States, 1872*, Pt. II, *Papers Relating to the Treaty of Washington* (Washington, 1872), II, 526; Fish Diary, May 18, 1872.

minute offer that represented yet another considerable concession: she would submit her summary subject to the proviso that she and the United States would ask the tribunal for an eight-months' adjournment, that this would be granted, and that she would give notice of her intent to withdraw from the arbitration if agreement on the indirect claims was not reached during the eight months.[13] Fish would not yield. "Such notice," he retorted indignantly, "would instantly terminate all further negotiations on the part of this Government."[14]

In six days the tribunal would meet. Great Britain and the United States seemed to have reached an impasse. The arbitration and the treaty appeared to be close to failure.

The tribunal convened at Geneva on June 15. Its five members were Count Frederic Sclopis (elected president) for Italy, Viscount d'Itajubá for Brazil, Jacques Staempfli for Switzerland, Sir Alexander Cockburn for Great Britain, and Charles Francis Adams for the United States. Lord Tenterden was the British agent and John C. Bancroft Davis the American agent; thus these two men—key figures, as will beome evident—occupied positions comparable to those they held during the sessions of the Joint High Commission.

Bancroft Davis formally submitted the American summary of argument; Lord Tenterden refused to submit the British summary; instead he announced that he would not submit it failing agreement on the indirect claims, and he asked for an eight-months' adjournment. Davis then asked for and was granted a two-days' adjournment so that he could get instructions from Washington.

The American agent's purpose was not so much to communicate with his superiors as to gain time in which to maneuver for the acceptance of a plan that he and Tenterden had devised the previous April. On the 15th of that month—about when Washington informed Charles Francis Adams of its desire to have the tribunal reject the indirect claims in return for a British promise never to advance such claims—Bancroft Davis and

---

[13] Schenck to Fish, June 8, 1872, *Foreign Relations, 1872*, Pt. II, *Papers Relating to the Treaty of Washington*, II, 561–62.

[14] Fish to Schenck, June 9, 1872, *ibid.*, 567.

Tenterden had met in Geneva to exchange the countercases, that is, the formal replies to the two cases presented the previous December. They were extremely pessimistic. Both men feared that the arbitration would not be held and that the Treaty of Washington, on which they had bestowed so much time and energy, would fail. But during their discussions that day and the next a ray of light appeared. They worked out a hopeful plan. It was this. If an agreement continued to elude the two countries, let the five arbitrators meet unofficially sometime before June 15 and express their views as to Britain's liability for the indirect claims. The two agents expected that the majority would declare that if they had formal jurisdiction over the claims they would find them invalid under international law. The United States would then have no reason to submit them to the tribunal and could afford, politically, not to do so; and Great Britain, with the claims disposed of, would proceed with arbitration.[15] This ingenious idea foreshadowed in outline what did in fact happen, as we shall now see, except that the arbitrators did not meet prior to mid-June.

Rather strangely, however, the plan made little immediate impact on Washington or London. Davis, of course, wrote to Fish about what had occurred, but the Secretary does not seem to have given the matter any consideration. Gladstone and Granville expressed themselves as very pleased with Tenterden's account of the plan, but apparently took no immediate steps to implement it. Probably both governments were so engrossed with the negotiations over the proposed bargain of April, mentioned above, regarding the indirect claims, that they had no time to give serious attention to the novel Geneva idea.

After the tribunal's adjournment on June 15, Davis and Tenterden proceeded to implement the essential features of their scheme. But first, Bancroft Davis had to deal with a complicaton introduced by Adams. The well-intentioned American arbitrator thought he knew how to save the situation: let the tribunal sim-

---

[15] Davis to Fish, April 15 and 17, 1872, John C. Bancroft Davis Papers, Alabama Claims, Letters from J.C.B. Davis, Library of Congress (Washington); Tenterden to Granville, April 15, 1872, and memorandum by Tenterden, April 15/16, 1872, Granville Papers, Public Record Office 30/29/106.

ply proceed with the direct claims while Washington and London continued to negotiate about the indirect claims.[16] Meeting with Tenterden later that day, Davis broached the suggestion, but the Englishman rejected it sharply; Britain, he said, would not arbitrate unless the indirect claims were abandoned.[17] This ended consideration of Adams's suggestion, and attention now turned to the Davis-Tenterden plan of April.

As soon as Davis left, Tenterden conferred about the April plan with Sir Roundell Palmer, one of the British counsel, and Sir Alexander Cockburn. The three men agreed on a statement, drafted by Palmer, to the effect that the tribunal could render nothing but an extrajudicial opinion about the indirect claims because these claims were not formally before it—only the request for an eight-months' adjournment was before it—and that an extrajudicial opinion would not, of course, be binding unless both London and Washington accepted it.[18] Armed with this paper, Davis conferred about it the next day (June 16) with the three American counsel (Caleb Cushing, William M. Evarts, and Morrison R. Waite) and with Adams. The counsel drew up a statement that followed the main lines of Palmer's draft.[19] According to the Englishman, it included the crucial pronouncement to be made by the arbitrators, that if the indirect claims had been submitted to them "they would have considered them, on juridical grounds, inadmissible." (This, it will be noted, was very similar to the statement envisaged by Davis and Tenterden in April.) Later that day Evarts examined the revised declaration with Sir Roundell, who found it acceptable.[20]

Now that the British and the American counsel were in agreement, it was necessary to get the consent of a majority of the arbitrators. The tribunal met on the 17th, but only long enough

---

[16] Frank W. Hackett, *Reminiscences of the Geneva Tribunal of Arbitration, 1872, the Alabama Claims* (Boston and New York, 1911), 240.

[17] Tenterden to Granville, June 15, 1872, Granville Papers, Public Record Office 30/29/106.

[18] *Ibid.*

[19] Hackett, *Geneva Tribunal*, 247–51. See also Martin B. Duberman, *Charles Francis Adams, 1807–1886* (Boston, 1961), 377–78.

[20] Memorandum by Palmer of conversation with Evarts, June 16, 1872, Granville Papers, Public Record Office 30/29/106.

to decide upon another two-days' adjournment. During the interval the arbitrators turned their attention to the proposed declaration. At their request the British drew up yet another draft, which the Americans amended. Evarts and Palmer then put it in final form. All five arbitrators and the counsel on both sides accepted it.[21]

The tribunal reconvened on April 19. The British summary of argument still had not been submitted and the request for an eight-months' adjournment was still standing. Count Sclopis opened the meeting by reading the Palmer-Evarts statement. It said that the arbitrators would not express an opinion on the question as to whether the Treaty of Washington gave them jurisdiction over the indirect claims; they would merely declare, extrajudicially, that

these claims do not constitute, upon the principles of international law applicable to such cases, good foundation for an award of compensation or computation of damages between nations, and should, upon such principles, be wholly excluded from the consideration of the Tribunal in making its award. . . .[22]

The tribunal, it was clear, was not going to make a judicial decision about the indirect claims.

It remained to secure the reaction of Washington and London. Would Washington now agree that the tribunal could omit the indirect claims from further consideration? Would London withdraw its request for an eight-months' adjournment and proceed with the arbitration? The tribunal adjourned to await the answers. Secretary Fish, persuaded at last that the tribunal would not take judicial cognizance of the indirect claims no matter how adamantly the United States insisted that it do so, agreed that they could be excluded. And Lord Granville agreed to submit the British summary of argument provided the arbitrators formally pronounced the indirect claims to be completely excluded from their consideration. This the arbitrators did, and Tenterden

---

[21] Memorandum by Cockburn, June 17, 1872, Foreign Office 5/1402; Tenterden to Granville, June 17, 18, and 19, 1872, *ibid.*; Palmer to Granville, June 19, 1872, Granville Papers, Public Record Office 30/29/67.

[22] The statement is in *Foreign Relations, 1872*, Pt. II, *Papers Relating to the Treaty of Washington*, IV, 19–20.

accordingly submitted the summary of argument on June 27, 1872. "British argument filed. Arbitration goes on."[23] So Davis cabled happily to Washington. He and Tenterden had seen the basic features of their April scheme come to fulfillment.

Although the indirect claims were thus disposed of for good and all, the outcome was not altogether satisfactory to either country. The United States had secured a statement from the arbitrators that would give her, as a future neutral, a measure of protection from claims for indirect damages. However, the statement did not refer to breaches of neutral obligations in general (as Fish and the Senate had wanted), but only to those claims put forward in the American case, that is, claims relating to vessels. Nor had the arbitrators assumed jurisdiction over the indirect claims and given the judicial opinion that Washington had demanded so unwaveringly. As for Great Britain, though the tribunal had declined to assume jurisdiction over the claims, she had not persuaded it to declare the claims outside the scope of the Treaty of Washington. Nevertheless both countries could take great satisfaction in the convening of an historic arbitration.

In mid-July the tribunal at last got down to hearing testimony. It considered each of the Southern cruisers in turn. Some two months later on September 14, 1872 Count Sclopis read the judgment. It found Great Britain failing in due diligence as regards the *Alabama,* the *Florida,* and the *Shenandoah* (the latter for part of her voyage only). For this it assessed Britain $15,500,-000, a large sum but far from half the cost of the Civil War. Loud applause followed the Count's closing words. The public, permitted to attend the last session, realized that it had witnessed a famous occasion in the peaceful settlement of disputes.

To many people in Great Britain the award seemed humiliating and unjustifiably large; Prime Minister Gladstone was severely criticized for his many concessions. Indeed the Treaty of Washington and the Geneva arbitration together constituted one of several reasons for the Liberal party's downfall in 1874. But Gladstone always defended the treaty and the great arbitration. More than any other person he must be given the main credit for

---

[23] Davis to Fish, June 27, 1872, *ibid.,* II, 580.

them, because it was his courageous authorization of major concessions that made them possible.

although we may think the sentence was harsh in its extent [he said
some years later], and unjust in its basis, we regard the fine imposed
on this country as dust in the balance compared with the moral value
of the example set when these two great nations of England and
America—which are among the most fiery and the most jealous in the
world with regard to anything that touches national honour—went in
peace and concord before a judicial tribunal to dispose of these pain-
ful differences, rather than to resort to the arbitrament of the sword.[24]

Americans were glad to have won the money, and surely they
were even gladder to be rid at last of the ominous *Alabama*
claims. But unfortunately events were to show that they had not
got rid of other issues affected by the Civil War and supposedly
settled by the Treaty of Washington. Partly because of that
cloudy accord a new phase of British-American contention was
to arise, centering not on expansion or neutrality, but on further
disputes between the United States and the Dominion of Canada.

---

[24] *Parliamentary Debates*, Third Series, CCLIII, 106 (June 16, 1880).

CHAPTER X

Halifax and the Fisheries

AFTER THE GENEVA ARBITRATION OF 1872 two parts of the Treaty of Washington still remained to be carried out. They concerned articles by which Great Britain and the United States agreed, first, to invite the other maritime powers to accept the three rules of due diligence; and, second, to arbitrate at Halifax, Nova Scotia, in order to decide what compensation, if any, was due British subjects in Canada and Newfoundland for the allegedly greater fishery concessions made by Britain as compared with those made by the United States.

It might seem simple enough to approach other countries about the three rules. But Great Britain naturally had doubts about rules that had led to the adverse award at Geneva. British people sharply criticized the tribunal's interpretation of the rules, and argued that Britain should sponsor them as understood, not by the tribunal but by her own experts. Discussion arose with Washington about submitting the rules with a covering comment expressing the British opinion as to their meaning. Washington saw no need for a comment, and neither country pressed the matter when a larger controversy arose about the Halifax arbitration.

According to the treaty each country would name a commissioner; if the two countries could not agree on a third commissioner within three months of the treaty's effective date (July 1, 1873), they would ask the Ambassador of Austria-Hungary at London to choose him. The difficulty of joint agreement soon became evident; the stakes were high, for the third commissioner could be expected to determine the decision.

One of the British suggestions for commissioner—the Belgian

Minister at Washington, Maurice Delfosse—should be noted. Nothing could be more definite than Secretary Fish's categorical rejection of him in 1873. He went so far as to assert that Delfosse would be sure to take the English side because Belgium was practically a British province, and that furthermore the Belgian was known to be anti-American.[1] Yet after standing firm in this attitude for several years, Fish reversed himself in 1877 and accepted Delfosse. The latter's casting vote at Halifax produced the unfavorable award the Secretary had foreseen. The history of the Halifax arbitration, therefore, turns essentially on Fish's unexpected change of front about the Belgian Minister.

The three months allowed by the Treaty of Washington for British-American agreement on the third commissioner ended on September 30, 1873. Britain then made the routine proposal that the Austrian Ambassador be asked to make the appointment. But Secretary Fish, presumably regretting what he had agreed to in the treaty and fearing that the Ambassador would make a pro-British appointment, hedged. He could do this the more easily because of a distraction that had arisen.

It had its origin in a suggestion made by the famous Senator from Massachusetts, Charles Sumner. The Senator had proposed to a British official that, instead of an arbitration, Canada might be satisfied with another reciprocity treaty similar to the defunct Marcy-Elgin Treaty of 1854. Canada had welcomed the idea, and Fish rather unenthusiastically had agreed to negotiate. Perhaps his main consideration was that this would relieve him from pressure to resort to the Austrian Ambassador. Ottawa appointed George Brown, editor of the Toronto *Globe*, to negotiate jointly with the British Minister at Washington, Sir Edward Thornton. The two men opened discussions with Fish in the spring of 1874.

By June they had drafted a treaty providing for free trade both in a large number of agricultural goods (as the earlier treaty had done) and also in many manufactured goods—the latter provision at American insistence. But by then the Secretary had become dubious about such an agreement. Sumner's death just when the negotiations started had removed one strong voice for reciproc-

---

[1] Fish to Thornton, Aug. 21, 1873, *Senate Executive Document* 44, 45 Cong., 2 Sess. (Serial 1781), 5.

ity; and various American business interests fearing adverse effects upon themselves—notably fishery, coal, wool, and lumber interests—had doubtless been deluging Washington with furious protestations. They were strong in such important Republican states as Massachusetts, Pennsylvania, Ohio, and Michigan, and could not lightly be alienated in 1874, a congressional election year.

Fish accordingly refused to sign the draft but, under British threats to break off the talks and press for the third commissioner, he sent it in mid-June to the Senate for its advice. With little ado that Republican-dominated body made the prudent decision to shelve the treaty until after the elections. Neither supporter nor enemy of reciprocity would be too irritated that way. Even the British went along, although Thornton again raised the bogey of the Halifax commission.

After the elections the Senate refused to recommend further negotiations. Angry over the months of lost time, and pushed hard by Canada, Great Britain now started demanding arbitration in dead earnest. Once more Fish had to cast about for some way to evade the perfectly clear injunction of the Treaty of Washington as to the appointment of the third commissioner by the Austrian Ambassador. The Secretary was even reduced to pleading that he could not act because the man Grant wanted as American commissioner was lost in Europe. Less absurd was his revival of the dispute about the rules of due diligence. He argued that if Britain refused to observe one section of the treaty by failing to submit the rules to the maritime powers, she could not blame the United States for disregarding another section. In March 1876 he gave formal warning that the United States would not arbitrate unless Britain agreed to recommend the rules.[2]

Nevertheless Fish soon reversed himself. In a long letter he told the surprised Thornton that the United States was appointing Ensign H. Kellogg, a minor Massachusetts politician, as her commissioner, and that she was ready to allow the Austrian

---

[2] Thornton to Foreign Secretary Derby, June 28, 1875, in memorandum by Francis C. Ford, April 1, 1876, Public Record Office (London), Foreign Office 5/1569; Thornton to Derby, March 9, 1876, *ibid.*

Ambassador to name the third commissioner. At the same time he blamed Britain for the delay over the three rules and said that before going ahead with the arbitration he wanted to have a final answer. Would Britain submit the rules to the powers or not?[3]

How is this strange behavior to be accounted for? Fish must have known that the delay over submitting the three rules, for which Britain was not solely responsible in any event, did not really balance the American refusal to meet the treaty terms regarding the third commissioner. Probably his immediate consideration was again political. He suspected that the Austrian Ambassador would make an unwelcome nomination and he did not want this to happen before the presidential election of 1876, which the Democratics threatened to win. Why, then, did he agree to arbitrate at all? The fact is that politics was not his only consideration. Both Fish and the President were inordinately proud of their treaty, one of the great monuments of Grant's eight years in the White House. They must have been supremely anxious to tie up its two loose threads before they left office, that is, they wanted to have decisions about the rules and about the Halifax arbitration. In short, if politics dictated a delay until November 1876, pride dictated a decision not later than the following March.

London more or less met Fish's condition regarding the three rules by again offering to submit them with a covering explanation. Fish fired off a final rejoinder.[4] Apparently this exchange satisfied him because he could now leave office, if not with the agreement he would have liked, at least with a clear-cut statement of his position. Nothing more of consequence was heard about the rules.

Not until after the elections, not in fact until February 1, 1877, when Grant was due to leave the White House in less than five weeks, did the Secretary finally approach Thornton about a third commissioner. Perhaps he had delayed in the hope of a last-minute British concession; perhaps the confusion attendant upon

---

[3] Fish to Thornton, May 8, 1876, *Senate Executive Document* 44, 45 Cong., 2 Sess., 19–21; *ibid.* 26, 45 Cong., 3 Sess. (Serial 1828), 76.
[4] Thornton to Fish, July 26, 1876, *Senate Executive Document* 26, 45 Cong., 3 Sess., 76–80; Fish to Thornton, Sept. 18, 1876, *ibid.*, 80–89.

the November presidential vote, which was still contested, prevented an earlier step. In any case, when he did at length act he did so in a most surprising way. He told Thornton that he wanted the Halifax commission to be appointed before Grant's term expired and that he therefore had "no great objection" to the selection of none other than Maurice Delfosse by the Austrian Ambassador. The startled British Minister blandly replied that he supposed the Ambassador could be prevailed upon to make this nomination.

In view of his earlier inflexible opposition to Delfosse, Fish's reversal seems at first almost incomprehensible. But in fact he had no other recourse because by February 1877 it was too late to reach agreement with Britain on any other person than Delfosse. In all probability this pressure of time was the Secretary's main consideration. A year later, however, he claimed to have had another motive, that is, that if he did not accept Delfosse the Austrian Ambassador, whose decision could not have been postponed much longer, might have nominated someone even worse.[5] This may not have been altogether an afterthought.

Events now proceeded rapidly. At the formal request of the United States and Great Britain that he appoint the third commissioner, the Austrian Ambassador named Maurice Delfosse on March 2, 1877.[6] Two days later Rutherford B. Hayes entered the White House, and William M. Evarts became Secretary of State. Just in time Grant and Fish had nailed down all the loose ends of their great treaty. The fate of the three rules had been determined, and the Halifax tribunal was ready to convene.

The tribunal met on June 15, 1877 at Halifax. Its three members were Delfosse, Kellogg, and Alexander T. Galt, a former Canadian Minister of Finance representing Great Britain. Galt was an able man. Kellogg had nothing to commend him; his stupidity and tactlessness weakened the American case. Great Britain argued that the fishery privileges given the United States by the Treaty of Washington were worth about $15,000,000

---

[5] New York *Tribune*, March 30, 1878.
[6] Fish to Edwards Pierrepont (Schenck's successor as American Minister at London), Feb. 13, 1887, *Senate Executive Document* 100, 45 Cong., 2 Sess. (Serial 1781), 9; Pierrepont to Fish, March 2, 1877, *ibid.*, 13.

more than those given Canada and Newfoundland for the minimum period of twelve years (1873–1885) during which the fishery section was to be in force. The United States contended that this figure was grotesquely high. On November 23, 1877, after many sessions, the commission awarded the British $5,500,000.

Since Kellogg and Galt each voted for his own country, the pro-British vote of Delfosse decided the verdict. Kellogg actually argued that the United States, not Canada, deserved compensation. He contended moreover that because the treaty did not specify a majority verdict (as it did for the Geneva tribunal) it required unanimity, and that therefore the commission could not legally render an award by a split decision.[7] The latter contention gained much credence in the United States. Everyone thought the award absurdly excessive, and almost as many believed that it was illegal as well. A great hue and cry arose against the commission.

Another Near Eastern crisis was just then at its peak, and this must have emboldened American critics. War seemed certain between Great Britain and Russia. In March 1878 the Foreign Secretary dramatically resigned, angered by Prime Minister Benjamin Disraeli's unbending policy. But later in the year the Congress of Berlin staved off a conflagration.

Inevitably the American excitement over Halifax embraced Delfosse. In March, at the height of the European crisis, Senator James G. Blaine, representing the fishing state of Maine and one of the most prominent men in the Republican party, introduced a resolution, passed by the Senate, calling for the correspondence about the Belgian's appointment. Some of it was published and Blaine claimed to see evidence of Britain's "very extraordinary efforts . . . to force Mr. Delfosse upon our Government." He also asserted that the treaty required unanimity, and had apt quotations from both the London *Times* and the Canadian Minister of Justice to support his position. He made one important point: that though the United States was honor bound to pay, she should make clear her conviction that the award was erroneous,

---

[7] *House Executive Document* 89, 45 Cong., 2 Sess. (Serial 1810), *Award of the Fishery Commission. Documents and Proceedings of the Halifax Commission, 1877* . . . (Washington, 1878), I, 76.

so as not to prejudice her case in any future negotiations.[8] Blaine also revived the *contretemps* over the three rules, blaming Great Britain for the failure to submit them to the powers and, again, calling for the correspondence.[9] But the rules, unlike the Belgian, attracted little public interest.

Almost everyone agreed with Blaine that the United States should pay, however unfair and illegal the tribunal's verdict. Congress authorized the President to make payment if, after corresponding with Britain, he should still consider this desirable. The ensuing correspondence, in which the United States reiterated the charges of excessiveness and illegality, changed no minds. The United States paid the award in November 1878, at the same time protesting (as Blaine had advised) that she did not consider that it truly reflected the fisheries' value.

The country did well to swallow its anger and to pay. To have refused would have been a dishonorable and provocative act. Americans were no more aggrieved over Halifax than Britons had been over Geneva; and it served the cause of good Anglo-American relations that each country promptly met its obligation. Nevertheless the Halifax award had harmful consequences that were enduring. In authorizing payment the Senate had attached an amendment expressing its opinion that the government should terminate the fishery section of the Treaty of Washington in 1885, the earliest legal date.[10] This the government did, as we shall see in more detail in the next chapter. It was all the more prepared to take this unwise and rather petty step because of two incidents that exacerbated the resentment over Halifax.

The first concerned a Canadian professor named Henry Youle Hind. While preparing an official index of the Halifax commission's proceedings, the professor happened upon some incorrect statistics in the British case. Soon he was busy writing letters to

---

[8] *Congressional Record*, 45 Cong., 2 Sess., 2021 (March 26, 1878). The published correspondence regarding Delfosse is in *Senate Executive Document* 44, 45 Cong., 2 Sess., and *ibid.* 100, 45 Cong., 2 Sess.

[9] *Congressional Record*, 45 Cong., 2 Sess., 3981–84 (June 1, 1878), 4015 (June 3, 1878). For the correspondence see *Senate Executive Document* 26, 45 Cong., 3 Sess.

[10] *Congressional Record*, 45 Cong., 2 Sess., 3979–98 (June 1, 1878), 4309 (June 8, 1878).

a large number of prominent English, Canadian, and American officials, charging Great Britain with deliberate fraud.[11] When James G. Blaine, who had his eye on the Republican presidential nomination in 1880, submitted a resolution in the Senate early that year asking the executive branch for information about the "alleged false statistics and fabricated testimony," and when Representative John S. Newberry of Michigan called upon England in early 1881 to defend herself "against the unheard of crime, national perjury and falsification of public records . . . ," a first-rate sensation seemed about to agitate the country.[12] Indeed, in view of Hind's inflammatory material, it is remarkable that this did not occur. The fact was, however, that few Americans on reflection believed that London had really stooped to fraud; and the administration, realizing that the tribunal's verdict had not been induced by occasional statistical errors, chose not to pursue the matter. As far as official activity was concerned, Hind's efforts fizzled out completely.

Nevertheless, among many Americans they must have raised persisting doubts; and even among those who dismissed the notion of British duplicity they must have fanned the dislike of Halifax. Americans found themselves more determined to get rid of the fishery articles that, they thought, had caused them to be assessed ludicrously for trifling benefits.

More significant in this regard was another incident. In March 1878, about when Hind started his campaign, Secretary of State Evarts complained to London about the rough treatment accorded some American fishermen at Fortune Bay, Newfoundland. On a Sunday the previous January several American fishing boats had been hauling in a school of herring with seines. A crowd of angry Newfoundlanders gathered, demanding that the fishing stop because it was illegal on Sunday, and destroyed some of the seines. The American boats, largely empty, sailed away.

For over three years Washington and London argued about the legal issues involved. The main points made were these:

---

[11] For some of his letters and activities see *ibid.*, 46 Cong., 3 Sess., 421–42 (Jan. 7, 1881); *Debates of the House of Commons . . . of Canada*, 4 Parl., 3 Sess., 905–907 (Feb. 9, 1881); New York *World*, Feb. 8, 1881.

[12] *Congressional Record*, 46 Cong., 2 Sess., 845 (Feb. 12, 1880); *ibid.*, 46 Cong., 3 Sess., 442 (Jan. 7, 1881), 683 (Jan. 17, 1881).

Secretary Evarts contended that the Treaty of Washington permitted fishing within Newfoundland waters; Foreign Secretary Lord Salisbury argued that the Americans had violated Newfoundland laws against Sunday fishing and against using seines for taking herring.[13] Evarts replied that local laws did not take precedence over treaty rights, and that in any case it was not up to a mob to enforce the law. He demanded reparations of $105,305.02.[14] To this Salisbury countered that the treaty privileges were, in the words of the treaty itself, "in common" with British subjects, and that therefore, since Newfoundland law bound Newfoundlanders, it also bound Americans. He flatly refused to pay any reparations at all.[15]

By this time two years had passed. Americans contrasted their prompt payment of the excessive and illegal Halifax award (as they considered it) with Britain's refusal to give trifling compensation to shamefully abused Americans. Of what benefit, they wondered, were treaty articles that imposed a heavy fine on Americans and yet gave them nothing at all for inexcusable British action?

What eventually broke the impasse was not the trans-Atlantic debate but a shift of power in England. In April 1880 Disraeli and the Conservatives were defeated in general elections. Gladstone, the chief architect of the Treaty of Washington and the Geneva arbitration, again became Prime Minister; and the conciliatory Lord Granville again Foreign Secretary. The Liberals wanted a settlement that would keep intact their Treaty of Washington. Furthermore, threats of American retaliation worried them. In response to Congressional resolutions President Hayes published the Fortune Bay correspondence on May 17, 1880, together with a recommendation that the duties on Canadian and Newfoundland fish and fish oil be reinstated and that the fishermen's losses be paid, if not by Britain then by the United States. Legislation was introduced to implement these proposals.

---

[13] Evarts to John Welsh (Pierrepont's successor at London), Sept. 28, 1878, *ibid.*, 21–24; Salisbury to Welsh, Aug. 23, 1878, *ibid.*, 19–20.

[14] Evarts to Welsh, Sept. 28, 1878, *ibid.*, 23–24; Evarts to Welsh, Aug. 1, 1879, *Papers Relating to the Foreign Relations of the United States, 1880* (Washington, 1880), 530–39.

[15] Salisbury to William J. Hoppin (Chargé d'Affaires, American Legation, London), April 3, 1880, *ibid.*, 570–73.

Reinstating the duties would constitute unilateral American repudiation of part of the Treaty of Washington. This could not help but undermine the entire treaty. Deeply worried, both Sir Edward Thornton and Lord Granville served warning of the danger.[16] It was fortunate that the end of the session was near. Congress adjourned in June without having acted on the proposed legislation.

About the same time a British governmental review of Lord Salisbury's legal arguments concluded that they were untenable. The First Lord of the Admiralty condemned the former Foreign Secretary in sharp terms: ". . . I do not think I ever read the history of an important and difficult transaction with greater regret as regards the manner in which it has been conducted on behalf of the British Government."[17]

After studying the matter Lord Granville was convinced. He told the new American Minister, James Russell Lowell, that Great Britain would pay reparations. Some delay was caused by the presidential election, and Washington and London did not reach final agreement until James A. Garfield was in the White House and that staunch champion of American fishermen, James G. Blaine, in the State Department. On June 2, 1881, almost three-and-a-half years after its inception, the Fortune Bay incident was closed when Sir Edward Thornton gave Secretary Blaine a bill of exchange for £ 15,000.

A few months later the British flag was saluted at the centennial celebration of the battle of Yorktown, and the President declared that Anglo-American goodwill had never been greater.[18] It must have appeared that the fishery altercations had had no lasting effect. This was not so. The anger over the Halifax award

---

[16] Thornton to Granville, May 24 and 31, 1880, Foreign Office 5/1826; Granville to Thornton, June 14, 1880, ibid.

[17] Memorandum by Northbrook, June 10, 1880, ibid. Other influential papers were: memorandum by Francis C. Ford, June 4, 1880, ibid.; memorandum by Sir Julian Pauncefote (soon to be Permanent Under-Secretary of State for Foreign Affairs), June 12, 1880, Foreign Office 5/1822; memorandum by Lord Tenterden (Permanent Under-Secretary of State for Foreign Affairs), June 14, 1880, Foreign Office 5/1826.

[18] Annual message, Dec. 6, 1881, James D. Richardson, ed., *A Compilation of the Messages and Papers of the Presidents, 1789–1897* (Washington, 1899), VIII, 38.

and the long delay in settling the Fortune Bay affair, along with the suspicions aroused by Professor Hind, had led to a general conviction in the United States that the fishery articles of the Treaty of Washington were inequitable and intolerable. The articles were doomed. With their demise further Anglo-American tension was certain.

CHAPTER XI

Parallel Troubles

By THE SUMMER OF 1881 four monetary awards had been paid by Great Britain and the United States as a result, direct or indirect, of the Treaty of Washington: the Geneva and Fortune Bay awards ($15,500,000 and £ 15,000 respectively) to American claimants and the Halifax award of $5,500,000 to British claimants. There was also an award of $1,929,819 to British claimants resulting from various private Civil War claims; these were minor enough not to require further description. All of these except the Fortune Bay award had been determined by arbitration. Furthermore, by the arbitral award of the German Emperor the United States had received San Juan Island. On balance the United States had done well.

Nevertheless the exasperation over the Halifax award, the years of argument over Fortune Bay, and some lingering suspicions that Henry Youle Hind's accusations had a germ of truth contributed, as we have seen, to widespread dissatisfaction with the fishery articles of the Treaty of Washington. The dissatisfaction was fanned and brought into sharp focus by a special business interest—commercial fishing.

As will be recalled, the Treaty of Washington gave Americans the privilege of fishing in Canadian and Newfoundland waters ("free fishing") in exchange for the duty-free admittance into the American market of the fish and fish oil of those British areas ("free fish"). American fishery interests would have liked free fishing without free fish, because duty-free fish ruled out the higher profits that could have been made under a protective duty. What made the situation altogether intolerable was that new fishing techniques—particularly the use of seines, which had fig-

149

ured in the Fortune Bay affair—were not generally adaptable to the inshore waters of the north, so that increasingly Americans fished outside the three-mile limit. Thus the *quid pro quo* of free fishing given at Washington lost most of its value. Even without the aggravations of Halifax and Fortune Bay, attacks on the Treaty of Washington from the fishery interests in Massachusetts and Maine would have been certain to bear down upon Washington; and since these states had powerful representatives in the capital—Senators George Frisbie Hoar and Henry L. Dawes of Massachusetts, Senators William P. Frye and Eugene Hale of Maine, and the most prominent figure in the Republican party and its presidential candidate in 1884, James G. Blaine of Maine— these attacks would have swayed policy in time. Halifax, Professor Hind, and Fortune Bay, by arousing national indignation, played into the hands of the special fishery interests largely restricted to two states.

The year 1883, ten years after the Treaty of Washington entered into force, was the earliest date when the two-year notice necessary for abrogation of the treaty's fishery articles could be given. Congress adopted a resolution directing President Arthur to give the notice on July 1, 1883; Arthur did so, and Congress immediately passed legislation providing for duties on fish when the articles expired in 1885.[1] If the United States banned free fish, Britain would be certain to terminate free fishing. The Convention of 1818, which closed the inshore waters to American fishermen except for the purpose of getting wood, water, shelter, and repairs, would again become effective. Accustomed to frequenting the northern waters as though they owned them, Americans would not easily be forced back into the tight mold of 1818. A recurrence could be expected of the clashes that had disturbed the inshore waters in the years around 1870.

The problem would be aggravated because the transition from the liberal regime of the treaty to the limitations of 1818 was scheduled to occur at the beginning of July, in the middle of the

---

[1] *Congressional Record*, 47 Cong., 2 Sess., 1041–42 (Jan. 10, 1883), 3055–56 (Feb. 21, 1883), 3298 (Feb. 26, 1883), 3673 (March 3, 1883); Harold A. Innis, *The Cod Fisheries, the History of an International Economy* (New Haven, 1940), 422.

fishing season. Even though a transition of some sort had become inevitable it would be less difficult if it occurred out of season. With this in mind Sir Lionel Sackville West, who had replaced Sir Edward Thornton as British Minister in 1881, twice proposed that if the United States would admit fish duty-free through 1885, Canada and Newfoundland would extend the inshore privileges through that year.

In March 1885 the Democratic administration of Grover Cleveland took office. Thomas F. Bayard, the new Secretary of State, answered the British suggestion by pleading lack of power to prolong duty-free treatment of fish; but he did say that if Canada and Newfoundland would allow free fishing through 1885, Cleveland would ask Congress for authority to establish a special British-American commission—that now-famliar Anglo-American device—that would try to arrange another broad settlement of the perennial fisheries problem.[2] Rather surprisingly Canada and Newfoundland accepted this unequal bargain, and Great Britain and the United States concluded a *modus vivendi* incorporating its terms on June 22, 1885. In July the fishery articles expired and the new American duties entered into force.

When Congress reassembled at the end of the year Cleveland, as promised, recommended a commission.[3] The chances of a favorable response were slight. The President had been ill-advised to use the word "commission," because the last thing American fishery interests wanted was another Anglo-American commission following the disastrous ones (in their view) of 1871 and 1877. Having just regained tariff protection, they were determined to keep it. Already these interests, meeting in their bastion, the fishing town of Gloucester, Massachusetts, had come out strongly for protection, and the American Fishery Union had protested to the administration against any agreement for low duties.[4] Moreover the Republicans controlled the Senate and

---

[2] *Senate Executive Document* 113, 50 Cong., 1 Sess. (Serial 2512), 488, 489.

[3] Annual Message, Dec. 8, 1885, James D. Richardson, ed., *A Compilation of the Messages and Papers of the Presidents, 1789–1897* (Washington, 1899), VIII, 332.

[4] Steele to Bayard, May 10, 1885, *Congressional Record*, 50 Cong., 1 Sess., 7535 (Aug. 14, 1888); *ibid.*, 49 Cong., 1 Sess., 702 (Jan. 18, 1886), 3440 (April 13, 1886).

would be most unlikely to let the Democratic administration settle so major a controversy. They showed their hand when Senator Frye sponsored a resolution (which included a sarcastic reference to Halifax) opposing a commission, and the Senate accepted it by a lopsided vote.

The *modus vivendi* had now expired; the fishing season of 1886 was at hand. That year was an especially difficult one in which to deal with trouble between Great Britain and the United States. In the latter country congressional elections were drawing near. Cleveland was the first Democratic President in twenty-five years, and Republicans were certain to strain every nerve to defeat the party still bearing the stigma of rebellion and civil war. They would not allow their opponents much leeway in seeking an accord with the British. "The Irish heart (the Irish *vote*) is to be fixed to increase the difficulty of settlement of the Fishery question," Bayard perceived.[5] To a still greater degree politics convulsed Great Britain. Lord Salisbury, whose inflexibility during the Fortune Bay affair we have observed, had become Prime Minister in 1885, but only for a few months. With Gladstone back in office, a fierce struggle arose over Irish home-rule. Feelings were at fever pitch. Gladstone resigned in 1886, and Salisbury was again Prime Minister. It was the third change of government within a year, not a situation conducive to constructive diplomacy.

Diplomacy, however, was sorely needed. Having lost the privilege of free fish, Canada was determined to ban free fishing. Her police ships were ordered to arrest Americans found within territorial waters. They seized three American fishing vessels; two of them were released, but the third was condemned and sold many years later. According to a Senate report no less than one hundred and sixteen American boats had encounters with Canadians during 1886.[6] Moreover Ottawa enacted legislation authorizing

---

[5] Bayard to Edward J. Phelps (American Minister to Great Britain), June 9, 1886, Charles C. Tansill, *The Foreign Policy of Thomas F. Bayard, 1885–1897* (New York, 1940), 229.

[6] *Senate Executive Document 55*, 49 Cong., 2 Sess. (Serial 2448); *Senate Miscellaneous Document 54*, 49 Cong., 2 Sess. (Serial 2451).

the capture and confiscation of fishing vessels not only when fishing but when even "preparing to fish" in Canadian waters. Britain approved and promised to send a warship to patrol the fishing waters during 1887.[7]

It is easy to imagine the anger of Gloucester and of the United States Congress. The fishery interests were persuaded that Canada's purpose was not so much to enforce her regulations as to drive the United States into another reciprocity agreement—that unvarying Canadian aspiration—that would restore at least the free American market for her fish.[8] As for Congress, both the Senate Foreign Relations Committee and the House Foreign Affairs Committee were conducting investigations. Fishermen testifying were nearly unanimous that they would be bankrupt without the duties and that the development of the seine had rendered the inshore fisheries valueless. Both committees issued reports in January 1887 urging retaliation; the House report went so far as to recommend that imports of Canadian fish be completely banned.[9]

Congress was only too willing to comply. On January 24, 1887 the Senate all but unanimously gave the President discretionary power to ban Canadian and Newfoundland ships and also to ban their fish "or any other product."[10] This was much too weak for the Democratic House of Representatives, which by a vote of 256 to 1 adopted an amendment further empowering the President to ban Canadian locomotives and also (if Canada violated a provision of the Treaty of Washington for duty-free shipment through Canada to the United States) to disallow duty-free shipment of Canadian goods through the United States.[11] The Repub-

---

[7] For the text of the law see *Senate Document* 870, 61 Cong., 3 Sess. (Serial 5930), 137–38. Donald G. Creighton, *John A. Macdonald, The Old Chieftain* (Toronto, 1955), 466.

[8] Charles S. Campbell, "American Tariff Interests and the Northeastern Fisheries, 1883–1888," *Canadian Historical Review*, XLV (1964), 216.

[9] *Senate Report* 1683, 49 Cong., 2 Sess. (Serial 2456), xv, 45; *House Report* 3648, 49 Cong., 2 Sess. (Serial 2500), 19.

[10] *Congressional Record*, 49 Cong., 2 Sess., 793 (Jan. 19, 1887), 929 and 952 (Jan. 24, 1887).

[11] *Ibid.*, 2127–28 and 2150 (Feb. 23, 1887).

lican Senate, where railroad and business interests were strong, refused to accept the amendment. In the end both houses passed the Senate bill, and Cleveland signed it on March 3, 1887.[12]

The fishing season opened soon afterwards. Would the threat of retaliation deter Canada? Fewer seizures of American fishing vessels occurred than during the preceding year, but it became evident that the Dominion was resolved, threat or not, to enforce the Convention of 1818 and the law of 1886 authorizing seizures of American vessels preparing to fish within its waters. The new incidents evoked another outburst of American anger. Cleveland, it seemed, would be sure to make the retaliatory moves for which he had been given discretionary power. Economic warfare across the international line would follow. And if Canada again enforced her measures during 1888, no one could be sure what dangerous explosion might not occur.

Matters were more perilous because a parallel situation existed in another area during those years of 1886 and 1887. A great fur-seal herd, the largest in the world, frequented the distant Bering Sea. If the fish were a valuable natural resource off one coast, so were the seals off the other coast. So far, the parallel held. But in the northeast, Canadians were arresting Americans; in the northwest, Americans were arresting Canadians. Each controversy aggravated the other.

As part of the Alaska purchase of 1867 from Russia, the United States had acquired the Pribilof Islands, four little islands in the Bering Sea. Every May the fur-seals gathered there during the breeding season; they remained until mid-November. On land they were defenseless against human hunters, who flocked to the islands lured by the easy profits to be made from seal skins. The principal American hunters joined together in 1868 to form the Alaska Commercial Company, which two years later secured from the government a twenty-year lease of the islands. In return the company agreed to pay an annual rental, plus a fee for each skin and gallon of seal oil taken, and not to

---

[12] *Ibid.*, 2166–67 (Feb. 24, 1887), 2452 (Feb. 28, 1887), 2554–63 (March 2, 1887); *Senate Report* 1981, 49 Cong., 2 Sess. (Serial 2458); *The Statutes at Large of the United States of America* (Washington, 1887), XXIV, 475–76.

kill over 100,000 male seals a year (a small number of males suffices to reproduce the herd), and these only in June, July, September, and October.[13] For the government the contract meant a welcome annual revenue and also a means of safeguarding the herd, which in default of regulated killing would have soon been exterminated, as most other herds already had been. For the Alaska Commercial Company it meant handsome profits; the price of seal skins mounted steadily, more than quadrupling from 1870 to 1880.

But thereafter the scene darkened. The company's monopoly was broken when sealing at sea—pelagic sealing, it was called—become more and more frequent. Large numbers of seals, females as well as males, were taken in the Bering Sea far from land; and even larger numbers were killed but not recovered. As these new skins entered the market, the price of skins fell; by 1885 it was about half what it had been in 1880. Conservationists predicted that the entire herd would be decimated under the double onslaught by land and sea.

One can be certain that the Alaska Commercial Company, faced with dwindling profits, bestirred itself behind the scenes to persuade Washington to suppress this inconvenient competition; presumably it kept in close touch with Grover Cleveland's Secretary of the Treasury, Daniel Manning, whose department had jurisdiction over the seals. Like the Commercial Company, the Treasury Department had reason to dislike pelagic sealers because its revenue would dwindle as the herd declined. At the beginning of August 1886 a Department revenue cutter seized three Canadian sealing vessels dozens of miles outside the three-mile limit in the Bering Sea. The vessels were taken to Alaska and left exposed on a beach. The captains and mates were put on trial before a United States District Court; the judge sen-

---

[13] *House Report* 623, 44 Cong., 1 Sess. (Serial 1712), passim; Great Britain, Foreign Office, *Blue Book, United States, No. 2 (1890): Correspondence Respecting the Behring Sea Seal Fisheries, 1886–1890* (London, 1890), 9–10. The lease is in *Fur Seal Arbitration, Proceedings of the Tribunal of Arbitration . . ., II, Appendix to the Case of the United States* (Washington, 1895), I, 104–106.

tenced them to a month in jail with fines of $500 for each captain and $300 for each mate.[14]

Just as the United States had protested against the interference with her fishing vessels in the northeastern waters—it was not long before the Bering Sea arrests that the three American boats had been apprehended—so now, with respect to the Bering Sea, Great Britain remonstrated and reserved rights as to compensation. The United States did not reply until November and then merely pleaded lack of information from distant Alaska. London waited two months and then, having heard no more, protested strongly, calling for "immediate and most serious attention" to the "grave" matter. But nothing but a temporizing response resulted.[15]

To people in Canada, Newfoundland, and Great Britain a violation of international law by the United States seemed self-evident. So did American hypocrisy. For at one and the same time Washington denounced arrests of American fishing vessels within undeniably Canadian waters, and yet ordered the seizure and confiscation of Canadian sealers scores of miles from land. The American position in the Bering Sea must have stiffened Ottawa's determination to stand firm in the northeast—just as America's abrogation of free fish had engendered the Canadian resolve to terminate free fishing. Yet Americans were no less indignant over what they considered to be British mistreatment of their fishermen. Each side denounced the other. A situation had arrived that, if unchecked, could have escalated dangerously.

But no more than the fisheries was the Bering Sea controversy to be eased in 1887. Within the Cabinet Secretary Bayard argued against further seizures, but apparently Manning opposed him, and Cleveland backed the latter. The Treasury Department's revenue cutters seized six British pelagic sealing vessels far from land in July and August 1887. They were sent to Alaska for trial

---

[14] Regarding the trial see *Senate Executive Document* 106, 50 Cong., 2 Sess. (Serial 2612), 17–48. One of the captains, who disappeared before the trial, was discovered dead near Sitka, *Blue Book, United States, No. 2 (1890)*, 29.

[15] Sackville West to Bayard, Jan. 9, 1897, *Blue Book, United States, No. 2 (1890)*, 37–38; Bayard to Sackville West, Jan. 12, 1887, *Fur Seal Arbitration*, V, 56.

before the same judge who had condemned the three ships arrested the year before. During the proceedings the judge confessed that he was relying upon information supplied by a certain N. L. Jeffries. Jeffries was none other than the Alaska Commercial Company's attorney. With such interested opinion to guide him, it is scarcely surprising that the judge pronounced the schooners liable to condemnation and the officers and crew to imprisonment. Cleveland ordered that the men be released, but the Alaskan authorities sold four of the schooners.

Just as the Canadian seizures of 1887, coming on top of those of 1886, seemed to indicate a settled policy, so did the American seizures of 1887 following those of the year before; and as Americans had reacted angrily to the incidents of 1887 in the fishing grounds, so now did the British to the renewed seizures in the Bering Sea. Lord Salisbury, always a person to stand up for British rights, denounced the seizures and demanded that they not be repeated. But Bayard, however willing personally, could give no promise. Manning and Cleveland still were overruling him.

By August 1887, then, both the American policy in the northwest and the British policy in the northeast had stiffened. Should further arrests take place in 1888, the state of Anglo-Canadian-American relations could deteriorate alarmingly. Even more could this happen if Cleveland invoked the retaliation act of March 3, 1887.

The similarities between the two Anglo-American maritime controversies were great in 1886 and 1887. They were not so great, though still fairly close, in 1888. Both controversies eased then; but whereas the fishery controversy was in fact if not in law settled permanently that year, the fur-seals dispute, deceptively pacified in 1888, flared up to its most dangerous peak in 1889 and continued to harass Canada, Great Britain, and the United States for many years thereafter.

As regards the fur-seals in 1888, little need be said. Secretary Bayard tried to persuade Canada and Great Britain to accept regulations that would safeguard the species. Ottawa rejected them. The Canadians, not believing that the existence of the herd was in danger, were unwilling to restrict their sealers while leaving the Alaska Commercial Company unrestrained (except by

United States law) on the Pribilof Islands. What they wanted was not restriction but damages for the seizures of 1886 and 1887. Lord Salisbury backed the Dominion, and the proposed regulations came to nothing. But if the Secretary of State's diplomacy failed on the international level, it succeeded at home. In 1888 it was Bayard, not Manning, who got Cleveland's ear; and in consequence the Treasury revenue cutters, although on patrol in the Bering Sea, did not arrest a single Canadian sealer. For the moment it looked as though the fur-seals controversy had ended.

Quite different was the road to a fishery agreement. About the time he was suggesting sealing regulations Secretary Bayard was busy also with a proposal to regulate fishing.[16] This proposal, too, came to nothing. Another fishing season was drawing near; and perceiving the dangers of new arrests, he suggested that he and British delegates meet at the earliest possible date.[17] Ottawa and London had no objection, and still another Anglo-American commission convened, this one at Washington on November 22, 1887.

The American commissioners were Secretary Bayard; James B. Angell, president of the University of Michigan; and William L. Putnam, a Maine lawyer. The British commissioners were Colonial Secretary Joseph Chamberlain, Sackville West, and Sir Charles Tupper, a prominent Canadian politician. Negotiations centered on Canada's demand for at least free fish, and preferably a broad reciprocity treaty. The British tried hard to get the bargain of 1871 restored—free fish for free fishing. But to no avail. With a low-tariff Democrat in the White House, who was pushing for an overall reduction of the tariff wall, and with the presidential election of 1888 approaching, not the slightest chance existed of the Republican Senate approving a treaty lowering even the fish duties.

After weeks of argument Britain in early 1888 withdrew her

---

[16] Bayard to Phelps, Nov. 15, 1886, *Papers Relating to the Foreign Relations of the United States, 1887* (Washington, 1888), 424–28.

[17] Bayard to Sir Charles Tupper (Canadian Minister of Finance), May 31, 1887, *Senate Document* 870, 61 Cong., 3 Sess. (Serial 5931), 942–44; Bayard to Phelps, July 12, 1887, *ibid.,* 945–47.

request for free fish. Not only that, but she indicated that pending ratification of the treaty under negotiation she would establish a *modus vivendi* opening the inshore waters to American fishermen who purchased annual licenses. The truth was that London had come to believe that the Dominion's enforcement measures were too harsh. Fearing that the Senate would not approve a treaty, Chamberlain wanted a *modus vivendi* as an alternative means of ensuring more lenient Canadian action.[18] He was ready to sacrifice the Canadians in order to improve British relations with the United States.

After these concessions agreement was quickly reached; the Bayard-Chamberlain Treaty was signed on February 15, 1888. It specified where Americans could fish in Canadian and New-foundland waters and what their rights and obligations would be. Article XV stated that if at any time the United States restored free fish, American fishermen could buy supplies, transship catches, and ship crews in Canadian and Newfoundland ports. With the treaty was a *modus* intended to last two years, pending the treaty's ratification: Americans buying annual licenses for $1.50 a ship ton could enter Canadian and Newfoundland waters for the three purposes mentioned in article XV; they could get licenses for nothing if the United States restored free fish; and fishing vessels were subject to confiscation only if fishing or preparing to fish in territorial waters.[19]

As Chamberlain had anticipated, the Senate rejected the treaty, by a vote of 27 ayes, 30 nays, far below the two-thirds needed for approval.[20] Undoubtedly the fishery interests had been exerting pressure. They had eagerly anticipated the application of the retaliation bill of March 1887; instead, they had been confronted by a treaty that, in article XV, threatened not retaliation but abolition of the fish duties. No wonder that the Gloucester Board of Trade wrathfully denounced the treaty as "detrimental to the

---

[18] Chamberlain to Salisbury, Dec. 22, 1887, Lord Salisbury Papers, Christ Church Library (Oxford).

[19] For the treaty see *Senate Miscellaneous Document* 109, 50 Cong., 1 Sess. (Serial 2517), 155–61; for the *modus* see *ibid.*, 164.

[20] *Congressional Record*, 50 Cong., 1 Sess., 7768 (Aug. 21, 1888). For reports of the Foreign Relations Committee see *Senate Miscellaneous Document* 109, 50 Cong., 1 Sess.

interests of the United States as a people, and injurious to its honor and dignity as a nation."[21] More crucial was the fact that the vote came in late August, about two months before the presidential election when politics dominated the scene. Instead of hailing the treaty as a welcome means of reaching an accord with Great Britain and Canada, the Republicans, hoping to garner the Irish vote, depicted it as outrageously pro-British.

Although the treaty was dead, the British *modus vivendi,* to the considerable annoyance of the fishery interests, was not. Throughout the 1888 season it worked smoothly. Consequently the problems of 1886 and 1887 did not recur, just as on the Bering Sea no arrest took place in 1888; and in default of fresh incidents it was impossible to whip up sentiment to ban British fish. Furthermore the standing British offer to give free licenses whenever the United States restored free fish created a temptation to abolish the fish duties that must have made Gloucester and other such centers extremely uneasy.

Whatever their unease, they had to adapt themselves to the new situation, for it turned out to be a lasting one. Originally envisaged as a two-year stopgap, the *modus vivendi* in point of fact was time after time renewed by Great Britain until it was replaced by a definitive settlement in 1912. The year 1888, then, witnessed a sharp turn in the long fishery controversy, a turn from clashes occurring over many years to peaceful conditions in the northeastern waters. In this respect the parallel between those waters and the Bering Sea broke down. Peace did return in both places after the conflicts of 1886 and 1887, but in the northwest it lasted only one season. Before considering the renewed troubles in the Bering Sea, however, mention must be made of an unexpected sequel to the fishery settlement that, for a while, undid much of the beneficial effect of the *modus.*

The political considerations involved in the defeat of the Bayard-Chamberlain Treaty have been mentioned. A series of maneuvers between the Republicans and Democrats ensued. Anxious for reelection, Cleveland could not take the Senate's

---

[21] Resolution of April 26, 1888, *Congressional Record,* 50 Cong., 1 Sess., 6062 (July 10, 1888). See also *ibid.,* 6061 (July 10, 1888), 8317 (Sept. 5, 1888); Tansill, *Bayard,* 304.

rebuff passively. As Sir Charles Tupper observed sourly, "Cleveland found that his supposed friendliness to England was killing his chances. . . ."[22] Two days after the treaty's defeat the President counterattacked. In a startling message to Congress he asked for drastic retaliation against Canada for mistreating American fishermen, retaliation going much beyond that authorized by the act of 1887, nothing less than a ban on the bonded transit of Canadian goods through the United States.[23] At one and the same time Cleveland was catering to the anti-British vote and directing a nasty blow at New England railroads and their Republican representatives in Congress. His request, if adopted, would have made the immensely valuable bonded trade dutiable. Undoubtedly that trade would have diminished, so that American railroads in the northeast would have suffered. No wonder that Republican Senators excoriated the President. The retaliation they favored (that of March 1887) was aimed at foreign fish, not American railroads, and was designed to benefit their section of the country, not injure it.

The Democratic House, by a one-sided margin, passed a measure in the sense of Cleveland's recommendation.[24] If the Republicans in the Senate followed suit, they would alienate their business supporters; if they did not, they would alienate the Irish vote. The dilemma was obvious; its resolution almost equally so. The Senate simply directed the Foreign Relations Committee to study Anglo-Canadian-American relations and report at the next session; thereby it shelved the delicate matter of retaliation until after the election and countered Cleveland's move to embarrass the Republicans.[25]

Nevertheless the President had regained some of the anti-British credentials that he had lost by supporting the fishery treaty, and this was disheartening to his opponents. By good fortune a chance for another shrewd move was now opportunely

---

[22] Tupper to Chamberlain, Sept. 4, 1886, Sir Charles Tupper Papers, Public Archives of Canada (Ottawa), IX.

[23] Message of Aug. 23, 1888, Richardson, *Messages and Papers*, VIII, 620–27.

[24] *Congressional Record*, 8439–40 (Sept. 8, 1888); 176 voted aye, 4 nay, 144 did not vote.

[25] *Ibid.*, 8644 (Sept. 17, 1888), 8979–80 (Sept. 27, 1888).

delivered to them. About the time that the Senate was postponing retaliation a man named George Osgoodby, but using the name Charles F. Murchison, wrote to Sackville West from Pomona, California. Calling himself a naturalized Englishman, he spoke of Cleveland as having usually been "so favorable and friendly towards England" that the retaliation message seemed out of character. In view of that message, whom should he and other naturalized Englishmen vote for, he asked.[26] The Minister's inept reply in effect recommended Cleveland—and this proved Sackville's ruination.

Osgoodby released the correspondence to the press; it was published throughout the country beginning on October 21, at the climax of the bitterly fought election. The evidence that no less a person than the British Minister thought well of Democrats was a terrible blow to them. Reports streamed in of masses of Irish-Americans switching to the Republican nominee, Benjamin Harrison.[27]

Sackville would have to go—that was obvious to the Democratic managers. Bayard was probably reluctant to take so abrupt a step but his decision to act was made easier by reports from the American Minister at London, Edward J. Phelps, that Lord Salisbury and the British press did not oppose dismissal. The Secretary handed the Englishman his passports on October 30. Sackville was the third British Minister whom Washington had told to go; Francis James Jackson had left in 1810, and John F. T. Crampton in 1856.

But Phelps had given bad advice. British newspapers denounced the American action and Salisbury, in a firm note, insisted that Sackville had done nothing to warrant "so striking a departure" from customary usage.[28] He refused to send another Minister to Washington until after Cleveland, defeated by Harrison (partly, it may be, because of Osgoodby), had stepped down from power in March 1889.

---

[26] The letter, dated Sept. 4, 1888, is in Foreign Office 5/2020. Regarding the incident see Charles S. Campbell, "The Dismissal of Lord Sackville," *Mississippi Valley Historical Review,* XLIV (1958), 635–48.

[27] Cleveland to Bayard, Oct. 26, 1888, Thomas F. Bayard Papers, Library of Congress (Washington), CXXXI.

[28] Salisbury to Phelps, Dec. 24, 1888, Public Record Office (London), Foreign Office 5/2031.

It was fortunate that the northeastern fisheries were no longer adding their own menace to good relations between Britain and America. The *modus vivendi,* so wisely instituted by Great Britain, had preserved the tranquillity of the fishing grounds throughout the stormy political events of 1888; and it would continue to do so long after the irritation over Sackville's dismissal quieted down. The fishery controversy, in the shape it assumed after the United States terminated the Marcy-Elgin Treaty in 1866, was the last one associated with the dangerous post-Civil War period. With its practical settlement, that period ended. One slight qualification should be made. As we have seen, the fisheries had exacerbated the Bering Sea dispute, and the most critical part of the latter was still to come.

CHAPTER XII

Clashes in the Bering Sea

A T THE END OF 1888 the controversy over the northeastern fisheries was substantially concluded; that over the Bering Sea fur-seals was shortly to enter upon its most dangerous phase. For this, Grover Cleveland was somewhat responsible. Two days before leaving the White House he signed an act requiring the chief executive every year to warn that pelagic sealers entering "all the dominion of the United States in the waters of Behring Sea" were liable to arrest.[1] Benjamin Harrison succeeded him on March 4, 1889, and James G. Blaine again became Secretary of State. Throughout his career Blaine had catered to the Irish vote, and in the fishery dispute had assumed a rather unconciliatory position. Since Harrison, too, was a resolute defender of American interests,· there was reason to expect a collision in the Bering Sea.

As required by Cleveland's law, Harrison issued the warning shortly after taking office. Was the arrest of pelagic sealers mandatory? It could be argued that since "all the dominion" was not defined, the phrase referred only to waters within the three-mile limit. But the new Republican administration did not so argue. During the 1889 season Treasury Department revenue cutters arrested five Canadian sealing vessels many miles from land. They all escaped. This must have happened by American design. Undoubtedly the administration hoped to frighten off the sealers by arresting them, while at the same time dampening down the reaction by letting them get away.

Spurred on by anguished cries from Ottawa, London pro-

---

[1] Act of March 2, 1889, *Statutes of the United States of America* . . . (Washington, 1889), 50 Cong., 2 Sess., 1009–10.

tested.[2] A protracted diplomatic debate followed, about which we need say little. Blaine's best point—he also made some dubious ones—was that pelagic sealing was "*contra bonos mores*" because it could exterminate the entire herd; Prime Minister Salisbury's that it was "an axiom of international maritime law" that seizures on the high seas were illegal.[3] He did admit privately that the American case was strong morally, if not legally.[4]

It will be recalled that in 1870 the Alaska Commercial Company had secured a twenty-year lease of sealing rights on the Pribilof Islands. When the lease came up for renewal in 1890 it went to another concern, the North American Commercial Company. This was surprising because the Alaska Commercial Company was powerful and well established. The principal explanation may be simply that the North American Commercial Company offered the government better terms. But it is also significant that two of the new company's five or six shareholders were closely connected with Secretary of State Blaine. One of them, Stephen B. Elkins, had been the Secretary's campaign manager in the presidential election of 1884 and was to be his Cabinet colleague as Secretary of War in 1892. The other was Darius Ogden Mills, a man of great wealth and father-in-law of Whitelaw Reid, owner of the influential New York *Tribune* and one of Blaine's most intimate associates over many years. The new lease, awarded on March 12, 1890, ran, like the former one, for twenty years. However it permitted only 60,000 seals to be killed the first year and, in subsequent years, a number to be determined annually by the Treasury Department.

---

[2] Lord Stanley (Governor-General of Canada) to Colonial Secretary Lord Knutsford, Aug. 8, 1889, Great Britain, Foreign Office, *Blue Book, United States, No. 2 (1890): Correspondence Respecting the Behring Sea Seal Fisheries, 1886–1890* (London, 1890), 296; Prime Minister Lord Salisbury to H. G. Edwardes (Chargé d'Affaires, British Legation, Washington), Aug. 22, 1889, *ibid.*, 300.

[3] Blaine to Sir Julian Pauncefote (British Minister to the United States), Jan. 22, 1890, *Papers Relating to the Foreign Relations of the United States, 1890* (Washington, 1891), 366; Salisbury to Pauncefote, May 22, 1890, *ibid.*, 420. The rest of the lengthy correspondence is in *ibid.*, 358–508, and *Papers Relating to the Foreign Relations of the United States, 1891* (Washington, 1892), 542–643.

[4] Salisbury to Pauncefote, March 28, 1890, Lord Salisbury Papers (Christ Church Library, Oxford).

While carrying on his legalistic debate with Salisbury, Secretary Blaine was taking other steps to curtail Canadian pelagic sealing. The Secretary was in a difficult position. On the one hand we may be sure that he was pressed by his friends in the North American Commercial Company to act against their Canadian competitors; but on the other hand he knew full well that Lord Salisbury would not tolerate illegal seizures by the revenue cutters. Blaine first suggested an annual closed season during which pelagic sealers would be banned from much of the Bering Sea, but he could not have been surprised when Canada rejected any such limitation out of hand.[5] The Secretary then turned to the new British Minister (at length appointed as Sackville West's successor), Sir Julian Pauncefote. In view of his own failure to satisfy Ottawa, he said, could not Sir Julian suggest something? The latter agreed to think about the matter.

He could do little without Canadian consent. By 1890 Great Britain was much more solicitous of her Dominion than she had been after the Civil War, Joseph Chamberlain's *modus vivendi* notwithstanding. Imperial sentiment had revived strongly. The consequence was that whenever an issue involving Canada arose between London and Washington, a time-consuming "wordy triangular duel" (so former Secretary of State Bayard had called it)[6] had to be embarked upon. Not until late April was Pauncefote ready with the requested proposal. He suggested that a joint commission be established for the purpose of reporting within two years on means to safeguard the fur-seals; and that meanwhile pelagic sealing be prohibited within ten miles of the Pribilof Islands in July, August, and September, and that in May, June, October, November, and December all sealing should be banned—on the Pribilof Islands as well as at sea.[7]

By then Harrison had issued his second annual warning to

---

[5] Charles H. Tupper (Canadian Minister of Marine and Fisheries) to Prime Minister Sir John A. Macdonald, March 3 and April 10, 1891, Sir John A. Macdonald Papers, Public Archives of Canada (Ottawa), XXX, XXXI, respectively; Pauncefote to Salisbury, Feb. 22, 1890, *Blue Book, United States, No. 2 (1890)*, 412.

[6] Bayard to Sir Charles Tupper (Canadian Minister of Finance), May 31, 1887, *Senate Document 870*, 61 Cong., 3 Sess. (Serial 5931), 942.

[7] Pauncefote to Blaine, April 29, 1890, *Blue Book, United States, No. 2 (1890)*, 455–57; see also *ibid.*, 457–59.

sealers against entering the American "dominion" in the Bering Sea. On May 22, after waiting over three weeks for an answer to his proposal, Sir Julian read in the newspapers that the administration had decided to reject it and to arrest pelagic sealers during the 1890 season. Greatly upset, he rushed off to the State Department. In a stormy interview Blaine insisted that there was no justification to ban killing on the Pribilof Islands and that the British proposal was therefore unacceptable. Back in his Legation, the Minister telegraphed London that seizures were likely.[8]

Whitehall reacted quickly and strongly. It decided to make a formal protest and to send four warships to the Bering Sea as soon as word came that the American cutters intended to arrest pelagic sealers.[9] Pauncefote delivered the protest on June 14: ". . . Her Britannic Majesty's Government must hold the Government of the United States responsible for the consequences which may ensue from acts which are contrary to the principles of international law."[10] Blaine was enraged. He had just learned about the order to the four warships. "We view it as a menace," he told Sir Julian, "and shall not defer on that account for a single day the departure of our cutters. It is a violent assertion of a right to share in a fishery to which the United States can show an exclusive title for 80 years."[11]

About this time Canadian sealers began to sail into the Bering Sea. So did a revenue cutter. The four warships were held in readiness outside that sea. London, Washington, and Ottawa waited anxiously to see what would happen. The outcome was anticlimactic. Though sealing occurred as usual, not a single arrest was made. Before the season ended, the four warships were assigned to service elsewhere.

---

[8] Pauncefote to Salisbury, May 22 and 23, 1890; *ibid.*, 465–66, 469–71; Blaine rejected the British proposal in writing on May 29, 1890, *ibid.*, 475–78.

[9] Salisbury to Pauncefote, May 23 and 31, 1890, Foreign Office 5/2107.

[10] *Blue Book, United States, No. 2 (1890)*, 507–508. Regarding this and other events of 1890 and 1891 see Charles S. Campbell, "The Anglo-American Crisis in the Bering Sea, 1890–1891," *Mississippi Valley Historical Review*, XLVIII (1961), 393–414.

[11] Pauncefote to Foreign Office, June 16, 1890, Public Record Office (London), Foreign Office 5/2108.

It seems clear that the administration had never intended to arrest sealers in 1890, though undoubtedly it did hope to frighten them away from sealing. Whereas in 1889 it had authorized seizures provided the ships were permitted to escape, in 1890 it merely acted menacingly. The British protest and threat to use force undoubtedly influenced Washington in the sense of making it somewhat more inclined to moderate its policy in the future, but the likelihood is great that they were not responsible for the failure to make arrests in 1890.

Harrison and Blaine had now seen two sealing seasons elapse without having been able to stop pelagic sealing and without having been able to do much for their friends in the North American Commercial Company. With the approach of the season of 1891, decisions about the Bering Sea again became necessary.

Blaine opened up negotiations with Pauncefote for a *modus vivendi*. He still hoped, though he could not have been sanguine, for an agreement prohibiting pelagic but not land sealing. Any faint chance of success disappeared in a cloud of embarrassing disclosures. In 1890 the Treasury Department had sent the leading American authority on fur-seals, Henry W. Elliott, to the Pribilof Islands to investigate. He estimated that since his last visit in 1876 the herd had diminished from some 4,700,000 to a mere 959,655.[12] In a secret report of late 1890 he attributed this dreadful decline to sealing on land just as much as to pelagic sealing; he recommended that pelagic sealing be stopped altogether and that land sealing be stopped for at least seven years.[13] About the same time four other reports, by the Treasury agents assigned to the Pribilof Islands, became public. All noted a great fall in the number of fur-seals; three put the blame on land sealing as well as pelagic sealing; and the report of the chief agent, Charles J. Goff, recommended that all killing be stopped indefinitely.[14]

---

[12] Hearings before the House Committee on Expenditures in the Department of Commerce, 63 Cong., 2 Sess., *Investigation of the Fur-Seal Industry of Alaska* (Washington, 1914), Appendix, 53.

[13] The full report was not released until 1896. *House Document* 175, 54 Cong., 1 Sess. (Serial 3421).

[14] *Senate Executive Document* 49, 51 Cong., 2 Sess. (Serial 2818), 6, 8, 9, 32.

Both the administration and the North American Commercial Company viewed these reports with dismay. The company's lease had proved a great disappointment. In 1890 Goff had authorized the slaughter of only about 21,000 seals, barely a third of the anticipated 60,000. Probably under pressure from Mills and Elkins, the Treasury in April 1891 dismissed Goff and gave the company a secret permit to take 60,000 skins during that year.[15] But soon afterwards Elliott, horrified by the permit, which he had learned about accidentally, made both it and part of his own secret report public. Thereafter any hope for an agreement banning only pelagic sealing vanished.

The best that Blaine could get was a *modus vivendi* prohibiting pelagic sealing but permitting the North American Commercial Company to kill 7500 seals on the islands to recompense it for expenses in taking care of the natives. Ottawa disliked the prohibition of pelagic sealing as much as the Commercial Company did the near-prohibition of land sealing, but finally gave a grudging and qualified consent. The *modus* was signed on June 15, 1891; it was to be effective until the following May 1.

Thus the perils of another sealing season had been surmounted. At the same time a less temporary remedy had come into view. In August 1890 Prime Minister Salisbury had suggested an arbitration treaty; negotiations for one had accompanied those for the *modus*. They lasted much longer but, in the end, the two countries agreed that seven arbitrators—two Americans, two British, and one from each of France, Italy, and Sweden and Norway—would meet in Paris to decide about five questions regarding the American claim to have exclusive jurisdiction in the Bering Sea and its seal fisheries. The tribunal was also to determine what regulations were necessary for the protection of the herd, and make decisions on factual matters regarding Canadian claims for the American seizures, but not on American liability. The treaty was signed on February 29, 1892.

Unfortunately the 1892 fishing season was drawing near, and this led to yet another altercation. The *modus vivendi* was due

---

[15] Hearings before the House Committee, *Investigation of the Fur-Seal Industry of Alaska*, 142–45; *Senate Executive Document* 49, 51 Cong., 2 Sess., 13–14, 26.

to expire on May 1, 1892, after which the Bering Sea would be open to unrestricted sealing. Lord Salisbury feared that the Canadians would accept no further restraints; however, he offered to ban pelagic sealing within thirty miles of the Pribilof Islands, leaving it unrestricted elsewhere in the Bering Sea, if land sealing was limited to 30,000.[16] Since Blaine was ill, Harrison assumed charge of the negotiations. The President was, on occasion, an intemperate person. Furious over Salisbury's suggestion of reopening most of the Bering Sea to pelagic sealing, he wrote a sharp reply virtually threatening the use of force: "certainly the United States can not be expected to suspend the defense, by such means as are within its power, of the property and jurisdictional rights claimed by it. . . ."[17] And when Salisbury replied with another unsatisfactory offer, Harrison flared up with such intensity that a member of his staff wrote: "The President today [March 22] finished his reply to Lord Salisbury's note refusing to renew modus in Bering Sea matter and the outcome means a backdown on the part of G.B., or war."[18]

Despite this melodramatic appraisal the danger of war was nonexistent. Neither the short-tempered President nor the imperturbable Prime Minister would have sanctioned hostilities over the fur-seals of the Bering Sea. At Sir Julian's strong advice, Salisbury agreed to renew the 1891 *modus vivendi* provided the Senate approved the arbitration treaty and provided the United States agreed that, if the arbitrators decided against her, she would compensate the pelagic sealers for their losses incurred by not sealing (Great Britain to compensate the United States and

---

[16] Pauncefote to Blaine, Feb. 29, 1892, Great Britain, Foreign Office, *Blue Book, United States, No. 3 (1892): Further Correspondence Respecting the Behring Sea Seal Fisheries* (London, 1892), 155; Salisbury to Pauncefote, March 11, 1892, Foreign Office 5/2174.

[17] William F. Wharton (Acting Secretary of State) to Pauncefote, March 8, 1892, *Foreign Relations, 1891*, p. 624.

[18] Diary of Everard F. Tibbott, March 22, 1892, cited in Albert T. Volwiler, "Harrison, Blaine, and American Foreign Policy, 1889–1893," *Proceedings of the American Philosophical Society*, LXXIX (1938), 647–48. For the Prime Minister's unsatisfactory reply see Pauncefote to Wharton, March 19, 1892, *Foreign Relations, 1891*, p. 625. For Harrison's note which alarmed Tibbott see Wharton to Pauncefote, March 22, 1892, *ibid.*, 625–28.

the North American Commercial Company if the decision went against Britain).[19] The Senate did approve the treaty on March 29. And back in the State Department again, Blaine met several times with Pauncefote to draft a final *modus vivendi*, similar to the preceding one. They signed it on April 18, 1892; the Senate approved it the next day.

Regular sessions of the arbitral tribunal began in Paris on April 4, 1893. The American arbiters were Supreme Court Justice John M. Harlan and Senator John T. Morgan of Alabama; the British arbiters were Lord Hannen of the High Court of Appeal and Sir John S. D. Thompson, Attorney-General of Canada. The three other arbiters were Baron Alphonse de Courcel, a French Senator and diplomat, who was elected the tribunal's president; Marquis Emilio Visconti Venosta, an Italian Senator and former Foreign Minister; and Gregers Gram, a Minister of State of Sweden and Norway. On August 15 the tribunal returned an award against the United States on all five questions. It also prescribed sealing regulations. Pelagic sealing was banned at all times in waters up to sixty miles from the Pribilof Islands, and from May 1 through July 31 it was also banned in waters north of the 35th parallel and east of the 180th longitude. These regulations were to be effective until changed by Anglo-American consent; their operation was to be reviewed by the two countries every five years.

The award ended the dangerous phase of the dispute. Nevertheless Americans resented it, though less so than they had the Halifax award, and their annoyance was intensified by the matter of damages. As will be remembered, the treaty authorized the tribunal to decide upon questions of fact related to Canadian claims but not upon American liability. The arbitrators found that American revenue cutters had arrested several British ships outside territorial waters. Consequent upon this, the United States and Great Britain reached agreement on August 21, 1894 for the former to pay $425,000 in damages. Congress, however,

[19] Salisbury to Pauncefote, March 26, 1892, *Blue Book, United States, No. 3 (1892)*, 165; for Pauncefote's advice see his notes to Salisbury of March 10 and 24, 1892, Foreign Office 5/2174.

at the end of 1895 refused to appropriate the money.[20] Accordingly the two countries appointed a joint commission of two to determine what sum America should pay. The two commissioners named a sum of $473,151.26 on December 17, 1897.[21] Americans were bitter over what they considered, again as in 1877, an inexcusably large award. But during the Spanish-American War, when no risk could be taken of alienating the British, Congress on June 15, 1898 made the appropriation.

Although Blaine's settlements of 1892 and the arbitration of 1893 ended Bering Sea perils, a good deal of Anglo-American-Canadian squabbling about the adequacy of the tribunal's regulations to preserve the herd took place over the years after 1893. The herd continued to decline, the North American Commercial Company continued to importune the government, the "wordy triangular duel" continued to preoccupy London, Washington, and Ottawa. Not until 1911 did Russia and Japan join Great Britain and the United States in a comprehensive settlement that imposed stricter regulations to safeguard the fur-seals.

---

[20] *House Executive Document* 132, 53 Cong., 3 Sess. (Serial 3319), 10–11; *Congressional Record*, 54 Cong., 1 Sess., 65–90 (Dec. 9, 1895).

[21] William M. Malloy, compiler, *Treaties, Conventions, International Acts, Protocols and Agreements between the United States of America and Other Powers, 1776–1909* (Washington, 1910), I, 766–70.

CHAPTER XIII

Détente Again: The British Guiana Boundary

WE HAVE NOTED the rise of better feelings in the late 1850s and the underlying factors that brought this about. In retrospect one can see that the dangerous British-American animosity during and after the Civil War could not long endure—provided, however, that those crucial years were surmounted without war. Bringing Britain and America safely through the tension of the late 1860s and early 1870s was the great achievement of the Treaty of Washington and the Geneva arbitration. With the critical phase of the post-Civil War period laid to rest, and the main Canadian difficulties greatly eased, the two English-speaking countries could be expected to resume relations at least as tranquil as those of the 1850s. And as a matter of fact, by the 1890s other forces, which we shall consider later, had come into play; and these were soon to bring a trans-Atlantic friendship immeasurably stronger than the transitory one forty years earlier.

But first, one more crisis had to be faced, the sharpest but not the most dangerous since the clash over the *Alabama* claims. Although once again, and for the last time, threats of war filled the air, the principal significance of this final crisis was its revelation that a deep feeling of British-American kinship had grown up. Despite the many disputes since the Civil War, Great Britain and the United States were suddenly seen to be much closer together than anyone had thought.

The new controversy related not to Canada but, surprisingly enough, to the distant jungle boundary of Venezuela and British Guiana. No agreed-on line existed, though a British surveyor, Robert Schomburgk, had drawn one acceptable to Britain. But

British claims reached into Venezuela considerably west of the Schomburgk line, and Venezuela asserted title to no less than two-thirds of present-day Guiana. Gold discoveries in the disputed zone in the 1870s attracted settlers and made a definite boundary more necessary. Appealing to the Monroe Doctrine, Venezuela began to solicit American aid. She broke diplomatic relations with Great Britain in early 1887.

Not until Grover Cleveland was in the White House for a second term did Washington do more than gently prod London. At first the administration merely recommended arbitration. Britain was willing to arbitrate so long as Venezuelan claims east of the Schomburgk line were excluded; considering them completely unjustified, she refused to expose British settlers to the risk of being turned over to Venezuelan rule as a result of a capricious judicial award. But Venezuela insisted that arbitration must cover the entire area under dispute; it would have to embrace all her claims, however far they extended into British Guiana.

In 1895 two developments caused Washington to intervene vigorously. A former American Minister at Caracas, William L. Scruggs, hired by Venezuela as a special agent, had written a pamphlet entitled *British Aggressions in Venezuela, or the Monroe Doctrine on Trial*, which he distributed widely in Washington. Its anti-British propaganda and Scruggs's personal lobbying publicized the hitherto rather unknown controversy and created sympathy for Venezuela. One of Scruggs's acquaintances was a Congressman from Georgia, Leonidas F. Livingston. Early in 1895 he introduced a House resolution, written by Scruggs. The House and Senate unanimously passed a slightly revised resolution and the President approved it on February 20. It "earnestly recommended" arbitration to Britain and Venezuela.[1] This was mild enough, but the unanimous vote suggested that trouble might be coming.

Nevertheless, more than Scruggs and Livingston was needed

---

[1] *Congressional Record*, 53 Cong., 3 Sess., 837 (Jan. 10, 1895), 2113 (Feb. 13, 1895), 2642 (Feb. 23, 1895). Regarding Scruggs see John A. S. Grenville and George B. Young, *Politics, Strategy, and American Diplomacy, Studies in Foreign Policy, 1873–1917* (New Haven and London, 1966), 127–33.

to produce the explosion that lay ahead. That could not have occurred without the death of Secretary of State Walter Q. Gresham, a cautious man who intended to handle the boundary question cautiously and tactfully, and his succession in June 1895 by Richard Olney, an altogether different type of man. The new Secretary was, according to his biographer, "like one of those modern war-tanks which proceeds across the roughest ground, heedless of opposition. . . ."[2] An impatient person, he was resolved to brook no opposition in getting the boundary determined forthwith. The controversy had dragged on far too long, he thought. It was time to tidy it up. Such was his hurry that he devoted his first three weeks in the State Department to writing a long instruction to Thomas F. Bayard, the former Secretary of State and since 1893 America's first Ambassador (his predecessors had the lower rank of Minister) to Great Britain. After being approved by Cleveland, it went off on July 20, 1895.

The "twenty-inch gun," as Cleveland called the note, was aptly named. Blunt and assertive, it was intended to end the dispute quickly. Olney took his stand upon the Monroe Doctrine, which he stated that Britain was violating. In any case, "three thousand miles of intervening ocean make any permanent political union between an European and an American state unnatural and inexpedient. . . ." To this he added the provocative *obiter dictum* that "To-day the United States is practically sovereign on this continent, and its fiat is law upon the subjects to which it confines its interposition." Olney asked Great Britain to decide whether she would or would not arbitrate the boundary question "in its entirety," and to do so in time for the President's annual message to Congress, to be delivered December 2.[3]

Bayard gave Prime Minister Salisbury this formidable note on August 7. After glancing through it, Salisbury said that he would need time to answer. In fact he took about four-and-a-half months, and his reply reached Washington only after Cleveland's message. The delay did not indicate discourtesy. The British did

---

[2] Henry James, *Richard Olney and His Public Service* . . . (Boston and New York, 1923), 12.

[3] Olney to Bayard, July 20, 1895, *Papers Relating to the Foreign Relations of the United States, 1895* (Washington, 1896), Pt. I, 556, 558, 562.

not yet appreciate the seriousness with which Olney—and soon Cleveland—viewed the petty dispute with Venezuela, and they were preoccupied with two international crises of gravest import. In 1894 and 1895 the Turks had slaughtered thousands of Armenians and again, as in 1854 and 1878, the perennial Near Eastern question was raising the specter of hostilities between Britain and Russia. So were events in the Far East. In October 1895, two months after Salisbury read Olney's note, reports reached London of Russian moves against China that threatened vital British interests. With such distractions, it is not surprising that Whitehall had little time for the obscure South American boundary.

The British reply to Olney left by ship on November 27. A copy was given to the American Embassy, and one wonders why the staff, who understood the administration's wish to have the reply before December 2, did not cable a summary. Unaware that the reply was on its way, Cleveland told Congress in his message that he had heard nothing, that British Guiana had been enlarged "against the will of Venezuela," and that the United States should insist on arbitration of "the whole controversy."[4]

Sir Julian Pauncefote (promoted in 1893 from Minister to Ambassador) gave Olney the reply on December 6. In it Salisbury denied that the Monroe Doctrine had anything to do with the boundary controversy, and even that it was international law at all. In effect he accused Olney of being prejudiced in favor of Venezuela. He reaffirmed his willingness to arbitrate part of the dispute, but not the extreme Venezuelan claims. Great Britain, he said, and this was his central and unwavering position throughout the whole debate with Washington, "can not consent to . . . submit to the arbitration of another Power or of foreign jurists, however eminent, claims . . . involving the transfer of large numbers of British subjects . . . to a nation of different race and language, whose political system is subject to frequent disturbance. . . ."[5]

---

[4] Annual message, Dec. 2, 1895, James D. Richardson, ed., *A Compilation of the Messages and Papers of the Presidents, 1789–1897* (Washington, 1899), IX, 632.

[5] Salisbury to Pauncefote, Nov. 26, 1895, *Foreign Relations, 1895*, Pt. I, 563–67, 575.

When the reply arrived, President Cleveland was away, shooting ducks in North Carolina. Reading Salisbury's bland dismissal of the Monroe Doctrine, Secretary Olney at once decided that nothing less than a special message to Congress was required. In great secrecy he drafted one. The President returned to the capital on December 15. Tired as he must have been, he stayed up all or most of the night revising the draft. He conferred with Olney the following day, told the Cabinet about the message on the 17th, and sent it to Congress that afternoon.

The President and his Secretary of State had written a sensational document. The Monroe Doctrine, Cleveland asserted, was international law and it most definitely concerned the boundary controversy. He asked for authority to appoint a commission that would determine the true line. When that line was known, the United States should "resist by every means in its power, as a willful aggression upon its rights and interests," any attempt by Britain to exercise jurisdiction over any territory which the commission had decided was Venezuela's. "In making these recommendations," he said grimly, "I . . . fully . . . realize all the consequences that may follow."[6]

That the consequences would be dangerous was likely indeed. No country could define the boundary of one of Her Majesty's colonies and then demand that Great Britain accept it, without considerable risk of war. A statesman asking for arbitration and receiving an offer of limited arbitration would ordinarily reply with further arguments, not abruptly terminate the discussion and send a warlike message to Congress. Even the mercurial Blaine had debated back and forth with Salisbury over the fur-seals arbitration. Why did the stolid Cleveland act so rashly?

Undoubtedly political considerations influenced him. His Democratic party had suffered severely in the elections of 1894, losing both houses of Congress, which it had previously controlled. The Republicans were making much of his alleged weakness in foreign policy. Angrily they had denounced him for withdrawing a treaty, negotiated by the previous administration, giving the United States the Hawaiian Islands. An unexpected

---

[6] Message to Congress, Dec. 17, 1895, Richardson, *Messages and Papers,* IX, 656–58.

revival of the old controversy over the Mosquito Indians gave them additional material. In 1894 Nicaragua had taken full control of the Mosquito Coast and had expelled some Britons. Great Britain demanded reparations. Nicaragua appealed to Washington in the name of the Monroe Doctrine, as Venezuela had done; but Secretary of State Gresham said that the doctrine was not involved. In April 1895 British troops occupied a Nicaraguan town—Corinto. Although a settlement was reached five days later and the troops soon departed, Republicans and much of the American press excoriated Cleveland for refusing to invoke the Monroe Doctrine and for what they depicted as his imbecilic attitude toward Britain.[7] In December 1895, with presidential elections due the next year, Cleveland must have seen that a strong stand for the Monroe Doctrine in Venezuela would take the sting out of Corinto. And as Postmaster General William L. Wilson perceived, it was difficult for the Republicans to argue foreign policy weakness after the Venezuelan message.[8]

Moreover the President believed that the national interest was at stake. In 1895 the country was suffering from the greatest depression in its history. Economic distress was acute; with it came social and political ferment that alarmed the established order. Two widely differing diagnoses of the parlous economy existed. Free silverites attributed the depression to an inadequate supply of money. The more accepted explanation, to which the administration subscribed, was overproduction. This could be relieved only by exporting the surplus. But where could it go? Only China and Latin America, so it was thought, could offer adequate markets and in Latin America Venezuela had crucial importance. For through that country flowed the great Orinoco River, which was believed to give access to the commerce of almost a third of the South American continent. Secretary Olney, in his twenty-inch gun, went so far as to portray the river as dominating "the whole river navigation" of the interior.[9] Holding such views, Americans were alarmed when Britain laid claim to

---

[7] *Public Opinion*, XVIII (May 2, 1895), 468–69.

[8] Wilson's diary, Jan. 3, 1896, Festus P. Summers, ed., *The Cabinet Diary of William L. Wilson, 1896–1897* (Chapel Hill, 1957), 4.

[9] Olney to Bayard, July 20, 1895, *Foreign Relations, 1895*, Pt. I, 559.

Point Barima at the Orinoco's mouth on April 5, 1895. Like Hong Kong, Singapore, Aden, Gibraltar, and other strategic British places, Point Barima was seen as controlling a great commercial empire.

Besides looking to the potential Latin American market, Washington anticipated the early construction of a canal across Central America. Britain's claim to Point Barima seemed to threaten not only the potential market but also the potential canal. So, for a few days, did the seizure of Corinto. Ready at hand was a convenient slogan for sugar-coating interest with morality, that is, the Monroe Doctrine. Cleveland later professed to be puzzled at the failure of Americans to understand that he had intervened so belligerently in Venezuela in order to vindicate that vital doctrine.[10]

Politics and the national interest swayed the President. Personal factors are always important, and they help explain Cleveland's intemperate behavior. Why, on returning to Washington from his shooting expedition, did he plunge into reworking Olney's draft, and then send the message to Congress scarcely two days later? There was no need for such haste. But Cleveland hated anything that looked like the bullying of a weak country by a strong one. This was evident in his reaction to the Hawaiian treaty, which he thought the United States had gained by strong-arm means. Instinctively he took Venezuela's side against Great Britain. Already irritated by Salisbury's delay in answering the July note, he was furious over the Prime Minister's cool denigration of the Monroe Doctrine. Cleveland's biographer has observed that often he "suddenly exploded" with astonishing force.[11] One can be sure that in December 1895 he lost his temper. Perhaps exhaustion after days of slogging through North Carolinan marches weakened his self-control. Just as the twenty-inch gun is explainable largely in terms of Olney's penchant for direct action, so the special message is attributable partly to Cleveland's explosive temper.

Were special business interests at work behind the scenes,

---

[10] Grover Cleveland, *Presidential Problems* (New York, 1904), 278–79.
[11] Allan Nevins, *Grover Cleveland, A Study in Courage* (New York, 1932), 629.

counterparts of the Gloucester fishery concerns or the North American Commercial Company? It is natural to suspect that Americans, with their eye on the gold in the disputed zone, wanted a boundary giving Venezuela possession of as many of the mines as possible. It is known that Venezuela, hoping to enlist their support, did give some American business men concessions in the disputed area. Were they at all responsible for Washington's intervention? The little available evidence does not permit a sure answer, although it does suggest that they played some part.

For two or three days after the message Cleveland enjoyed massive support. Speedily and unanimously Congress appropriated $100,000 for the investigatory boundary commission he had requested. Surveying the press, *Public Opinion* found it strongly behind the government.[12] During that short period a war scare gripped the country. Ambassador Pauncefote observed "in Congress and among the Public a condition of mind which can only be described as hysterical."[13] A flood of selling swept over the New York stock exchange. Hostilities seemed inevitable.

But just as quickly the excitement subsided. With share prices collapsing and gold streaming out of the country, business men and financiers denounced Cleveland for damaging the already tottering economy. On Sunday the 22nd the clergy, in pulpit after pulpit, roundly rebuked him. Soon the press had second thoughts. Across the country people turned away in revulsion from the prospect of fratricidal war that had opened before them so unexpectedly.

At that very moment another international incident flared up. On January 3, 1896, following the capture of some British subjects raiding the Transvaal, the Kaiser telegraphed congratulations to the Boer President. The telegram was intended to be a warning to Great Britain to moderate her South African policy, and the British press reacted with a torrent of abuse hurled at Germany. During the ensuing agitation the great majority of Americans took Britain's side. As for Britons, all at once they

---

[12] *Public Opinion*, XIX (Dec. 26, 1895), 837–43.
[13] Pauncefote to Salisbury, Dec. 24, 1895, Foreign Office 80/364.

realized how friendless they were in Europe, and the consequent importance of reaching an accommodation with the United States.

Like Americans, the British had reacted with horror when for a fleeting moment war with America over Venezuela seemed likely. They listened with sympathy when Arthur Balfour, Salisbury's nephew and Leader of the House of Commons, predicted in January that "some statesman of authority, more fortunate even than President Monroe, will lay down the doctrine that between English-speaking peoples war is impossible," and when the powerful Colonial Secretary, Joseph Chamberlain, declared: "While I should look with horror upon anything in the nature of a fratricidal strife, I should look forward with pleasure to the possibility of the Stars and Stripes and the Union Jack floating together in defence of a common cause sanctioned by humanity and by justice."[14]

The "Message may turn out a 'boomerang,'" Pauncefote had predicted.[15] Nothing showed his perception so well as the extraordinary outburst of demand in both Britain and America for some kind of permanent arbitration system that would banish for ever all possibility of Anglo-American war. In early 1896 a flood of letters and resolutions poured down upon London, and a large number upon Washington. An "Anglo-American Memorial" with several thousand British signatures resolved that "all English-speaking peoples united by race, language, and religion, should regard war as the one absolutely intolerable mode of settling the domestic differences of the Anglo-American family," and it asked for a permanent arbitration tribunal. Another such resolution had over 5000 signatures and still others in great number were adopted by various British churches and other associations.[16] Similar petitions were signed by thousands of Americans, including such prominent men as Marshall Field, Philip D. Armour, George M. Pullman, and Cyrus H. McCormick.[17] At many meetings in the United States resolutions were

[14] Blanche E. C. Dugdale, *Arthur James Balfour, First Earl of Balfour, K. G., O.M., F.R.S., Etc.* (London, 1936), I, 226; London *Times*, Jan. 27, 1896.

[15] Pauncefote to Salisbury, Dec. 24, 1895, Public Record Office (London), Foreign Office 80/364.

[16] Foreign Office 96/200, 5/2302, 5/2303, 5/2010, and 80/367.

[17] Foreign Office 5/2316.

passed asking for permanent arbitration.[18] Partly because of this pressure, London and Washington began negotiations (which we shall describe below) for a general arbitration treaty in March 1896. These paralleled the more urgent negotiations required to repair the damage done by the President's intemperate message.

For despite the quick passing of the war scare, the boundary controversy could not be allowed to drift. Cleveland had appointed his investigatory commission on January 1, 1896 and it soon got down to work. If no British-American accommodation were reached before it decided upon the true line, an extremely dangerous dilemma would confront the two countries. Either the United States would have to back down from Cleveland's demand that Britain accept the line, or else Britain would have to allow the United States to define the boundary of one of her colonies. On the other hand, successful negotiations were difficult to envisage. Olney and Cleveland had sided with Venezuela in insisting that Britain arbitrate the entire area in dispute, whereas Lord Salisbury had firmly refused to do so. A minor problem was that Salisbury contended that, because he had written the last communication (his answer to the twenty-inch gun that had so enraged Cleveland), the next formal move was up to Olney; but the latter hesitated to make one.

Negotiations did resume, but at first they were informal. In London Lord Playfair, who had an American wife and knew the United States well, met several times with Bayard. Playfair suggested arbitration on the condition—Salisbury's unvarying point —that British and Venezuelan settlements be excluded. Olney refused; he would only consent that long-lasting settlement of territory be "given all the weight belonging to it in reason and justice, or by the principles of international law."[19] On this basic disagreement the talks ground to a stop.

Similar conversations took place in Washington between Secretary Olney and George W. Smalley, an American who was the United States correspondent of the London *Times* and an acquaintance of many high British and American officials. Exasperated by Salisbury's silence in the face of Cleveland's boundary

---

[18] *Nation*, LXII (Feb. 27, 1896), 169.
[19] Olney to Bayard, Jan. 14, 1896, James, *Olney*, 229.

message and by the slow pace of events (over six months had elapsed since the twenty-inch gun was dispatched), the Secretary used Smalley to conduct a strange negotiation through the latter's articles in the *Times* and editorial responses inspired by Salisbury. Again the dilemma about settled districts arose. A Smalley article reiterated that the United States agreed that occupation should have "all the weight belonging to it in reason, justice, or international law" (almost Olney's exact words quoted above), but Salisbury's editorial rejoinder was that this would not sufficiently safeguard the settled districts.[20] The Olney-Smalley-Salisbury talks made no more headway than had those between Bayard and Playfair.

Informal diplomacy had failed. Increasingly impatient to get results, Secretary Olney yielded in late February to Salisbury's wish that the next diplomatic move be made by Washington. He instructed Bayard to propose formally, not through Playfair or the *Times*, that negotiations be commenced in Washington; he also asked London to explain what it meant by settled districts. Salisbury, of course, was agreeable, but he reiterated that settled districts must be excluded from arbitration.[21] Olney would not accept this, and the negotiations lapsed. Formal diplomacy, like the informal talks, had come to grief over the question of settled districts.

By the summer of 1896 almost a year had passed since Secretary Olney had decided to make Britain accept a satisfactory boundary. He had accomplished nothing. Great was his exasperation as Salisbury refused to budge. Abruptly in the middle of July the Secretary abandoned his insistence that Venezuela's entire claim be arbitrated. He asked whether Britain would submit all the disputed territory to unrestricted arbitration on the understanding that areas settled for at least two generations, or sixty years, would be excluded.[22] His unexpected reversal virtually ensured an early termination of the controversy.

---

[20] London *Times*, Feb. 18 and 21, 1896.

[21] Olney to Bayard, Feb. 26, 1896, Charles C. Tansill, *The Foreign Policy of Thomas F. Bayard, 1885–1897* (New York, 1940), 759; Salisbury to Pauncefote, Feb. 27, 1896, Foreign Office 80/369.

[22] Olney to Pauncefote, July 13, 1896, *Papers Relating to the Foreign Relations of the United States, 1896* (Washington, 1897), 253–54.

It is not easy to account for the Secretary's retreat, but probably the approaching presidential election was a major factor. The Democrats, jettisoning Cleveland's wing of the party, had just nominated the radical free silverite, William Jennings Bryan. Soon the Populists would do the same. Economic conditions had steadily deteriorated ever since the alarming message to Congress and were now catastrophic. To a conservative man like Richard Olney the American scene appeared gloomy indeed. Probably he concluded that the controversy with Britain must be terminated before the elections; otherwise free silverites, inveterate haters of gold-standard Britain, might inflame it dangerously with wild campaign rhetoric.

During the summer both Pauncefote and Olney were away from Washington and negotiations were suspended. When the two men returned, they readily agreed that fifty years of settlement was sufficient for exclusion. On November 12, 1896 they signed an agreement specifying the terms of a treaty to be made by Britain and Venezuela. The treaty would provide for an arbitral tribunal to define the boundary. The tribunal would meet in Paris and be composed of two members nominated by the U.S. Supreme Court, two by the British supreme court of justice, and one selected by either these four or by the King of Sweden and Norway. A minimum of fifty years of settlement, or of political control (a point introduced by Joseph Chamberlain during a September visit to America), would convey title; and claims to territory settled for a shorter period would be given such weight "as reason, justice, the principles of international law, and the equities of the case" indicated (Olney's old point).[23]

The boundary commission, no longer serving any useful purpose, discontinued its efforts to determine the line.

In Britain and America the treaty was greeted with a sigh of relief, although some British queries were raised as to whether a dangerous precedent had not been set by the United States superseding a Latin American disputant and taking charge of its negotiations with Great Britain. Venezuela, on the other hand, was incensed at being told to sign a treaty in the negotiation of which she had not participated. She was only slightly mollified

---

[23] *Ibid.*, 254–55.

when London and Washington decided to let her appoint one of the arbitrators originally designated for American appointment, provided he was not a Venezuelan. (She named the American Chief Justice, Melville W. Fuller.) She and Great Britain signed the treaty on February 2, 1897.

The British-Venezuelan arbitral tribunal deliberated in Paris during the summer of 1899. Besides Fuller, it had two British judges appointed by Great Britain: Lord Chief Justice Russell and Lord Justice Collins; the United States appointed Supreme Court Justice David J. Brewer. These four selected as the tribunal's fifth member and president a Russian expert on international law, Feodor de Martens. Rather trustfully, Venezuela had four Americans as her counsel, one of them former President Benjamin Harrison. The unanimous award of October 3 laid down a boundary that followed the Schomburgk line quite closely. It gave most of the disputed territory to British Guiana; but Point Barima, the mouth of the Orinoco River, and several thousand square miles in the south went to Venezuela.[24]

By that time the fate of the British-American general arbitration treaty, mentioned above, had been decided. It will be recalled that negotiations for this treaty accompanied those for

---

[24] In 1944 Severo Mallet-Prevost, one of the Americans representing Venezuela, wrote a memorandum that was published five years later after his death. According to it, de Martens told the other four judges in Paris in 1899 that he wanted a unanimous award and threatened that if the American judges did not vote for a compromise line (the one of the eventual award), he would vote with the British jurists, giving Venezuela a less favorable boundary. Although the American judges thought the compromise line unfair to Venezuela, they felt impelled to do as de Martens wished. Mallet-Prevost wrote that he believed that Britain and Russia had made a secret "deal." In 1962 Venezuela asked the United Nations to investigate. Perhaps a new boundary is in the making at the time of this writing. See Otto Schoenrich, "The Venezuela-British Guiana Boundary Dispute," *American Journal of International Law*, XLIII (1949), 523–30; Clifton J. Child, "The Venezuela-British Guina Boundary Arbitration of 1899," *ibid.*, XLIV (1950), 668–93; William C. Dennis, "The Venezuela-British Guiana Boundary Arbitration of 1899," *ibid.*, 720–27; *United Nations, Official Records of the General Assembly, Seventeenth Session, Annexes*, III, 1–15, Agenda Item 88; *ibid., Seventeenth Session, Plenary Meetings*, I, 244–46, III, 1098; *ibid., Seventeenth Session, Special Political Committee*, 119–21.

the Venezuelan agreement. By June 1896 they, like the boundary talks, had become deadlocked; the difficulty was that Olney wanted more binding, comprehensive provisions than Salisbury did.[25] But in time a compromise was reached, and Pauncefote and Olney signed a general arbitration treaty in Washington on January 11, 1897. The two countries agreed to submit all their disputes to arbitration; a decision by simple majority would be binding for minor matters, but territorial claims and questions of vital interest would go through elaborate procedures that would enable either country to block an unfavorable award.

Enthusiastic applause greeted the accord. Editorials, peace societies, and leaders in both countries hailed it as a turning point for mankind. Both the outgoing Democratic President, Grover Cleveland, and his Republican successor, William McKinley, urged the Senate to approve the treaty; and hardly anyone doubted that it would do so.[26] Instead, the Senate drastically amended it, and then defeated it in May 1897 by a vote three short of the needed two-thirds.

Did this indicate a recrudescence of anti-British sentiment? A good deal of such sentiment still existed of course. Almost half the adverse vote came from states where free silverites were strong; probably their vote is to be explained in large part as an irrational attempt to strike at Britain. But these states were very scantily populated, and there is no reason to attribute the remainder of the negative vote to Anglophobia. Although Irish and other anti-British elements opposed the treaty, the great majority of Americans apparently supported it.

Indeed the truly significant thing is not that the treaty was defeated but that it was signed and nearly approved. No one would have dreamed of general arbitration with Britain at an earlier date, not even in the relatively friendly years just before

---

[25] See Salisbury's explanation in Hansard's *Parliamentary Debates*, Fourth Series, XXXVII, 53 (Feb. 11, 1896).

[26] *Public Opinion*, XXII (Jan. 21, 1897), 68–70; *Literary Digest*, XIV (Jan. 23, 1897), 356–58; Cleveland's message to Congress is in James D. Richardson, ed., *A Compilation of the Messages and Papers of the Presidents . . .* (New York, 1397–1916), XIV, 6178–79; McKinley's message is in *ibid.*, 6242. A general account is Nelson M. Blake, "The Olney-Pauncefote Treaty of 1897," *American Historical Review*, L (1945), 228–43.

the Civil War. The close vote on the treaty, along with the revulsion from the war scare following Cleveland's boundary message, showed that a remarkable change had come over British-American relations. All at once it was plain that the people in both countries were much better disposed to each other than had been supposed.

Perhaps the better disposition should have been anticipated. Not for many years had the United States moved aggressively toward Canada, and Britain had long ago ceased opposing American expansion. The two countries had peacefully surmounted the somber perils during and after the Civil War, and the many subsequent altercations. For these and other reasons conditions were ripe in the 1890s for a rapprochement.

CHAPTER XIV

Rapprochment

A FEW MONTHS BEFORE Secretary of State Richard Olney wrote his twenty-inch gun another rebellion broke out in Cuba. As in the 1870s, various incidents threatened to bring the United States to war with Spain. There were many reasons why Great Britain could be expected to side with the latter country in its developing quarrel with America. The Spanish Queen-Regent was Queen Victoria's niece; and Prime Minister Salisbury was typical of ruling-class Britons in instinctively preferring the ancient European monarchy to the *nouveau riche* republic. Yet to their surprise and delight, Americans found not only the British people but also the government sympathizing with them.

The sympathy became more marked in 1898 as the Spanish-American War drew near. In February the American press published a private letter written by the Spanish Minister at Washington, Dupuy de Lôme, describing President McKinley in unflattering terms. Such torrents of abuse fell on him that the Minister resigned. The affair must have stirred memories of Sackville West's dismissal a decade earlier, but the British expressed little sympathy for the disgraced diplomat. In that same month an explosion sunk the U.S. warship *Maine* at Havana, causing great loss of life. The outpouring of British sorrow was extraordinary. A London newspaper thought that "the calamity will send a pang through every British heart"; it attributed the reaction to a feeling of "community of race."[1] Should war come, another paper predicted, "we shall not of course forget, whilst maintaining the duties of neutrality towards both [countries],

---

[1] London *Daily News*, Feb. 17, 1898.

that one of them is knitted to us yet more closely by the ties of blood."[2]

War was very close by April. The leading Continental powers were anxious to mediate, but Britain was unwilling to join them without American consent. Accordingly Ambassador Pauncefote sounded out President McKinley and then showed Assistant Secretary of State William R. Day the text of a joint note the powers intended to present to Washington. Day asked for changes that Pauncefote succeeded in having made. Consequently the note as presented on April 5 was inoffensive. A few days later the European diplomats in Washington, including Pauncefote, again considered mediation. Again London refused to cooperate, and the plan was dropped.[3] Twice Great Britain had saved the United States from embarrassment.

In late April the long-threatened war broke out. Britain, though of course proclaiming neutrality, did little to conceal her hope for American victory. Public officials and writers in newspapers and magazines expressed sentiments friendly to America. Even the government, so Spain complained, was not truly neutral. It was universally believed that a British warship had stood with Rear-Admiral George Dewey in Manila Bay against a threatening German squadron. The story, though greatly exaggerated, was repeated for years to come, evoking cheers for England. And it was quite true that Whitehall, reversing its pre-Civil War opposition to American expansion, encouraged the United States to annex Hawaii and the Philippines. Having gone to war with some apprehension, Americans were vastly relieved at Britain's support; it was the more welcome because it contrasted sharply with Continental backing of Spain. An explosion of friendly feeling for Great Britain resulted. Pauncefote, a cautious reporter, called it "the most exuberant affection"; and the London *Times* believed that "a revolution in American sentiment" had occurred.[4]

---

[2] London *Times*, March 28, 1898.

[3] Alexander E. Campbell, *Great Britain and the United States, 1895–1903* (London, 1960), 140–46; Charles S. Campbell, *Anglo-American Understanding, 1898–1903* (Baltimore, 1957), 31–36.

[4] Pauncefote to Salisbury, May 16, 1898, Lord Salisbury Papers, Christ Church Library (Oxford); London *Times*, Jan. 17, 1899.

To a surprising extent, the Britsh people responded in kind, though much less effusively. Britain, too, was feeling lonely in a hostile world, and she welcomed the change of mood across the Atlantic. John Hay, Bayard's successor as American Ambassador at London, discovered greater friendliness for the United States than he had encountered in many previous visits to England.

So marked was the trans-Atlantic affection that it gave rise around the world to rumors of a secret alliance. A widely quoted remark by the Colonial Secretary, Joseph Chamberlain, fed the speculation: "And I even go so far as to say that, terrible as war may be, even war itself would be cheaply purchased if in a great and noble cause the Stars and Stripes and the Union Jack should wave together over an Anglo-Saxon Alliance."[5] Chamberlain and not a few others would have welcomed an alliance, but however exuberant the affection observed by Pauncefote, neither America nor Lord Salisbury's Great Britain was yet ready for so drastic a break with tradition.

In any event the exuberance should not be overemphasized.[6] Although genuine enough for a while, it could not have lasted. It had surged up too suddenly. Inevitably it dwindled as easy victory after victory increased American self-confidence. The cooler temper became evident when Britain and America tried to take advantage of the wartime mood in order to clear up some remaining issues.

Two disputed matters needing further attention we have already described. We have seen that peace reigned in the northeastern fisheries only because Great Britain periodically renewed the *modus vivendi* of 1888; and that, although the Bering Sea was much calmer, London, Ottawa, and Washington were continuing to argue about the sealing regulations. More pressing were two other controversies. The unpopular Clayton-Bulwer Treaty of 1850 will be remembered. By its terms the United

---

[5] Speech at Birmingham, May 13, 1898, London *Times*, May 14, 1898. Regarding the rumored alliance see Campbell, *Anglo-American Understanding*, 47–49; Lionel M. Gelber, *The Rise of Anglo-American Friendship, a Study in World Politics, 1898–1906* (London, 1938), 21–23.

[6] Charles S. Campbell, "Anglo-American Relations, 1897–1901," in Paolo E. Coletta, ed., *Threshold of Internationalism, Essays on the Foreign Policies of William McKinley* (Jericho, New York, 1970), ch. 6.

States could not construct an American canal. Long before the war with Spain, Washington had argued that the prohibition was out of date and several times had vainly asked Great Britain to modify it. After that conflict, with nationalistic sentiment running high and newly acquired Caribbean and Pacific colonies needing to be linked together by a canal, the United States was in no temper to wait much longer. The other dispute was about the Alaskan-Canadian boundary. Having wrangled over every inch of the international line from the Passamaquoddy Islands off the east coast to San Juan Island off the west coast, Great Britain and the United States in 1898 turned to the far northwestern line, the only one still unclear. Its uncertainty had not mattered much until the Alaskan gold rush of the late 1890s suddenly attracted thousands of rough-and-ready men to Alaska and the Yukon. Drawing the boundary then became imperative; with much at stake, it also became difficult.

Britain and America began two sets of negotiations during the war: one concerning the Canadian issues, the other the Clayton-Bulwer Treaty. As regards the former they resorted again to that well-tested device, a joint commission. The new Joint High Commission met from August 1898 to February 1899, first in Quebec, later in Washington. It reached substantial agreement about the fisheries, fur-seals, and several less important matters, but Alaska proved a stumbling-block. Canada demanded an Alaskan boundary giving her access to the open sea; the United States insisted that she was not entitled to it. The unfortunate upshot was that the British delegation refused to sign anything unless agreement was reached on everything. Consequently the commission disbanded in utter failure. Later reports of fighting between American and Canadian gold miners so alarmed Washington and London that they signed a *modus vivendi* in October 1899 drawing temporary lines in some of the disputed areas, but not until 1903 was a definitive boundary agreed upon.

John Hay, who hopefully believed that "a sanction like that of religion" bound together the two English-speaking countries in a "sacred mission of liberty and progress,"[7] became Secretary

---

[7] John Hay, *Addresses of John Hay* (New York, 1906), 78–79; he made these remarks while Ambassador, on April 21, 1898.

of State on September 30, 1898. No other Secretary had been such a lover of England and so determined to foster British-American amity. Hopes were then still high for the Joint High Commission, and the new Secretary decided to deal with the Clayton-Bulwer Treaty as well. He requested Pauncefote, who was an expert on international law concerning canals, to draft a treaty amending the one of 1850 so as to enable the United States to build the waterway she was now urgently demanding. Hay accepted Pauncefote's draft with a few changes; it went off to London, and from there to Ottawa. There it struck a snag. The Canadians made the same condition they had just made to the Joint High Commission: nothing was to be settled unless everything was; in other words, no American canal without an Alaskan boundary settlement.[8] Lord Salisbury felt unable to overrule the Dominion. To enthusiastic extenders of hands across the sea it must have seemed in early 1899 as though the new-found Anglo-American affection was being ground to bits in the frozen wastes of Alaska.

That this did not happen was perhaps the ironical consequence of the Boer War, which started in October 1899, just when the Alaska *modus* was concluded. At first Britain suffered one humiliating defeat after another, and a chorus of abuse from the Continent added to her discomfiture. Among the powers only the United States, mindful of Britain's help during the Spanish war, stood by her; and even that support came more from the administration than from Congress or the American people. Congress, in fact, did not scruple to use Britain's plight to American advantage. During her most perilous moment, that of "Black Week" in South Africa, Representative William P. Hepburn introduced a measure for canal construction in total disregard of the Clayton-Bulwer restrictions.[9] This forced Britain to yield on Pauncefote's canal treaty as the lesser of evils, Canadian wishes notwithstanding. She agreed to go ahead with the treaty. But all to no avail because the Senate made amendments that London,

---

[8] Campbell, *Anglo-American Understanding*, 132–33.

[9] *Congressional Record*, 56 Cong., 1 Sess., 151 (Dec. 7, 1899); Hay to Ambassador Joseph H. Choate (his successor at London), Jan. 15, 1900, Tyler Dennett, *John Hay, from Poetry to Politics* (New York, 1933), 252.

no matter how hard pressed in South Africa, would not accept. Not until November 1901 did the Hay-Pauncefote Treaty at length supersede the Clayton-Bulwer Treaty and permit the United States to build her canal.

It is obvious that the exuberant wartime affection was no match for self-interest. Nevertheless Anglo-American friendship was solidly based at the end of the century. Trans-Atlantic sentiment had changed out of all recognition from the beginning of the century when Britain and America were on the slope to war, from the dangerous post-Civil War years, and from many other tense occasions. Although deadlocks existed over Alaska and Central America in 1899, both controversies were on their way to settlement within a few years. And in two other regions, in Samoa and The Hague, Americans and Britons were cooperating in a way their ancestors would have found incredible.

Out on the Pacific Ocean a small civil war over the succession to the Samoan throne broke out in 1899. The three western countries with the greatest interests in Samoa supported rival claimants: Germany, a chief named Mataafa; America and Britain another chief, Malietoa. Mataafa was at first victorious. But in the spring of 1899 American and British soldiers, fighting side by side, defeated him and made Malietoa king. The war with Spain had ended by then, but the exciting partnership in distant Samoa must have rekindled some of the British-American fervor. It was significant enough to convince the German Foreign Minister, for one, that despite the Alaskan and canal disputes the rapprochement was very much alive.[10]

A degree of cooperation between the two countries occurred soon afterwards at The Hague. There many countries, including the United States and Great Britain, met in May 1899 in an endeavor to mitigate the horrors of war. The collapse in 1897 of the proposed general arbitration treaty had not lessened British-American interest in some permanent arbitration arrangement, and at The Hague a Permanent Court of Arbitration was established. The court was largely a British but to some extent an

---

[10] Memorandum by Bernhard von Bülow, March 14, 1899, Edgar T. S. Dugdale, ed., *German Diplomatic Documents, 1871–1914* . . . (London, 1928–1931), III, 53.

American creation, and the American delegates took a leading part in persuading Germany to accept it. It would be absurd to portray this small affair as evidence of much trans-Atlantic friendship; and in fact Britain and America did not always stand together at The Hague. All the same, their limited cooperation would have been improbable even a decade earlier; and like the Samoan partnership it helped offset the failure of the Joint High Commission and of Pauncefote's canal treaty.

Something should be said about developments in the Far East at the century's close because these were commonly, though erroneously, interpreted as evidence of British-American collaboration in matters of enormous gravity, much more important than affairs in Samoa or The Hague. We have seen that before the Civil War both countries wanted to open China to western trade. We have also seen that the accepted explanation of America's economic distress in the 1890s was overproduction at home and that the accepted remedy was to increase exports to Latin America and, even better, to China. If the potential isthmian canal was one major objective of United States foreign policy at the turn of the century, the potential Chinese market was another. In that market Great Britain was already well established; no less than a sixth of her foreign trade was with China, and her investments there were enormous. With Britain established and America hoping to be, grounds for a common policy existed, a policy of open trade beneficial to both. Richard Olney, scarcely a notorious Anglophile, virtually advocated an alliance with Great Britain in order to prop open the Chinese door.[11]

We have mentioned Russia's moves against China in 1895. Two years later a Russian fleet sailed into Port Arthur, and German soldiers landed at Kiaochow. The already-tottering Chinese empire seemed about to collapse. In March 1898 London inquired whether the United States would help save the great market.[12] Washington declined, as it would undoubtedly have done even had the Spanish-American War not been imminent.

---

[11] Richard Olney, "International Isolation of the United States," *Atlantic Monthly*, LXXXI (1898), 580.

[12] Foreign Office to Pauncefote, March 7, 1898, Public Record Office (London), Foreign Office 5/2364.

Similarly it rejected a British request of January 1899 for "conjoint action" against the French in Shanghai.[13] Nonetheless the very fact that Britain made the overtures was indicative of a new relationship. Never in an earlier day would she have considered enlisting American help in Asia against three great powers.

John Hay's open-door notes of September 6, 1899 to Great Britain, Germany, and Russia (followed later by notes to France, Italy, and Japan) asked each country to agree that, as regards any sphere of influence it had in China, it would permit China to levy her own tariff, would not interfere with any treaty port or vested interest, and would not impose discriminatory harbor dues or railway charges. Each country conditioned its assent, which in no instance was complete, on acceptance by all the others; and Russia's reply was evasive. Nevertheless Secretary Hay formally announced that they had all accepted his requests.

On the surface Great Britain's answer welcomed the American overture. The notes had, so it seemed, something of a British origin. Secretary Hay had depended for their drafting on his Far Eastern adviser, William W. Rockhill, and Rockhill in turn had asked an English friend, Alfred E. Hippisley, to help him. The notes incorporated some of Hippisley's ideas and wording. Then too, another Englishman, Lord Charles Beresford, Member of Parliament, had made several speeches across America in early 1899 strongly urging British-American cooperation to keep the door open. Altogether it was natural to see Hay's *démarche* as in effect, if not overtly, the sort of conjoint action twice solicited by Great Britain. Writers drew a parallel with the Monroe Doctrine, depicting both it and the Open Door Policy as classic examples of British-American collaboration against Continental powers: just as John Quincy Adams had worked for objectives in Latin America that were British as well as American, so John Hay had done in the Far East.

In reality the Open Door Policy, like the Monroe Doctrine, was essentially American. Far from acting with Great Britain, Washington had moved unilaterally, treating Britain exactly like the Continental countries. Hippisley was not a British agent, and

---

[13] Pauncefote to Hay, Jan. 8, 1899, John Hay Papers, Library of Congress (Washington), Box 21.

Rockhill considered Britain "as great an offender in China as Russia itself."[14] Beresford probably had no influence on policy. Nevertheless such facts were little appreciated at the time. Generally speaking, people in America, and in Britain too, viewed the September notes as conclusive evidence of close trans-Atlantic ties. The myth of Anglo-American cooperation in the Far East gained widespread credence; undoubtedly it contributed to the rapprochement.

Short-lived wartime affection, joint action on a remote tropical island, minor cooperation mixed with disagreement at The Hague, and a misinterpreted policy in China—these are not the stuff of solid, enduring friendship. No more, of course, were the quarrelsome Joint High Commission of 1898–1899 and Pauncefote's spurned canal treaty. Yet such a friendship did come into being near the end of the century. How can it be accounted for?

We have previously noted that aggressive activity by the U. S. government against British North America ended with the Oregon settlement, and that in the late 1850s Great Britain pretty much abandoned her efforts to contain American territorial expansion. Thereafter British-American relations improved for a few years. We have noted, too, that the resurgence of animosity during and after the Civil War was not likely to endure, given good diplomacy; more probable was the recurrence of relations at least as good as those of the late 1850s. And in fact amity between the two countries did grow, as was disclosed by the reaction to President Cleveland's special Venezuelan message. Well before the Spanish-American War broke out, this amity existed in all its essential elements, although the demonstrative displays of it occurred only during that conflict.

We have also seen, however, two Anglo-American wars and a near-war during the dangerous years from 1861 through 1872, as well as many other instances of discord and occasional war scares. But this has not been the main theme. The United States and Great Britain had a remarkable diplomatic record. What a

---

[14] Paul A. Varg, *Open Door Diplomat, The Life of W. W. Rockhill* (Urbana, Illinois, 1952), 29; Rockhill to Hay, Aug. 28, 1899, Alfred L. P. Dennis, *Adventures in American Diplomacy, 1896–1906* (New York, 1928), 186.

series of comprehensive treaties—the Jay-Grenville Treaty, the Webster-Ashburton Treaty, the Oregon Treaty, the Clayton-Bulwer Treaty, the Marcy-Elgin Treaty, the Treaty of Washington, the Bering Sea Treaty, the Venezuelan Treaty, and others. And what a list of joint commissions—from the four established by the Jay-Grenville Treaty to the Joint High Commission during the war with Spain, with several others in between. Even the *modi vivendi* reflected a willingness to compromise seldom found in international affairs.

Moreover the United States and Great Britain had an arbitration record that no other two countries could rival. The commissions of the Jay-Grenville and Ghent treaties were pioneer undertakings arbitral in nature; more extraordinary were the six full-scale arbitrations held during what may be called the heyday of arbitration, from 1872 through 1899. Five of them concerned disputes that, left unsettled, could have had grave consequences —disputes over the *Alabama* claims, the San Juan boundary, the fishery articles of the Treaty of Washington, the Bering Sea fur-seals, and the Venezuelan boundary (the arbitration of this was formally between Britain and Venezuela). The private Civil War claims, although less dangerous, were by no means inconsequential.

The simple fact is that on the whole Anglo-American diplomacy was good. Notwithstanding occasional bombastic talk particularly in America, London and Washington dealt with most of their disputes prudently and patiently (except those leading to the War of 1812). Time after time they settled serious controversies without hostilities. Many clashes occurred, it is true. Along the Canadian-American border, in the northeastern fishing grounds, in the Bering Sea, and in Alaskan gold fields, Britons, Canadians, and Americans shot at each other or came close to shooting. But these incidents led not to war but to peaceful settlement. The long years of peace after 1814 gave time for the bitterness engendered by the Revolution and the War of 1812 to die down; and when American anger against Britain mounted again in the Civil War period, it too dwindled in the absence of hostilities. The avoidance of a third war was all-important for the rise of friendship; and much of the credit for this must go to the diplomats.

Many years of peaceful relations are usually an essential prelude to enduring international amity. But the mere absence of fighting cannot produce the amity. Other, more positive factors are necessary. In British-American affairs during the nineteenth century such factors were present; and most of them became stronger as the years passed. They help elucidate the diplomatic and arbitral successes. An adequate account of them, however, would require another volume, and here a sketchy treatment must suffice.

One such factor was the common heritage—the shared language, culture, political institutions, and tradition of common law. To what extent did this create a bond between the United States and Great Britain? Richard Olney believed that because of "the close community . . . in origin, speech, thought, literature, institutions, ideals—in the kind and degree of the civilization enjoyed by both," the two countries would stand side by side whenever danger threatened.[15] Although the "close community" had not prevented two wars and frequent tension, similarities so basic do tend over the long run to create sympathy between countries. Certainly they worked to bring the two English-speaking countries together. But even though the common heritage was a pervasive and persistent influence making for amity, it was not sufficient by itself to bring about a reconciliation.

Reference has often been made to trans-Atlantic economic ties, and to their restraining influence whenever thoughts turned to war (except for a while during the Civil War). In the 1890s Great Britain was by far the principal market for American goods (out of all comparison more important than the potential Latin American and Chinese markets), and the chief supplier of imports and capital. In 1890 Britain took $448,000,000 worth of American goods, whereas the second largest market, Germany, took only $86,000,000 worth; total exports were valued at $858,000,000. In 1898 the corresponding figures were $541,000,000, $155,000,000, and $1,231,000,000. As for American imports, in 1890 Great Britain supplied $186,000,000 worth, and Germany (the next largest supplier) $99,000,000 worth; total imports

---

[15] Olney, "International Isolation of the United States," **588.**

amounted to $789,000,000 worth. Eight years later the figures were $109,000,000 (well below the average), $70,000,000, and $616,000,000. The United States was similarly important to Great Britain. For the five-year period 1890–1894, 11 percent, on the average, of all British exports went to America; for 1895–1899, 8.6 percent. For the former years no less than 23.4 percent of British imports came from America; and for the latter years 24.4 percent.[16] At the end of the century a large community of business men and financiers moved back and forth between the two countries, at home in both. Their fortunes depended on the Atlantic economic connection and therefore on good Anglo-American relations. Such men enjoyed public esteem; governments heeded their counsel. As economic ties deepened, so did British-American friendship.

During the century's last decade or so the British became uneasily aware that their power was declining. Russia exerted a nearly unbearable pressure, not only in the Near East as she had for long, but in the Far East as well. German strength had grown alarmingly. Britain's splendid isolation had come to seem much less splendid. American power too had increased, but the United States did not endanger Great Britain. Although American and British vital interests did not coincide except in their economic relations, they did not clash—once Britain had abandoned her opposition to American expansion, and the United States had renounced any serious intent of taking Canada. Americans, too, were apprehensive about Russia and Germany. They feared that the former's expansion in the Far East would jeopardize the potential market; they saw German steps in Latin America as threatening the Monroe Doctrine and the potential canal. It would be a mistake to depict Britain and America as falling into one another's arms from fears of the Continental powers. Nevertheless many British leaders, notably Joseph Chamberlain, looked longingly across the Atlantic for an ally; and though Washington did not respond, there was, as Henry

---

[16] U.S. Bureau of the Census, *Historical Statistics of the United States, Colonial Times to 1957* (Washington, 1960), 550, 552; Harry C. Allen, *Great Britain and the United States, A History of Anglo-American Relations (1783–1952)* (London, 1954), 61.

Cabot Lodge observed, "a very general and solid sense of the fact that . . . the downfall of the British Empire is something which no rational American could regard as anything but a misfortune to the United States."[17]

The widening of the franchise by electoral reform bills had greatly altered the British social structure. No longer in 1900 was Britain the aristocratic and somewhat arrogant nation that had so irritated republicans like Thomas Jefferson and James Madison one hundred years earlier. And if a more democratic Britain had greater appeal for the ordinary American, the United States no longer seemed a subversive rabble-rousing republic to upper-class Britons; on the contrary, with her written constitution and Supreme Court she seemed to many of them a welcome element of order and stability in a turbulent world.

The upper classes of the two countries had much in common, including marriages. Typically the union was between an American heiress and a British aristocrat or high governmental official. In 1895 Joseph Chamberlain; Lord Playfair; Sir William Harcourt, leader of the Liberal party; Sir Michael Herbert, who succeeded Pauncefote at Washington; Lord Randolph Churchill; George Curzon, a future Foreign Secretary; and the Duke of Marlborough, all men of considerable power, were married to Americans. Such trans-Atlantic unions doubtless had wide influence on policy.

At another social level, the Irish had become much less disruptive. A new generation, born in the United States, were not so mindful of their ancestral land as their fathers had been. Never would the young Irish-American of the 1890s have raided into Canada with Hunters or Fenians. Anti-British free silverites, too, lost most of their impact in the last years of the nineteenth century.

It may be that the most immediately important bond of all was the most ephemeral. In the 1890s Americans of Anglo-Saxon descent stood dominant, quite unchallenged in almost all walks of national life. These Americans and most Britons were ex-

---

[17] Lodge to Theodore Roosevelt, Feb. 2, 1900, Henry Cabot Lodge, ed., *Selections from the Correspondence of Theodore Roosevelt and Henry Cabot Lodge, 1884–1918* (New York and London, 1925), I, 446.

tremely race conscious, proud of being Anglo-Saxons. Enormously important was the widely held conception of a shared Anglo-Saxon race. We have seen that it accounted for most of the feeling of horror at the prospect of a fratricidal war during the war scare of 1895 and for much of Britain's sympathy for America against Spain in 1898. Arthur Balfour expressed the conception unforgettably in 1895: "We have a domestic patriotism as Scotchmen or as Englishmen or as Irishmen, or what you will. We have an Imperial patriotism as citizens of the British Empire. But surely, in addition to that, we have also an Anglo-Saxon patriotism. . . ."[18] Three years later, as the United States neared war with Spain, Richard Olney echoed Balfour: "There is a patriotism of race as well as of country—and the Anglo-American is as little likely to be indifferent to the one as to the other."[19] Although the influence of Anglo-Saxon race patriotism cannot be measured with precision, it must have been very great indeed. Without it there would have been no such rapprochement as occurred around 1900.

The common heritage, the close economic relations, the absence of clashing vital interests, the rise of British democracy and of admiration for American institutions, the dwindling of Irish and free-silver fanaticism, and Anglo-Saxon race patriotism —these were positive forces moulding the British-American relationship. Diplomacy and arbitration had held off war and mitigated tension; more positive forces had then made themselves felt. As early as December 1895, when Britain and America recoiled from the specter of war raised by President Cleveland's special Venezuelan message, the two countries were evidently much better disposed to each other than had been suspected. Pauncefote's "most exuberant affection" of the Spanish-American War was a fleeting phenomenon, but at the end of the century Anglo-American friendship had replaced the long years of hostility.

---

[18] London *Times*, Jan. 16, 1896.
[19] Olney, "International Isolation of the United States," 588.

Bibliographical Essay

FOOTNOTE REFERENCES are not mentioned in this essay, except for a few indispensable works. These references, along with the citations listed below, constitute the immediate sources for this book. The joint list provides material for additional study. It does not, however, necessarily include the best works and is far from being exhaustive.

For the most part, titles will be listed under the headings of the chapters to which they are pertinent; but it is desirable first of all to name several publications because they are particularly important as being relevant to most or all of the chapters in this volume. Harry C. Allen's comprehensive study, *Great Britain and the United States, A History of Anglo-American Relations (1783–1952)* (New York, 1955), has both a chronological account and an analytical section, the latter treating such matters as economic, social, and cultural relations; although occasionally erroneous on small points and exaggerating the friendliness of the relationship, the book has many stimulating interpretations, especially in the analytical section. John Bassett Moore's books, *A Digest of International Law* . . . (Washington, 1906) and *History and Digest of the International Arbitrations to Which the United States Has Been a Party* . . . (Washington, 1898), are important multivolume sources of information; the latter work is indispensable for the international arbitrations mentioned in the present volume. Hunter Miller, ed., *Treaties and Other International Acts of the United States of America* (Washington, 1931–1943), another multivolume indispensable work, gives not only the text but also detailed information about the background and negotiation of all the treaties through 1863 described in this volume; for later treaties William M. Malloy, compiler, *Treaties, Conventions, International Acts, Protocols and Agreements between the United States of America and Other Powers, 1776–1909* (Washington, 1910), has the text but no background information. James D. Richardson, ed., *A Compilation of the Messages and Papers of the Presidents, 1789–1897* (Washington, 1899), gives the text of the Presidents' inaugural addresses, proclamations, and annual and other messages to Congress. For a representative selection of British-American diplomatic correspondence beginning in 1861 see the State Department series, *Papers Relating to the Foreign Relations of the United States* . . . , successive volumes of which were published in most years (1861–1900), each one bringing the correspondence up to date; from 1861 to 1870 this series was entitled *Papers Relating to Foreign Affairs.* . . . A similar selection of the correspondence from 1789 through 1828 is in *American State Papers, Foreign Relations* (Washington, 1832–1859), part of the collection *American State Papers, Documents, Legislative and Executive of the Congress of the United States* . . . (Washington, 1832–1861). An enormous amount of information on a wide range of topics can be found in the United States Congress's Serial Set. The debates of Congress and of the British Houses of Parliament are in, respectively, the *Congressional Record* (before 1873 called the *Congressional Globe* and other names) and Hansard's *Parliamentary Debates*. The British Foreign Office's *British and Foreign State Papers,* published annually in London, has much information on Anglo-American treaties and other agreements. U. S. Bureau of the Census, *Historical Statistics of the United States, Colonial Times to 1957* (Washington, 1960), is invaluable for statistics about Anglo-American trade.

As regards material pertinent to only one or, at most, a few chapters, it should be observed that considerably more books and articles have been published relating to the years 1783–1865 than to the post-Civil War years. The following citations should be supplemented by the footnote references in each chapter.

CHAPTER I.   THE CONTINUING STRUGGLE
FOR INDEPENDENCE

The classic account is Samuel F. Bemis, *Jay's Treaty: A Study in Commerce and Diplomacy* (New York, 1924; revised edition, New Haven, 1962); it should be supplemented by Alfred L. Burt, *The United States, Great Britain and British North America from the Revolution to the Establishment of Peace after the War of 1812* (New Haven, 1940), a book with many new interpretations; and by Jerald A. Combs, *The Jay Treaty: Political Battleground of the Founding Fathers* (Berkeley and Los Angeles, 1970). Regarding the Indians see Orpha E. Leavitt, "British Policy on the Canadian Frontier, 1782–92: Mediation and an Indian Barrier State," Wisconsin State Historical Society, *Proceedings of the . . . Sixty-Third Annual Meeting* (Madison, 1916), 151–185.

CHAPTER II.   IDEOLOGY, POLITICS, AND WAR

A perceptive and detailed account of British-American relations around 1800 is Bradford Perkins, *The First Rapprochement, England and the United States, 1795–1805* (Philadelphia, 1955). Henry Adams, *History of the United States of America . . .* (New York, 1890), critical of Jefferson and Madison, is the one indispensable study of the coming of the War of 1812; Alfred T. Mahan, *Sea Power in its Relation to the War of 1812* (Boston, 1905), is another classic account. Four more recent surveys suplement these works. Bradford Perkins, *Prologue to War, England and the United States, 1805–1812* (Berkeley and Los Angeles, 1961), is traditional in stressing the maritime grievances, but pays more attention to chance and emotion than did the older historians, who mainly examined rational motives. Reginald Horsman, *The Causes of the War of 1812* (Philadelphia, 1962), also finds British maritime policy as the main irritant to the United States, but at the same time gives considerable weight to the Indian problem. A study which treats conventional explanations lightly and concludes that the Republican party went to war to save republicanism is Roger H. Brown, *The Republic in Peril: 1812* (New York and London, 1964). Patrick C. T. White, *A Nation on Trial: America and the War of 1812* (New York, 1965), is a short survey that sees the American nation having to fight "because the sovereignty of the state itself was at stake." Irving Brant's monumental biography, *James Madison . . .* (Indianapolis and New York, 1941–1961), strongly defends the President's policy. Julius W. Pratt, *Expansionists of 1812* (New York, 1925), is the classic appraisal of the influence of the frontier in bringing on the war. James F. Zimmerman, *Impressment of*

American Seamen (New York, 1925), gives a detailed account; Anthony Steel, "Impressment in the Monroe-Pinkney Negotiations, 1806–1807," *American Historical Review*, LVII (1952), 352–369, deals with the subject in a smaller but crucial context. Louis M. Sears, *Jefferson and the Embargo* (Durham, North Carolina, 1927), is sympathetic toward the President's embargo policy. George R. Taylor, "Agrarian Discontent in the Mississippi Valley Preceding the War of 1812," *Journal of Political Economy*, XXXIX (1931), 471–505, argues that economic difficulties made the West more war minded. A provocative interpretation of Canadian-American relations in the post-war (and later) years is Charles P. Stacey, "The Myth of the Unguarded Frontier, 1815–1871," *American Historical Review*, LVI (1950), 1–18.

CHAPTER III. SETTING THE STAGE FOR EXPANSION: THE MONROE DOCTRINE AND WEST INDIAN COMMERCE

Kenneth Bourne's able and informative book, *Britain and the Balance of Power in North America, 1815–1908* (Berkeley and Los Angeles, 1967), concerns British policy as related to considerations of a possible war with the United States, not only in the time period of the present chapter but for the rest of the century as well (except 1872–1895). One part of the American impact on Great Britain that angered many upper-class Britons is examined in David P. Crook, *American Democracy in English Politics, 1815–1850* (Oxford, 1965). J. Fred Rippy, *Rivalry of the United States and Great Britain over Latin America (1808–1830)* (Baltimore, 1929), is a general survey; William W. Kaufmann, *British Policy and the Independence of Latin America, 1804–1828* (New Haven, 1951), is a fine study from the perspective of London. Charles K. Webster, *The Foreign Policy of Castlereagh, 1815– 1822, Britain and the European Alliance* (London, 1925), ably examines Castlereagh's European policy; Webster, ed., *Britain and the Independence of Latin America, 1812–1830, Select Documents from the Foreign Office Archives* (London, 1938), is useful for documents. Dexter Perkins, *The Monroe Doctrine, 1823– 1826* (Cambridge, Mass., 1927), is the classic account; it must be considered along with Samuel F. Bemis, *John Quincy Adams and the Foundations of American Foreign Policy* (New York, 1949), an outstanding study. Additional material regarding the controversy over West Indian commerce may be found in F. Lee Benns, *The American Struggle for the British West India Carrying-Trade, 1815–1830* (Bloomington, 1923), and Vernon G. Setser, *The Commercial Reciprocity Policy of the United States, 1774–1829* (Philadelphia, 1937).

CHAPTER IV.   BORDER DISPUTES

Frederick Merk, *Manifest Destiny and Mission in American History, A Reinterpretation* (New York, 1963), is a more penetrating interpretation than Albert K. Weinberg's interesting *Manifest Destiny; A Study of Nationalist Expansionism in American History* (Baltimore, 1935). Two carefully done books consider, respectively, American anger over the attitude of British visitors and British anger over the American repudiation of state debts: Max Berger, *The British Traveller in America, 1836–1860* (New York, 1943), and Reginald C. McGrane, *Foreign Bondholders and American State Debts* (New York, 1935). Bourne, *Balance of Power* (cited p. 208), and Bemis, *John Quincy Adams* (cited p. 208), are illuminating on the controversies over Texas and Maine. Oscar A. Kinchen, *The Rise and Fall of the Patriot Hunters* (New Haven, 1956), has detailed information. Hugh G. Soulsby, *The Right of Search and the Slave Trade in Anglo-American Relations, 1814–1862* (Baltimore, 1933), is the standard monograph; see also Richard W. Van Alstyne, "The British Right of Search and the African Slave Trade," *Journal of Modern History*, II (1930), 37–47. Ralph W. Hidy, *The House of Baring in American Trade and Finance, English Merchant Bankers at Work, 1763–1861* (Cambridge, Mass., 1949), is a comprehensive study of the banking house, frequently influential in British-American affairs, of which Lord Ashburton was a member.

CHAPTER V.   WESTWARD EXPANSION: TEXAS, CALIFORNIA, AND OREGON

Bourne, *Balance of Power* (cited p. 208), is useful for Britain's reaction to American policy toward Texas and Oregon. Regarding Texas, Ephraim D. Adams, *British Interests and Activities in Texas, 1838–1846* (Baltimore, 1910), is a thorough account. Jesse S. Reeves, *American Diplomacy Under Tyler and Polk* (Baltimore, 1907), is useful chiefly for details; more penetrating are Charles G. Sellers, *James K. Polk, Jacksonian, 1795–1843* (Princeton, 1957), and *James K. Polk, Continentalist, 1843–1846* (Princeton, 1966). Norman A. Graebner, *Empire on the Pacific, A Study in American Continental Expansion* (New York, 1955), interprets expansion to the Pacific Ocean in terms of the desire of business interests to get ports, a thesis vigorously attacked by Shomer S. Zwelling, *Expansion and Imperialism* (Chicago, 1970). The authoritative book on Oregon is Frederick Merk, *The Oregon Question, Essays in Anglo-American Diplomacy and Politics* (Cambridge, Mass., 1967); see also his *The Monroe Doctrine and American Expansionism, 1843–1849* (New York, 1966). Wilbur D. Jones, *Lord Aberdeen and the Americas* (Athens, Georgia, 1958), is good on the Foreign Secretary's policy. For different interpretations of McLane's report of February 3, 1846 see, besides Merk, *Oregon Question,* Julius W. Pratt, "James K. Polk and John Bull," *Canadian Historical Review,* XXIV (1943), 341–349, and Wilbur D. Jones and J. Chal Vinson, "British Preparedness and the Oregon Settlement," *Pacific Historical Review,* XXII (1953), 353–364.

CHAPTER VI.   CRISIS AND DÉTENTE: CENTRAL AMERICA

The standard survey of a century of British-American relations in Central America is Mary W. Williams, *Anglo-American Isthmian Diplomacy, 1815–1915* (Washington, 1916). For British policy see Mark J. Van Aken, "British Policy Considerations in Central America before 1850," *Hispanic American Historical Review,* XLII (1962), 54–59; Robert A. Naylor, "The British Role in Central America Prior to the Clayton-Bulwer Treaty of 1850," *ibid.,* XL (1960), 361–382; and Mario Rodríguez, *A Palmerstonian Diplomat in Central America, Frederick Chatfield, Esq.* (Tucson, 1964). For the American filibuster see William O. Scroggs, *Filibusters and Financiers, the Story of William Walker and His Associates* (New York, 1916). James M. Callahan, *Cuba and International Relations: A Historical Study in American Diplomacy* (Baltimore, 1899), is useful for details. Richard W.

Van Alstyne, "Great Britain, the United States, and Hawaiian Independence, 1850–1855," *Pacific Historical Review*, IV (1935), 15–24, describes Anglo-American friction in Hawaii. Dexter Perkins, *The Monroe Doctrine, 1826–1867* (Baltimore, 1933), throws light on many topics of the 1850s, including Central America, Hawaii, and Santo Domingo. James M. Callahan, *American Foreign Policy in Canadian Relations* (New York, 1937), has much detail; more interpretative is the chronologically narrower study by Lester B. Shippee, *Canadian-American Relations, 1849–1874* (New Haven, 1939). There are two adequate accounts of the Marcy-Elgin Treaty: Donald C. Masters, *The Reciprocity Treaty of 1854* . . . (London, 1937), and Charles C. Tansill, *The Canadian Reciprocity Treaty of 1854* (Baltimore, 1922). Further information about the slave trade controversy is in Soulsby, *Right of Search* (cited p. 209), and two articles: Harral E. Landry, "Slavery and the Slave Trade in Atlantic Diplomacy, 1850–1861," *Journal of Southern History*, XXVII (1961), 184–207, and Van Alstyne, "British Right of Search" (cited p. 209).

CHAPTER VII.   REGROWTH OF ANIMOSITY:
THE CIVIL WAR YEARS

The standard account is Ephraim D. Adams, *Great Britain and the American Civil War* (London, 1925); Donaldson Jordan and Edwin J. Pratt, *Europe and the American Civil War* (Boston and New York, 1931), though not restricted to Great Britain, has much material about British policy. Three good articles analyze British public opinion: Wilbur D. Jones, "The British Conservatives and the American Civil War," *American Historical Review*, LVIII (1953), 527–543; William M. Rossetti, "English Opinion on the American War," *Atlantic Monthly*, XVII (1966), 129–149; and Arnold Whitridge, "British Liberals and the American Civil War," *History Today*, XII (1962), 688–695. Spencer Walpole, *The Life of Lord John Russell* (London, 1889), is useful for the Foreign Secretary. Charles Francis Adams, "The Trent Affair," *Proceedings of the Massachusetts Historical Society*, XLV (1911), 35–148, *ibid.* (1912), 522–530; and Thomas Le G. Harris, *The Trent Affair* . . . (Indianapolis and Kansas City, 1896), are thorough accounts of a dangerous incident; see also Bourne, *Balance* of *Power* (cited p. 208). Regarding the *Peterhoff* see Stuart L. Bernath's valuable monograph, *Squall Across the Atlantic: American Civil War Prize Cases and Diplomacy* (Berkeley and Los Angeles, 1970). Good accounts of the British role in the intervention in Mexico are in Carl H. Bock, *Prelude to Tragedy, The Negotiation and Breakdown of the Tripartite Convention of London, October 31, 1861* (Philadelphia, 1966), and Perkins, *Monroe Doctrine, 1826–1867* (cited p. 211). Brooks Adams, "The Seizure of the Laird Rams," *Proceedings of the Massachusetts Historical Society*, XLV (1911), 243–333, is still a valuable study, but Wilbur D. Jones, *The Confederate Rams at Birkenhead: A Chapter in Anglo-American Relations* (Tuscaloosa, Alabama, 1961), has fresh interpretations. Regarding British North America see the fine comprehensive account by Robin W. Winks, *Canada and the United States: The Civil War Years* (Baltimore, 1960).

CHAPTER VIII.   DAGGERS ACROSS THE SEA

Shippee, *Canadian-American Relations* (cited p. 211), gives the general framework in so far as Canada was directly concerned. Charles Francis Adams, Jr., *Lee at Appomattox and Other Papers* (Boston and New York, 1902), has material on United States policy. For a key figure see Edward L. Pierce, *Memoir and Letters of Charles Sumner* (Boston, 1878–1893), Moorfield Storey, *Charles Sumner* (Boston and New York, 1900), and especially the fine study by David H. Donald, *Charles Sumner and the Rights of Man* (New York, 1970). A good biography of an influential figure in Britain politics is T. Wemyss Reid, *Life of the Right Honourable William Edward Forster* (London, 1888). The best study of the northwest boundary controversy is James O. McCabe, *The San Juan Water Boundary Question* (Toronto, 1964). The standard book about the Fenians is William D'Arcy, *The Fenian Movement in the United States: 1858–1886* (Washington, 1947); more directly pertinent is Brian Jenkins, *Fenians and Anglo-American Relations during Reconstruction* (Ithaca, 1969). A. H. U. Colquhoun, "The Reciprocity Negotiations with the United States in 1869," *Canadian Historical Review*, VIII (1927), 233–242, is helpful regarding the background of the Treaty of Washington.

CHAPTER IX.   A CLOUDY ACCORD

Allan Nevins, *Hamilton Fish, The Inner History of the Grant Administration* (New York, 1937), although unduly laudatory, is a splendid biography and has much material on the Treaty of Washington; Goldwin Smith, *The Treaty of Washington, 1871, A Study in Imperial History* (Ithaca, 1941), is also helpful. McCabe, *San Juan Water Boundary Question* (cited p. 212), is useful. Reid, *Life of Forster* (cited p. 212), is a good biography of a man who worked for British concessions in order to gain an agreement with the United States. Regarding Canada see Donald G. Creighton's sympathetic biography, *John A. Macdonald, The Old Chieftain* (Toronto, 1955), and Donald F. Warner's able study, *The Idea of Continental Union: Agitation for the Annexation of Canada to the United States, 1849–1893* (Lexington, Kentucky, 1960).

CHAPTER X.   HALIFAX AND THE FISHERIES

For the general background see Robert C. Brown's excellent monograph, *Canada's National Policy, 1883–1900, A Study in Canadian-American Relations* (Princeton, 1964), and Charles C. Tansill's detailed *Canadian-American Relations, 1875–1911* (New Haven, 1943). There are several biographies of the statesmen involved in the Halifax and other controversies: Chester L. Barrows, *William M. Evarts, Lawyer, Diplomat, Statesman* (Chapel Hill, 1941); Lady Gwendolen Cecil's sympathetic *Life of Robert, Marquis of Salisbury* (London, 1922–1932); Creighton, *Macdonald* (cited above); the standard biography by John Morley, *The Life of William Ewart Gladstone* (New York, 1903); Nevins, *Fish* (cited above). See also two biographies of prominent Canadians: Oscar D. Skelton, *The Life and Times of Sir Alexander Tilloch Galt* (Toronto, 1920), and Dale C. Thomson, *Alexander Mackenzie, Clear Grit* (Toronto, 1960).

CHAPTER XI.   PARALLEL TROUBLES

Tansill, *Canadian-American Relations* (cited above), gives the background and has considerable detail. David M. Pletcher's careful study of *The Awkward Years, American Foreign Rela-*

tions Under Garfield and Arthur (Columbia, Missouri, 1961), although mainly dealing with other topics, has material regarding Canada in the early 1880s. James L. Garvin's fine biography, *The Life of Joseph Chamberlain* (London, 1932–1934), is informative on Chamberlain's visit to Washington. Alice F. Tyler, *The Foreign Policy of James G. Blaine* (Minneapolis, 1927), is the only book on the subject.

CHAPTER XII. CLASHES IN THE BERING SEA

There is a little information in Tyler, *Foreign Policy of Blaine* (cited above), and Albert T. Volwiler, ed., *The Correspondence between Benjamin Harrison and James G. Blaine, 1882–1893* (Philadelphia, 1940). For the negotiations leading up to the arbitration see Charles S. Campbell, "The Bering Sea Settlements of 1892," *Pacific Historical Review*, XXXII (1963), 347–367.

CHAPTER XIII. DÉTENTE AGAIN: THE BRITISH GUIANA BOUNDARY

Alexander E. Campbell, *Great Britain and the United States, 1895–1903* (London, 1960); John A. S. Grenville, *Lord Salisbury and Foreign Policy, the Close of the Nineteenth Century* (London, 1964); Walter LaFeber, *The New Empire: An Interpretation of American Expansion, 1860–1898* (Ithaca, 1963); and Dexter Perkins, *The Monroe Doctrine, 1867–1907* (Baltimore, 1937), are excellent studies with interesting interpretations. Biographies of people involved in the boundary dispute are: Garvin, *Chamberlain* (cited above); Matilda Gresham, *Life of Walter Quintin Gresham, 1832–1895* (Chicago, 1919); Robert B. Mowat, *The Life of Lord Pauncefote, First Ambassador to the United States* (Boston and New York, 1929); and T. Wemyss Reid, *Memoirs and Correspondence of Lyon Playfair, First Lord Playfair of St. Andrews, P.C., G.C.B., LL.D., F.R.S., Ec.* (New York and London, 1899). Two articles should be consulted: Marcus Baker, "The Venezuelan Boundary Controversy and its Work," *National Geographic Magazine*, VIII (1897), 193–201, and Joseph J. Mathews, "Informal Diplomacy in the Venezuelan Crisis of 1896," *Mississippi Valley Historical Review*, L (1963), 195–212.

CHAPTER XIV.   RAPPROCHEMENT

Robert G. Neale, *Great Britain and United States Expansion: 1898–1900* (East Lansing, 1966), has considerable detailed information on British policy. A definitive article is Thomas A. Bailey, "Dewey and the Germans at Manila Bay," *American Historical Review*, XLV (1939), 59–81. William R. Thayer, *The Life and Letters of John Hay* (Boston and New York, 1915), is useful for the letters. A fine biography of an influential British statesman is Blanche E. C. Dugdale, *Arthur James Balfour, First Earl of Balfour, K.G., O.M., F.R.S., Etc.* (London, 1936). For the Hague Conference see Calvin DeA. Davis, *The United States and the First Hague Peace Conference* (Ithaca, 1962), and James B. Scott, ed., *The Proceedings of the Hague Peace Conferences . . .* (New York, 1920–1921). Charles S. Campbell, *Special Business Interests and the Open Door Policy* (New Haven, 1951), has material on the potential Chinese market; A. Whitney Griswold, *The Far Eastern Policy of the United States* (New York, 1938), analyzes other important aspects of American policy. Bradford Perkins, *The Great Rapprochement, England and the United States, 1895–1914* (New York, 1968), considers briefly some of the underlying factors in Anglo-American relations.

Index